THE CASE OF THE LEGLESS VETERAN

The case of the legless veteran

JAMES KUTCHER

PATHFINDER
New York London Montreal Sydney

ISBN 0-87348-939-X paper (formerly 0-913460-17-6);
ISBN 0-913460-16-8 cloth
Library of Congress Catalog Card Number 73-77556
Manufactured in the United States of America

First British edition, 1953
First United States edition, expanded, 1973
Third printing, 2002

Cover design by Toni Gorton

Pathfinder
410 West Street, New York, NY 10014, U.S.A.
Fax: (212) 727-0150
www.pathfinderpress.com
E-mail: pathfinderpress@compuserve.com

PATHFINDER DISTRIBUTORS AROUND THE WORLD:
Australia (and Southeast Asia and the Pacific):
    Pathfinder, Level 1, 3/281-287 Beamish St., Campsie, NSW 2194
    Postal address: P.O. Box K879, Haymarket, NSW 1240
Canada:
    Pathfinder, 2761 Dundas St. West, Toronto, ON, M6P 1Y4
Iceland:
    Pathfinder, Skolavordustig 6B, Reykjavík
    Postal address: P. Box 0233, IS 121 Reykjavík
New Zealand:
    Pathfinder, P.O. Box 3025, Auckland
Sweden:
    Pathfinder, Domargränd 16, S-129 47 Hägersten
United Kingdom (and Europe, Africa, Middle East and South Asia):
    Pathfinder, 47 The Cut, London, SE1 8LL
United States (and Caribbean, Latin America, and East Asia):
    Pathfinder, 410 West Street, New York, NY 10014

CONTENTS

ILLUSTRATIONS

PREFACE

This book tells the story of a battle for workers' rights and civil liberties during the height of the cold war witch-hunt in the United States.

In 1948 James Kutcher, a worker who had lost both legs in World War II, was fired from his job as a clerk with the Veterans Administration. The stated reason was Kutcher's membership in the Socialist Workers Party (SWP), which had been included on a list of "subversive" organizations compiled by the U.S. attorney general the year before. Later the government revoked Kutcher's disability pension and tried to evict him from public housing.

In response to these attacks, defenders of democratic rights launched the Kutcher Civil Rights Defense Committee, winning support from hundreds of organizations and thousands of individuals holding many different political views. After a long and hard-fought battle, the case ended in victory in 1956 when Kutcher was ordered reinstated in his job. He subsequently was awarded back pay.

This eight-year fight was waged from within the labor movement—the central target of the McCarthy-era witch-hunt—reaching out broadly to all supporters of democratic rights. During a period of political victimizations and of relative quiet within the unions, the Kutcher case dealt a blow to the witch-hunters and opened valuable space for working-class fighters to function within the labor movement.

The Case of the Legless Veteran was first published in 1953, as the fight was still going on. In 1973, when the book was republished, two chapters (18 and 19) were added to complete the story. The following year the attorney general's list of subversive organizations—one of the justifications for the attack on Kutcher—was abolished. In 1986, after a thirteen-year court fight, a federal judge declared in a landmark ruling that the government's massive, decades-long efforts to spy on and disrupt the SWP were illegal and constituted a violation of the socialists' constitutionally protected rights. James Kutcher remained a member of the Socialist Workers Party until 1983; he died in 1989.

In today's world of wars, capitalist depression, and deepening social conflicts, the fight for democratic rights is a vital part of the struggle by working people internationally to defend their interests. *The Case of the Legless Veteran* offers an invaluable account of one such battle that ended in victory.

January 1995

|

We have choices to make

In most respects, I am an ordinary man. I have no special talents. I never showed any capacity for leadership. In school my marks generally put me in the middle sections of my class, sometimes lower. I never rose above the rank of Pfc. in the army. Often, when I get into a discussion, I don't think of the right point to make until hours afterward. I was active in a political organization for over ten years and never made a speech in all that time. I am a "Jimmy Higgins" by nature, the fellow who collects tickets at the door and sweeps up the hall after the meeting. People like me usually get their names in the papers twice—when they come into the world and when they go out.

And yet I have become a public figure of a sort. A thousand separate items about me have appeared in large newspapers and small mimeographed bulletins from New York to California. Hundreds of organizations representing millions of people have taken time out from their regular business to discuss and pass resolutions about me. Lawyers have labored long hours drawing up involved legal documents for or against me. The highest court in the land may some day hand down a ruling that will have important effects not only on my future but on the liberties of the whole American people. I, who used to be too shy to make a motion to adjourn, now have made hundreds of speeches at meetings and over the radio; and the astonishing thing about it to me is that while I still have no special oratorical abilities, people have shed tears, lost their tempers or risen to their feet cheering when I talked to them about my struggle with high officials of the government of the United States.

This change was not sought by me; it happened almost independently of my will. We like to think that we are the captains of our fate, that we make the major decisions in our lives ourselves. In a certain sense we do, but we are not free to do or become any old thing. Conditions beyond our individual control push and pull us into situations we never expected to meet. The bigger and more complicated society becomes, the smaller the role of the individual seems to shrink.

My life has been shaped by three catastrophes: the depression, the war and the cold war. The depression, beginning with the stock market crash of 1929 when I was seventeen years old, deprived me of a chance to settle down in a job; but it provided me with a new outlook on the world. The war cost me my legs; this made me feel "different" from most people and turned my thoughts and activities inward; but it also brought me a job I expected to keep for the rest of my life and, for the first time, I also got a sense of personal security. The cold war cost me my job and struck a blow at my civil liberties; but these events helped to tear me out of a routine that was becoming more and more self-centered and reawakened my interest in the world at large and in my relations to it.

These three man-made disasters combined to make me into a symbol for one of the crucial conflicts of our time. Usually it is the great men and women who serve as our symbols of significant ideas, movements and controversies. But I refuse to delude myself into thinking that I personally am important because I serve as a symbol. I know very well that often it is otherwise insignificant and obscure people who are chosen by accident to serve that function. If I have to compare myself with a figure of the past, it would be with Dred Scott, a Negro and a slave, who accidentally became a symbol for the great struggle over slavery that was dividing this nation during the first half of the nineteenth century. Dred Scott happened to sue for his freedom at a time when the U.S. Supreme Court was preparing to deliver some vital constitutional opinions on the slavery issue and found it convenient to hinge its decisions around his suit. Otherwise, no one would remember Dred Scott's name today.

Let no one misunderstand me, however. I do *not* believe that we are mere puppets moved by some inscrutable force, or that our acts are rigidly predetermined and therefore essentially meaningless, or that the individual counts for nothing because he is not able by himself alone to decide what he shall be or do.

We are the products of our environment, our heredity, our heritage (good and bad) from the past. These influence what we think and do, but they don't determine what we think and do under all circumstances. We still have choices to make; and we are not relieved of responsibility for our actions. We are compelled to operate within certain limits, but within them we make our own history. The individual is important; under favorable circumstances he can change the course of great events; when the time is ripe, even a small group equipped with correct ideas can alter the thinking and conduct of millions; man has the power to get control of the natural and social conditions that have controlled him in the past and to remake the world. Those are my firm beliefs, and I have tried to live in accord with them whenever possible.

Even in a world we never made, I repeat, we have decisions to make. Dred Scott certainly had. Some people become symbols entirely against their will—for example, prisoners unjustly arrested and convicted, who have nothing to lose by fighting for their exoneration and liberation. Not much is known about Dred Scott, but I am sure he had to think the matter over carefully before he decided to go to court. We cannot tell what was the main factor in his decisions—a personal desire to secure freedom, a belief that through his suit he might help improve the lot of his fellow slaves, or some other consideration—and it doesn't matter too much in this connection. But he must have known that his act would incur the wrath of many slaveholders and that if he should ever fall into the hands of one of these the rest of his life could be made into a living hell. Whatever his reasons were, his decision required courage, moral courage; it was a moral act. No matter why other people remember Dred Scott, I for one will remember him from now on primarily for the decision he made.

I had a decision to make myself. I wasn't looking for one, I would have been much happier if one had never come up, but the gun was put to my head and I made it. Because it affected me first of all, I had to make it by myself. But I think the same issue confronts every American and sooner or later every American will have to make a decision too. That, rather than an attempt to justify myself, is why I am writing the story of the circumstances that led up to my decision and what has happened since I made it.

2

The depression

Students being graduated from high school today are concerned mainly with the question of the draft. It was different with my generation. The big question facing us was: How am I going to get a job? Young men today may think that, all things considered, we had the better of it because unemployment is not as serious or dangerous as military service, either in a "police action" or a regularly declared war. But I am not sure they are right, and I have experienced both. The depression affected the old as well as the young, women as well as men, and it produced plenty of wounds and scars that have not healed to this day.

When the stock market crashed in 1929, I was going to the Central High School in Newark, New Jersey, where I was born. I remember my father shaking his head as he read the newspaper one morning: "This means trouble." The remark remained in my memory only because he kept reminding me of it as the depression developed and deepened and seemed on the way to becoming a permanent feature of our lives.

At that time I was more interested in the sports page than the front page. Later I learned that the chief characteristic of the Roaring

Twenties was supposed to be an all-pervading frenzy to get rich quick. I was never gripped by it, maybe because I was too young, maybe because I grew up in a working class family where the memory of my father's unemployment during the early 1920s was still fresh.

Whatever the reason was, I did not expect to become either an athlete or a banker when I went out into the world. What I wanted to be was a teacher. I am afraid now I probably would not have been a very good teacher after all. But then I was an idealistic boy, and it seemed to me that no profession was nobler or more useful than helping young people to find their way to the truth. Perhaps this ambition was originally fostered by my parents who had come to this country with little schooling and who had the immigrant's traditional respect for education. Perhaps it was partly the result of my gratitude to those teachers who took a genuine interest in their work, did not easily become discouraged with slower students like myself, and opened new horizons for me.

I had not decided yet what kind of subject I wanted to teach, although American history and English attracted me the most. Even before the depression my parents did not have enough money to pay my way through college. But I was sure that I would become a teacher anyhow—for I had already learned in school that ours is a land of infinite opportunity, where hard work and determination are well rewarded and where there is "always more room at the top." Since my ambition was modest, I had no doubt about succeeding in it. The stock market crash and the unemployment that followed may have worried Wall Street and my father, but it didn't seem to concern me.

Before long I learned that I was wrong. My father, a fur worker, was laid off more frequently and for longer periods. My mother began to watch our budget more closely, and started to dip into savings built up by twenty years of skimping, scraping and haggling with shopkeepers. My weekly allowance was cut in half. I had to take a lunch to school instead of buying it in the cafeteria. And then came the time in 1932, when I was about to be graduated, that my parents sat me down and broke the news: It would be impossible for them to help me go to college; what was more, they felt I ought to put it off a year or two and get a job to help the family out through the "hard times."

It was a scene I will never forget. My father sat across the table from me, a short man with shoulders bowed from a lifetime of toil, prematurely old, a stubble of gray on his face. He gestured earnestly as he tried to explain things to me, some sweat appeared on his brow from the effort he made to explain them so that I would understand. My mother sat turned away from the table; in a little while, she began to cry and got up and went into another room.

I should have realized even then how painful the whole thing was for them. It meant dashing not only my hopes but theirs as well. But I was not thinking about them, I was thinking only of myself. I became bitter—not against the depression, but against my father. I felt that he was a failure, that he had let me down. If there was no work in his own trade, then why didn't he get another job? That, I told myself, was what I would do in his position. He was selfish, thoughtless, indifferent to what became of me. And this hurt as much as the prospect of postponing college.

It seems incredible now that in the third year of the depression I should really have thought that my father could get a job in another trade merely by deciding that he wanted to. I liked school, and hoped to devote my life to education, and yet the school I went to had not equipped me with the faintest notion of economic realities. Nobody knows for sure how many Americans were unemployed in 1932, but it is agreed that the figure was over thirteen million. I soon learned from my own experience that my father was not to blame, and it was not long before I liked him as much as ever.

But that was later. Walking off the graduation platform holding my diploma, I was still full of grievances. When the class valedictorian made a speech about how we were going out to conquer the world and make it a better place to live in, I thought: "Maybe you will, and maybe I will too, but not right now. The world will have to stay unconquered and unimproved for a while, so far as I am concerned, because it so happens that rich women aren't buying as many fur coats as they used to."

Leaving school to look for work, I began my real education. Not having any special training, I did not expect a very good job. To my dismay I found there was no job at all for me.

I thought at first the fault must be mine. Maybe I wasn't getting up early enough. Maybe I didn't look eager enough. Maybe I wasn't looking hard enough. I consulted friends and neighbors and tried to correct my "approach." It was no use. Nobody wanted me. I was young, strong, fairly well educated, willing to tackle almost anything. But nobody was interested.

Getting up earlier in the morning, I began to see new things, or to see old things in a new light. When I was going to school, I sometimes used to see men and women rooting in garbage cans. I felt sorry for them but assumed they were derelicts or drunks who did not want to work. Now I observed the same scene more frequently, not only in my own neighborhood but in other "better" districts throughout the city. When I was downtown, I saw people standing in lines in the cold to get a handout of soup and bread. Once I saw two men get into a fist fight about which one had seniority rights to the corner where both had been trying to sell apples.

Another time, standing outside of a factory, a man started crying uncontrollably; when he realized that the rest of us were watching him, he ran away, tears still running down his cheeks. A veteran jeered at him. He said he had been to Washington with the Bonus Army the year before, and they had been "run out" by the army. "But they ran us out, by God, we didn't quit on our own." I had never heard of the Bonus Army before this, and I thought he was making it up until my father told me more about it.

A family that lived across the street from me was evicted one summer; their name was Schmidt, I think. All their belongings were set out on the sidewalk because they were behind in their rent and failed to move out when ordered. My mother offered to take in the two small children and some of the more perishable equipment, but Mrs. Schmidt refused. She said she would not move an inch, and would scandalize the landlord. They stayed there all day and night, her husband sitting in a chair at their table, saying nothing, the two kids jumping around like at a picnic. They had a daughter about my age, a thin pretty girl who worked as a typist, the only employed member of the family. She came home after work, took a look at what had happened, made some of her clothing into a parcel and went away without answering a single thing her mother told her. My mother says the Schmidts never heard of her again. The next day it looked like rain, and a wagon finally came and the Schmidts moved away. Later in the depression there was a great deal of resistance to evictions; friends and neighbors used to get together and move things back into the same apartment from which the authorities had removed them.

Once a friend and I answered a vaguely worded advertisement asking job-seekers to report to the Newark Armory. When we got there, we were turned over to a sergeant who tried to talk us into joining the National Guard. He told us that we would enjoy being in uniform, that Guard service was really like a paid vacation, that we would be sent to a summer encampment for maneuvers, and that the president of the United States, no less, would come to watch us pass in review. We got out of there in a hurry. My father never tired of telling how he had fled czarist Russia in 1909 in order to escape military service and come to the land of the free, where no man had to bear arms against his will in peacetime. Antimilitarism, or anyhow nonmilitarism, was a family as well as a national tradition, and I had no intention of ever becoming a soldier. But I knew two fellows who joined the National Guard at this time mainly because of the small allowance. I think it was $1.50 that they were paid for drilling one or two nights a week.

I lowered my sights and took a job as a delivery boy for a butcher. But even this didn't last; the butcher replaced me with a relative after a few weeks. I got a job in a five-and-ten as a stock clerk during the Christmas season. I worked in the ballpark selling scorecards for a whole summer. The best job I got was as a sales clerk in a paint store. This paid $1 a day for six days a week, and lasted about six months, until the business went bankrupt. I kept going around to factories, but never with any success. Why should they hire an inexperienced boy when there were so many skilled workmen standing at the gate, hungry enough to work at almost any wage?

For a while I thought of going to night school to continue my education. But there didn't seem any point in it. I was bewildered and disgusted. Bewildered to find the world so different from what I had expected; disgusted with myself for not getting ahead somehow, although I was beginning to suspect that it was not altogether my fault.

Somewhere I have read about the great number of man-hours of work that the depression cost our country, and was impressed to learn how many homes, schools and hospitals could have been built with that wasted manpower. But these were only a part, a small part, of the total expense. I saw some families broken up, and I knew a number of couples who never got married. I knew others like myself who could not go to college, and some who started but had to drop out. I saw at least one of my schoolmates take to a life of crime and end in the penitentiary. I heard of girls who became prostitutes because that seemed the only way they could earn enough to keep alive. I am sure that malnutrition took a heavy toll in sickness and disease. I observed what demoralization and apathy were spread among workers like my father who asked nothing more than the right to earn their living by the sweat of their brow. It is hard to express these things in statistical tables, but all of us who were mature or growing into maturity during the depression saw these things with our own eyes, and most of us never forgot them.

The suffering was great, the casualties many, but the results were not all bad or negative. The depression taught many Americans to think in broader terms. It shook us out of our towers, ivory or otherwise, and compelled us to look around and work together for common ends with other people in the same plight as ourselves. It made us reconsider some of our concepts and prejudices about the role of government and the sacredness of our economic system. It made us take politics more seriously. (Anybody who wants to understand why the American workers are so loyal to their unions, even though most of them play little part in its day-to-day activities, should begin by studying the impact the depression had on their thinking.)

It was inevitable that we who started by doubting and blaming ourselves should turn after a while to doubting and blaming external conditions and institutions. It was inevitable that radicalism should be one of the by-products of the depression. That is how it happened with me. My idealism, my love of my country and its people, and the shock of the depression combined to convince me that fundamental changes were needed in the United States, and that it was my duty to help bring them about.

I don't write this apologetically. At the age of forty I am still a socialist, and expect to be one for the rest of my life. Almost every day another ex-radical appears before a congressional committee, confessing and repenting the beliefs and associations he formed during the 1930s, and begging forgiveness for the error of his ways. I don't know these people, I don't know the details of their experience. Maybe one of them—a famous playwright—was telling the truth when he explained that he had joined the Communist Party because he was living on ten cents a day. If that was really the reason, then it is understandable that he changed his views when his income rose. But most of the radicals I knew did not join merely because of their personal situations—unemployment, poverty, etc.; most of them became radicals because they were stirred by a feeling of solidarity with all victims of exploitation and oppression and a wish to help abolish such evils. I have the impression that even for most of these repentant witnesses, their conversion to radicalism was the most sincere and unselfish act of their lives, and that few of them will ever do anything of which they will have as much reason to be proud.

I, at any rate, am proud of what I did and became. I think my life has been fuller and richer and more meaningful because of my radical beliefs, associations and activities. If I had a chance to do it over again, I would do substantially the same thing. And I firmly believe that most Americans are going to share my views sooner or later.

One day, toward the end of 1932, I heard that there was going to be a symposium at the Y, and I went there. H.V. Kaltenborn, the radio commentator, defended capitalism; Norman Thomas, the Socialist Party's candidate for president, defended socialism; and Scott Nearing defended communism. A lot of what they said went over my head. But when Kaltenborn said it wasn't fair to judge capitalism by what it looked like during a crisis because that was not its normal condition, and Thomas poked fun at this, my sympathies were with Thomas.

Looking for new books at the library after this, I became acquainted with Upton Sinclair's novels about social injustice. I read many of them, but the one that impressed me most was *Boston,* a novel about the Sacco-Vanzetti case. I was shocked after finishing it to learn that two such men had actually lived and been railroaded to the electric chair although their only "crime" was to advocate a different kind of society. I was beginning to learn a little about economic and labor conflicts—and to remember that as a small boy I had been taken by my father to his union meetings—but it seemed "un-American" to me that people should really be imprisoned and even executed in this country because they exercised their right of free speech. Sinclair's two books about the educational system also fascinated me.

Another writer who influenced me at this time was Will Rogers, the actor. For some reason I then had the impression that he was a radical too. Recently when some of his articles and speeches on politics were collected and published in a new volume, I was surprised to see that he was actually a Progressive Bull Moose and later a Democrat. In spite of that, he helped to educate me about politics and to indoctrinate me with a healthy dose of skepticism about the two-party system.

A year later, another three-sided symposium was held in Newark, again with Thomas and Nearing, and with Drew Pearson defending capitalism. This time I was definitely in Thomas' corner. I thought he was a great orator, and that everything he said made good sense. I liked some of what Nearing said too, but I vaguely understood that communism had something to do with dictatorship, and I didn't want any of that. I still did not know much about socialism, but I had reached the conclusion that capitalism was not the last word by a long shot, and that changes of some kind were overdue.

Even so, I did not join any organization until 1935. I kept looking for a steady job, without luck. Our family managed to survive without going on relief, thanks to a job my younger brother got and to the last of my parents' savings. I thought of enlisting in the CCC (Civilian Conservation Corps) but was barred because of my non-relief status. For the same reason I was never able to get employment with the Public Works Authority and other governmental work relief agencies.

In the fall of 1935 I started going as a student to Essex County Junior College, an institution holding evening sessions which was organized chiefly to help unemployed teachers. I attended for two years, still looking for a job in the mornings. I ran into some students with socialist ideas, and through them was introduced to the Young People's Socialist League, the youth organization of the Socialist Party. The first time they asked me to join, I said I wanted to think it over for a while. But actually I did not have much to think over. I was already a rebel. Why waste time when I could join an organized movement to change the world? So I joined.

I met many fine people in the YPSL and the Socialist Party. Throwing myself eagerly into work with them, I became an active campaigner in the 1936 elections, getting petitions signed, passing out leaflets, selling literature. I was thrilled when we got a capacity audience at the Laurel Garden for our presidential candidate, Norman Thomas, who delivered a fighting speech under a huge banner with our slogan, "Socialism in Our Time." Bitterness about my personal situation had been replaced by great hopes and enthusiasm for the future and a growing desire to learn more about socialism and how to get it.

Two big events in 1936 contributed to my political education. One was the civil war in Spain, where the fascists led by Franco were trying to overthrow the legally elected republican government of the People's Front, which was supported by both the Socialist and Communist parties. Up to then I thought that socialism would be achieved through the process of gradually electing more and more socialists to office until they were a majority. But now I saw it was not quite so simple, because the enemies of socialism might refuse to abide by the democratic will of the majority and might resort to force and violence in order to thwart their will—as was happening in Spain. Like many others, I became an active partisan of the Loyalist cause. Some of the YPSL members talked about going to Spain to join the armies fighting the fascists. I just could not conceive of myself as a soldier, however, and confined my activities to spreading propaganda and raising funds for the antifascist cause.

Around the same time came the Moscow Trials, where the Stalin government accused several of the leading Russian revolutionists, including the exiled Leon Trotsky, of being agents of fascism and executed as many of them as it had in its power. Studying these strange proceedings convinced me that the trials were frame-ups, every bit as reactionary as the Sacco-Vanzetti case in this country. I also began to get a clearer understanding of Stalinism. Previously I had thought that the members of the Communist Party were more revolutionary than I was. But now, watching them defend the purges in Russia and seeing them support Roosevelt in the 1936 election, I came to realize that their policies were not revolutionary at all. Their members may think that they are working for socialism, but the main mission of the Communist Party leaders is to promote the interests of the bureaucratic dictators who have destroyed all democratic liberties in the Soviet Union and are concerned only with remaining in power on the backs of the people.

I also learned much from the internal disputes inside the Socialist Party. Under the influence of the depression, the rise of fascism in Germany, and the influx of new members, the party took a more radical position on many questions than it had taken in the 1920s. This led to a conflict with the "Old Guard," who wanted to support Roosevelt in the 1936 campaign. They split away and formed the Social Democratic Federation for just that purpose shortly after I joined.

But this split did not end the factional fights between the right wing of the party, led by Norman Thomas, and the left wing, whose members were called "Trotskyists." I had been warned not to have anything to do with the latter because they would try to convert me to their ideas. But the left wingers seemed more serious than the other members, better educated in socialist theory and history, and more interested in spreading the socialist message among the workers, unemployed and Negro people. For them "Socialism in Our Time" was not just a slogan but a goal they really expected to achieve.

I became friendly with some of them, and especially with one who has been my best friend ever since, George Breitman. He was a couple of years younger, but I always looked up to him as a model of what a socialist should be. He was a hard and conscientious worker, willing to undertake any task, from cleaning out the furnace to running for public office, from mimeographing a leaflet to organizing a picket line. He wasn't very talkative around party headquarters, unlike some of the other comrades, but I noticed that he was listened to with close attention by members of the unemployed movement, the Workers Alliance, in which he was elected state organization secretary. We were alarmed once when he was falsely arrested for "inciting to riot" during a WPA strike in South Jersey and held in jail for a week before the charges were dropped; we greeted him on his return with a social affair at which we presented him with a book by Leon Trotsky. He had the respect of almost everyone who knew him, even of the Stalinists who fought our people in the Workers Alliance, and I learned a great deal from him.

It was through George that I made my first acquaintance with the labor movement. The CIO was being organized in those days and George, as a Workers Alliance official, would help some of the CIO organizers by getting Alliance members to distribute leaflets and walk on picket lines. One day I got a card from him, asking me if I would join a CIO picket line in one of the Newark suburbs that afternoon. To tell the truth, I was a little afraid to go. The Memorial Day massacre had just taken place in Chicago, where police had shot down a number of defenseless CIO pickets. But I went anyhow.

A line of pickets was walking in a circle in front of the plant when

I arrived. A number of big burly policemen stood around outside the circle, swinging their clubs. I stopped dead in my tracks; the whole atmosphere was charged with tension. "What am I walking into here?" I asked myself. But I saw George and got into the line beside him. He explained that the strikers' morale was low, and that was why additional pickets were needed. But I only half listened to him. Every time I walked by one of the cops with his swinging club, I kind of winced inside, wondering what he would do with it. At five o'clock some scabs came out of the plant, there was some name-calling back and forth, and then the picket line broke up. George kidded me about looking pale around the gills, but said I had acquitted myself well. I felt good about this.

After that, I wasn't afraid any more, and I spent some time working with two other socialists who were CIO organizers. We would pass out leaflets and make visits to workers' homes. The police arrested me twice, once outside an aluminum plant in Edgewater, and the second time at an auto plant in Linden. They drove us to the stationhouse, took away our leaflets, and told us to get out of town. The plants were unionized just the same.

The Socialist Party vote declined drastically in 1936 because many who had formerly voted socialist now became New Dealers. (Instead of cursing Franklin D. Roosevelt as a "socialist" the capitalist class should have been deeply grateful to him because through his reform program he did more to keep this country from going to the left than anybody who ever sat in the White House.) The lowered vote produced moods of pessimism and skepticism in the party; many of the leaders began to think that perhaps the Old Guard had been right in refusing to oppose the Democrats who were then at the height of their popularity with the workers.

When 1937 came, therefore, Norman Thomas and others proposed that the party should not run a candidate against Fiorello LaGuardia in the New York mayoralty election. This sharpened the struggle in the party because the left wing insisted that wherever possible socialists should oppose the candidates of the capitalist parties as a matter of principle. The factional atmosphere was also heightened by a controversy over Spain, where the Loyalist government had taken punitive measures against workers who were demanding a more radical policy from the government. Our left wing condemned such measures as reactionary and wanted our party to do the same.

Finally, the whole thing came to a head when the right wing expelled the leaders of the left wing because they insisted on expressing their criticisms in the party. I protested against this, and then was presented with an ultimatum: either agree to go along with the expulsions or get out. The idea of leaving the YPSL, which had become the center of my life, was a bitter pill. But I had learned that loyalty to principles comes first, and the wrench of leaving was softened by the fact that most of the Socialist Party and YPSL members in Newark sided with the left wing. I went with them, and when they set up a new organization, the Socialist Workers Party, at the beginning of 1938, I was a charter member.

The depression introduced me to socialism, but I found socialism was a way of life and an answer to more problems than unemployment. I like to think that if there had been no depression, I would eventually have become a socialist anyhow. But who knows?

3

War

For ten years the government tried to end the depression, but despite some ups and downs in the industrial cycle it did not succeed—until World War II broke out in Europe. Even with pump-priming we could not get organized for maximum production in peacetime. It took the evil of war to liquidate the evil of unemployment.

The factories began to hire, but I was turned away from several because I did not have any skill. So in the fall of 1940, I enrolled in a school set up by the government in Verona, New Jersey, to provide young people with industrial training. I took a machine shop course, learning how to operate a lathe. We lived in dormitories, were paid $10 a month, and were allowed to go home for the weekends. For the first time I saw a steady job within my reach.

But the job I got was not the one I expected. The war in Europe not only brought armament, it also brought peacetime conscription. My number came up near the top of the list, and I was among the earlier ones to be drafted. I asked to be deferred a month or two to finish my training, but it was refused. After many years of not being wanted at all, I was now wanted so urgently that no delay could be brooked. I was sworn into the army in January 1941. It turned out to be the longest job I ever held.

At this point I must explain just what my attitude was to the draft, the army and the war. I find this necessary because on numerous occasions during the last few years I have seen or heard myself described as a "hero." In part, this comes from a loose habit of thinking and talking that spreads among civilians during wartime. To them, everyone who wears a uniform, or goes overseas, or engages in battle—no matter how reluctantly—automatically qualifies for the title of "hero." When in addition the serviceman gets wounded or decorated, all restraints are thrown overboard and the word "hero" gets bandied about as freely as references to "free enterprise" at a convention of the National Association of Manufacturers.

I was a soldier, I fought in battle, I was wounded, I was decorated—but I was not a "hero" and I don't want any sympathy based on misconceptions. I was drafted, I did not volunteer. What's heroic about doing something you are forced to do?

When I first became a socialist, I was a pacifist, against all wars and military service on principle. As a college student, I joined the Student League for Industrial Democracy which later became a part of the American Student Union, and like other members I participated in antiwar demonstrations and took an antiwar pledge. I assumed that if war came, I would be a conscientious objector, preferring to go to prison rather than into the armed forces, as many socialists did in World War I.

But after I joined the Socialist Workers Party, my views on this matter underwent a change. I came to realize that not all wars are wrong and bad—that some are necessary, just and progressive. For example, the war of a colonial country for its independence. If I had been alive in 1776 when the American colonies fought to throw off British domination, I would gladly have participated in that struggle—just as in more recent times I have supported the wars of the colonial people for independence from imperialism. Each war, I decided, must be judged on its own merits.

Furthermore, I developed a new attitude toward conscientious objection as a means of expressing protest against a reactionary war. I still sympathize with principled conscientious objectors. They often show courage greater than those who don't want to go to war but submit to the draft anyhow. But I now believe that their method of protest is futile and accomplishes little or nothing toward the elimination of war. For socialists, such a policy is self-defeating because it gets them jailed and isolated from the very people they are trying to convince that socialism is the way to abolish war. The Socialist Workers Party rid me of my pacifist ideas and convinced me that socialists of military age should "go with their generation," accepting the draft even in a war they cannot support politically, and trying to become "the best soldiers" in an effort to win the respect of their fellow draftees.

I was politically opposed to World War II, before it began and while it was going on. I did not believe that it would bring the spread of the four freedoms proclaimed by President Roosevelt, or that it was part of a people's revolution as asserted by Vice President Wallace, or that it was a war of national liberation as the Stalinists claimed after Hitler attacked the Soviet Union and they suddenly became the most vociferous supporters of the war. To me it seemed essentially a repetition of the first World War, a struggle over markets and raw materials and spheres of influence and not a crusade for democracy or moral principles.

The Communist Party denounced us as agents of fascism and Hitlerite saboteurs because we refused to give political support to the war. But that was a lie. We socialists were a minority of the population and most of the people did not hear or would not listen to our antiwar warnings and appeals; when the war came, there was nothing we could do about it but go along as a minority, without changing our views on the causes of the war and how to eliminate them and without surrendering our right to advocate our socialist program. We neither favored nor practiced sabotage; our task, in wartime as in peacetime, was to convince a majority of the people of the need to establish socialism if they wanted to achieve peace and security.

And so I went into the army, even though I did not believe in the justice of the war and even though I did not expect anything worthwhile to be accomplished by it. I hated fascism, but I did not expect the war to abolish fascism or its causes. I had nothing against the German or Italian soldiers, who had been conscripted like myself and had nothing to say about whether or not there should be a war. I had no use for the authorities who put me into uniform to risk death for a cause I could not share. In certain respects I felt something like the Irish aviator in Yeats' poem who fought for the British in World War I:

> Those that I fight I do not hate,
> Those that I guard I do not love

I was put into the infantry, and happened to serve with the two outfits that saw the most combat and had the heaviest casualties of the U.S. forces in the early years of the war—the 9th Division and the 3rd Division. After being inducted I was assigned to the 39th Infantry Regiment, K Company, attached to the 9th Division at Fort Bragg, North Carolina.

The training was sometimes hard and painful, but I did not mind so long as it contributed to teaching me how to remain alive in the war I was sure we would enter sooner or later. I never regretted my resolve to learn everything I could. After we got into battle, I saw many soldiers, including officers, killed or wounded for failing to take the most elementary precautions.

Some of the training was valuable, but some of it was useless, with the stress in the wrong places. For example, they taught us four positions for firing a rifle—prone, sitting, standing and kneeling. The kneeling position was especially difficult for me. You were supposed to kneel until you were sitting on the heel of your right foot, with your left foot extended; you kept the stock of the rifle jammed into your right shoulder with the right elbow held high to keep it steady. My trouble was that I couldn't sit down on the heel without getting fierce pains shooting through to the right knee which rested on the ground. It never seemed a steady position for firing anyhow.

But because "the book" said everyone had to master all four positions, they devoted special attention to me *for a whole week,* showing me how to kneel, with and without the rifle in my hands. They
seemed to think that the whole military program depended on my
success with the kneeling position. Needless to say, I never fired a
rifle from that position in combat. I don't remember seeing anyone
else use it either, except from behind a fence, where the rifle rested
on something—which altered the position considerably.

At the same time, really important things were neglected, probably because they did not receive as much emphasis in "the book."
Later on, in Italy, I watched in horror from a hill as a lieutenant who
had just joined our company, a twenty-one year old youth fresh from
officers school, directed six of our men into an exposed position
where they were shot down one by one. He then followed them and
was killed instantly. It was probably his first battle. He did not know
the first thing about combat, but I am sure he was versed in all the
niceties of saluting. He might still be alive if he had received as much
instruction on what to do in an exposed position as I got in the
kneeling position.

I hated most aspects of what they called military discipline. The
good soldier is the one who does as he is told, and God help the man
who deviates from an order—that idea was drummed into our heads
over and over again. Once in a while we were also told that initiative is a good thing. But initiative is almost impossible in an atmosphere where blind obedience is held up as the highest virtue.

There was little effort to train us through persuasion, through
genuine education. We were taught to do things because we would
be punished if we didn't. On top of this it seemed to me there was a
deliberate effort to break our spirits. We were given foolish, unnecessary tasks to do—tasks that our officers knew we knew were foolish
and unnecessary—like sending us out to police up the grounds before dawn, when it was so dark that we could not possibly see all the
matchsticks and scraps of paper on the ground. The only purpose
for apparently purposeless things like that was to show us that what

we thought was unimportant, and that our job was to obey, not reason why. We were never permitted to forget about the Articles of War or the fearful consequences of a court-martial. They called this training, but I thought a better name for some of it was terrorization.

I was older and more experienced in some ways than most of the soldiers in my outfit, but I was intimidated too during the first months of my service. One night I was walking guard duty in a restricted area in camp, under strict orders to keep everyone out who had no business there. I saw a soldier in deep conversation with an old man, probably his father, walking in my direction. I accosted them in the customary manner but they were so immersed in their talk they did not hear me. I called to them three times as I was ordered to do and they still kept coming. I shouted at the top of my voice, but it seemed to have no effect.

Then I found myself bringing the rifle to my shoulder and taking aim. I am generally calm and self-controlled, but at that moment I was swept by panic. I kept asking myself frantically why don't they stop, will I have to shoot, what will happen to me if I disobey orders and don't shoot? I tried to aim away from them, but I couldn't. After what seemed like a hundred years the soldier saw me at last, stopped and halted his companion too. I told them they were in a restricted area and to get out. They left without a word. Cold sweat covered me all over. I knew they had meant no harm, and yet I had almost fired at them out of an unreasoning obedience to orders backed up by severe disciplinary measures. I understand that for killing under such circumstances the penalty is a court-martial, a $500 fine and transfer to another post. But the penalty for disobeying orders on guard duty can be much more drastic.

This incident cured me of an excessive fear of military discipline. I knew that I would never again risk hurting innocent bystanders even if I had to pay heavily for not abiding by the strict letter of my orders. It also set me to wondering. Why was the army run from top to bottom this way? Why was so little attempt made to create or arouse the kind of discipline that comes from within, that arises from understanding rather than fear? From my studies of history I knew that during the American Revolution and the Civil War many of the military units elected their own officers by democratic vote. Such a practice would be ruled out as unthinkable today, but the soldiers of 1776 and 1861 were just as valorous and disciplined in battle as the soldiers of 1941. Why was that?

I came to the following conclusion. You don't have to frighten men who volunteer to fight, or men who know what they are fighting for and are enthusiastic about fighting for it. It is different with an army of youthful conscripts who know little about political or international affairs, and care less—such as the draftees of 1941 were by and large. This was before Pearl Harbor, of course, and the situation changed when war was declared. But it did not change basically. Most of the troops I knew never did have a clear idea of what the war was about, and they paid little attention to the official explanations and orientation talks. They fought to save their lives and get it over with so that they could go home. I don't blame them, and I know that discipline is necessary in every enterprise, but I still say you can't make good soldiers or good members of society primarily through intimidation.

The chief topics of conversation among my fellow soldiers were sports and women. I never ran across any soldier who agreed fully with my socialist ideas, which I did not conceal but which naturally I did not go around flaunting either. I often felt isolated and lonely among them, especially after discussions that showed how politically uninformed and uninterested they were. But despite their general political inexperience I found that they were capable of acting courageously and vigorously in situations where they clearly saw their rights and interests were affected.

For example, the draft law passed in 1940 had set our term of service at one year. But near the end of the first year, the military and political authorities in Washington decided that we should be kept in the service for another eighteen months. This produced a surprising wave of indignation and protest among the ranks, something like the we-want-to-go-home demonstrations that exploded at the end of the war.

The proposed extension seemed like a breach of contract to most of the men, and especially to those who had volunteered so they could get their year's service out of the way before getting married or starting college. Notices appeared on the bulletin board prohibiting any letters to Congress, and our first sergeant assembled us to say: "Any of you guys have a complaint, you bring it to me. Anybody caught sending letters to the president or signing petitions will get a court-martial sure as hell." But the draftees kept writing letters and signing petitions of protest, and it was common to hear soldiers vowing that they would go over the hill in October, when the first year of the draft ended. I don't know how many made good on this threat, but I got a new respect for my fellow soldiers. The furor did not die down until Pearl Harbor and the declaration of war by Congress.

My company stayed in training at Fort Bragg until October 1942, when we sailed overseas. Just before we sailed I got a sad letter from my mother. My father had suffered a stroke and the doctor said that he would probably never be able to work again. I wrote back, expressing my grief and my remorse over the one serious quarrel I ever had with him, and telling my mother to spend any or all of the allotment checks she had been saving for me.

We spent a week in North Ireland, another in Scotland, and then we sailed off with a huge convoy. On our fifth day at sea they let us know our destination was North Africa. We landed in Algeria on November 8, 1942. I lasted exactly one year and one day after that.

Our ship, the *Leedstown,* was bombed right after we landed and went down before most of our equipment could be unloaded. We marched inland toward our first objective, an airport called Maison Blanche. On the way, a French seventy-five hit in front of us and we hit the ditch. It was our first battle, but it did not amount to much. The French held us up but the next day they surrendered. That night, as we were getting ready to bed down, someone took a few potshots at us and disappeared. I don't think he was a soldier, but an Arab or a Frenchman with a gun who resented our presence. Ordered out to get him, we crossed a field to a house where he might (or might not) have gone. A sergeant threw a grenade at the corner of the house, tearing a hole in the bedroom wall. The occupants were scared out of their wits but they could give us no information about the sniper. I felt ashamed of the damage done to their home, which struck me as needless and callous. Later such incidents became so frequent that I never bothered to think about them.

The next day our outfit surrounded a small French garrison in a village whose name I don't remember. The big question was whether they would surrender or fight. Our company commander, Captain Hutchinson, got the French commander to discuss the question. Meanwhile, we tried to talk to their troops. Our objective was to get some good wine from them, and since I had studied a little French and German in school, I acted as would-be interpreter. Finally, they understood what I was saying, and brought the wine. Captain Hutchinson had similar success, and the garrison surrendered without trouble. Drinking the wine and fraternizing, we thought war might not be so bad after all.

But war with the Germans was another story. Their morale was still high, and their planes, which seemed to be bombing and strafing everywhere we went, produced plenty of casualties. In fact, once we got a taste of them we never had another hour of confidence or ease until the whole North African campaign was finished. My company marched back and forth, did guard duty at railroads and supply depots, and dug in deep to escape the aerial and artillery bombardments. During this time I had a chance to get a look at the Arabs. From the way they acted, they didn't seem to think the war was any of their affair, or in their interest. Many were so poor that they lived in makeshift shacks in the fields; the only covering some had for their bodies was an old potato sack slipped over their heads. They had the idea that all Americans are rich and they were always after us for shoes. But they did not seem to have any idea that their terrible conditions would be different, no matter who won the war.

We were still green troops in February 1943 when we reached Kasserine Pass by convoy. It was our first direct encounter with the Germans and they beat us badly. For four hours we crouched and shook under a deadly artillery bombardment, and then we were routed out of our positions. Retreating out of the pass, we came out on a great open plain, cut across by deep ravines and surrounded by mountains. The plain was about fifteen to twenty miles long and wide. As I reached it, I saw thousands of our men running wildly in different directions. It was no orderly withdrawal—we just ran, throwing away all of our equipment except rifle, cartridge belt and canteen. I was soon separated from my company. The Germans came after us, on foot, in captured jeeps and by plane. It was a beautiful sunny day—perfect weather for strafing by the German planes.

I stopped for a minute in the middle of all the panic, trying to reason out a course of action as coolly as possible. I made up my mind to stick to the top of the plain as much as possible because there I could at least see where I was going. About half the men chose the ravines, which were ten to twenty feet deep and as wide as an ordinary street at home. I had to go down into them five or six times before I got across the plain, but I always went back up again. I also decided to stay by myself as much as possible, rather than gang up with others and make a more inviting target to the planes. I passed an officer trying to round up men for an orderly retreat, but I pretended I didn't hear him when he called in my direction. I got through all right and later learned that many who went into the ravines had been ambushed.

After night fell, I was picked up by a jeep and returned to my own outfit. All the next day stragglers kept coming in. Our company lost twenty-four men, killed or captured, almost one-eighth of our strength. One of the dead was Sergeant Tansey of New York City. His wife bore him a child after we went overseas and he had told us many times about the celebration he was going to throw when he saw the baby the first time. Unfortunately, he had never applied for GI government insurance. We took up a collection of $500 and sent it to his widow.

Just thinking about that year still wearies me. At first I tried to keep up with what was going on in the world, to follow the political maneuvers with the French, the Russian war news, reports of the coal strikes at home and so on. But it was too much of an effort. We were tired all the time, and our nerves began to go bad. I got thinner; there was not an ounce of fat on my body. Sometimes, as I hugged the ground and waited for a shell to land, everything took on a dream-like quality and I expected to wake up in my own bed at home any minute. But it went on with few interruptions for an entire year.

After Kasserine, our next big action was at El Guettar in the spring. There was a young fellow in my platoon named Andres, I believe his first name was Robert. He was only about twenty, a Regular Army man who had joined up before I was drafted. We used to sit and talk a lot, and I became fond of him. He told me about his home in Louisiana, a small farm, and why he had left it to join the army. I said, "I'll bet you're sorry now." But I don't think he was. He didn't like marching and fighting—he wasn't looking for something glamorous—it was just that he had been so unhappy and poor on the farm that any change seemed for the better.

We got orders to dig in at a bank along a road when we came under heavy shell fire near El Guettar. The fire was coming at right angles to the road, so naturally we dug into the bank which was not facing the direction from which the firing came. But Andres crossed the road and dug into the bank there. We shouted at him to come back, we told him what a foolish and dangerous thing he was doing. But he refused. "I'll be all right here, this is good enough." Half an hour later his hole suffered a direct hit, and after the battle we threw the pieces of mangled flesh and bone back into the hole and covered it up before moving on. The poor devil had dug his own grave. After that I hardened myself, swearing I would not become too friendly with anyone who might be dead tomorrow; it was easier to march with a minimum of emotional baggage.

Near El Guettar too there was a strafing attack that missed me by a few seconds. In the dusk those screaming planes swooping down and spitting fire resembled big bats out of hell. They followed us, haunting and keeping us awake through the final days of the drive that ended German power in Africa, and kept on harassing us even after the fall of Bizerte. We bivouacked near Oran until they got ready for the next invasion. The rest period we got was all too short, and then we were given another period of basic training. Once, when we were on a course to condition us to live fire—we wondered what madman had dreamed that one up—an artillery shell fell short, wounding a dozen men. Some of the men said they were glad to get away from the retraining and onto the ships for the invasion of Sicily, which came early in July.

Sicily was the same story over again. We knew how to fight better, but the terrain was worse, the enemy more stubborn, the casualties bigger. Our company commander was shot squarely between the eyes. I was pinned down once for an entire half-hour under crossfire from rifles, mortars and machine guns, and owed my life to a slight depression in the ground that I happened to roll into. Men began to crack up. Not the worst nor the weakest necessarily—but often the best, the kindest, the most considerate. I am a slow thinker with a poor imagination; maybe these shortcomings saved me. But I no longer could see ahead. I lived just for the moment and in the moment, shutting everything else out of my mind. When I saw others get wounded, I would say to myself, "But I don't have a charmed life," and then I would refuse to follow the thought further.

The worst comes out in a man under such conditions; the best too. I saw men succumb to cowardice, and thereby endanger the lives of others; I also saw men risk their lives consciously, deliberately, to protect a buddy; sometimes it was the same men, in the same hour. Man is capable of all kinds of things—the vile and the noble; a great deal depends on the conditions around him. When we get control over our conditions, when we abolish war and quit acting by the law of the jungle, I am confident that man will think and act as differently from us as we do from the ape.

Every once in a while we would hear about another soldier shooting off a toe or finger to get himself sent to the hospital. I even saw one soldier shoot himself in the toe. "It was an accident," he cried when I went up to him. Of course, everyone said that on the five or six occasions that it happened in my or nearby companies. It may have been in some cases; nobody could prove otherwise. A few times I thought of doing the same thing, but I just couldn't. I guess I lacked either the nerve or the initiative to inflict a wound on myself.

Just before the Italian invasion early in September 1943, I was transferred to the 3rd Division, 15th Infantry, K Company. We landed below the Salerno beachhead and marched inland, up the peninsula until we came to the Volturno River. The Germans were waiting for us again when we waded across one night, and the monotony of battle, digging in and marching was resumed. My escapes became more narrow, but it was the weather I cursed most of all from then on. It was always raining, we were always wet. I never seemed to get enough rest. Once I was so fatigued I just had to sleep whatever happened. It was raining heavily, and my foxhole dug in a hill was quickly filled with water. I couldn't fall asleep there, so I crawled out and lay on the ground where I fell asleep though the water continued to run under me like a brook. Later, when I woke up and found that the Germans had been sending over shells for some time, I knew I was getting careless. But I seemed to be losing control over myself.

The farther we went up the peninsula and the closer we got to Germany, the more the resistance hardened. Before, the Germans, after losing an action, used to withdraw a distance before standing and fighting again. Now they always left small groups behind to delay our advance. It was costly to dig them out, and demoralizing never to know when someone behind us would start sniping.

We were out on a small patrol along the bed of a stream once when a young German soldier practically walked right into our arms. He surrendered without any trouble at all, and then broke down and cried like a baby. I don't know if it was because he suddenly found himself without a friend in the world and facing an uncertain future, or out of relief at the thought that for him the war was now over.

I noticed my platoon sergeant watching our prisoner closely as he wept with his head on his hands at the side of the stream. This sergeant was a first-rate soldier, but there were times when he seemed ready to begin crying himself. When we met extra heavy resistance or suffered extra heavy casualties, he would begin to discuss the situation with a peculiar catch in his voice. I figured he was beginning to wonder if he would make it.

In a few minutes we got into a fight with the comrades of our prisoner. It is hard to tell if you have hit a man you fire at, and I never knew all through the war if I had killed anyone; you could never be positive because you were hardly ever the only one firing. But in this engagement I think I killed a German soldier. He went over on his side after I fired and did not move any more. We were driven back and I never knew for sure. I hope I didn't kill him.

I was attached to our headquarters bazooka squad when we reached the San Pietro area early in November. My job was carrying the ammunition for the bazooka. We came to a mountain with a rounded top that was occupied by the Germans and gave them a good position to command the whole area. Our officers told us we would have to drive the Germans off the mountain, or find some way of bypassing it. It didn't seem to me that they could be dislodged by anything but planes, but I didn't spend much time worrying about that. I was more concerned at that time in trying to get dry, or not wetter.

We were sent out along a trail in an effort to bypass the mountain, but after an hour artillery and mortar shells poured down on us, and we had to dig in. For some reason I felt extra jumpy. I left the hole I had dug, moved away and dug another. The next morning, I found that a dud shell had landed exactly on the spot I had left.

That morning some German planes came over to strafe us. I was watching one plane which skimmed along the tree tops when suddenly it came plummeting straight to the ground, crashing not far away. Its motor had been shot clean out of it. We heard that in falling it had killed our battalion major. Not long after, I was called back to company headquarters. Waiting nearby, I dug a hole against a wall and covered it with my shelter-half to form a canopy against the rain. Then I looked around and discovered the major's body in a ditch a few feet away, face down, with the motor resting squarely in the center of his back. I felt too tired to get up and go somewhere else, and I just sat there staring at him for a while. A mortar shell struck close by. After a while, I began to feel wet. I looked up and saw the mortar shrapnel had riddled my shelter-half like a sieve.

The shelling got worse, and we moved back to our starting point to try another route, through a deep ravine along a stream and then out across a field strewn with huge coils of barbed wire. The wire was unfastened and lay in loose coils all over the field. Fearing a trap, we had to cross the wire on the double. It was difficult to run and not get tangled up in the wire, and I fell flat on my face several times.

After crossing the field and beginning to climb a small mountain, we ran into an attack. I saw men getting wounded all around me. I passed Sergeant Stiles, in charge of my squad. He lay on the ground bleeding from a wound in his neck. I stopped to see how he was, although we had never gotten along well together. He was still alive, looking shocked and surprised, as though he had never expected such a thing to happen to him. We had to go on, however, because the Germans opened up from brush piles ahead of us. We lost a number of officers there too.

We retreated and advanced up and down that small mountain, or maybe it was really just a big hill, for another day or two. One morning we were ordered part way up it again, and told to dig in and wait. The man in the hole with me was from Brooklyn, and I am sure his name was Schulman. I hadn't known him long. He had been a milk truck driver and was a little older than me. He was married, although not for long, and all he ever talked about was his wife and how much he wanted to see her. He said he'd give anything in the world to get back to her and start raising a family, although he wasn't sure that he could do it now, the army had pooped him so.

He talked a lot, and then I decided to catch a nap. He may have slept too. When I woke up, I asked the time and he said three. I said, "The butler must have forgotten to announce when dinner was served. I'm hungry—let's eat." Our movement in reaching for our packs must have attracted someone's attention because a mortar shell hit right behind us. First I heard the noise of the shell landing, and then I felt a sharp blow on the back of my legs, roughly the same kind of feeling you would get if someone hit you there hard with a baseball bat when you weren't expecting it. I found myself sitting on the ground outside our hole and leaning forward rather dazed. My helmet flew off into space and I never saw it again. Schulman was stretched out full length beside me. He was wounded fatally and soon died. If he hadn't been between me and the shell, I probably would have been killed too.

I was lucky to get medical aid almost immediately. The medic who came in response to my calls examined me, applied something and said, "Well, they'll take you back to a hospital where they'll amputate your legs and then when you get back to the States the army will give you a new pair." I didn't know whether to believe him or not; sometimes combat humor can be pretty grim. But I suppose he was trying to be kind, to assure me that I would live.

It was dark before men came with litters to carry me to an ambulance which drove me to a field hospital. I was examined by two different doctors at the same time. They told me my legs were in pretty bad shape and both would have to be amputated. I told them to go ahead and so they operated on me simultaneously, and they both came off around the same time.

A few months later I happened to read an item in Walter Winchell's column about a woman who had written to General Mark Clark in Italy asking him if he would please send her husband home for a few days. She said she had not seen him for a long time and missed him terribly. She got a letter back from the general, courteously saying that he was very sorry but her husband was badly needed and could not possibly be spared at that time. The next day she got a telegram from the War Department announcing that her husband had been killed in action. That was Schulman.

4

The third catastrophe

After the operation, they put me to bed in a hospital ward. The only thing I remember thinking before falling asleep was, "Now, at last, I am going to get a real rest." I stayed at this field hospital for about ten days until the doctors thought I was strong enough to travel again. I must have still been in a daze, because although I was conscious a good part of the time, I don't remember thinking about anything. A British field artillery unit stationed nearby fired at the Germans every once in a while and I would just lie there listening to the whine of the shells as they passed over. Suddenly, after about a week, my mind started functioning normally again. I then realized for the first time that the war was over for me, that I would soon get away from it all, from the noise and the wetness, the marching, the tension and fatigue. "I made it, I'm coming out alive!" The thought excited me so much that I almost burst out laughing. The excitement did not keep me awake long, however, and I soon fell asleep again to the melody of the shells.

But the next morning everything appeared different. Alive—sure, but what kind of life? A picture came to my mind of a legless man who used to sit in a boy's wagon outside of a five-and-ten in Newark, selling pencils. I don't know if he was a veteran, or just wore an army shirt to arouse sympathy. I thought of my father and mother. They were depending on me to help take care of them, and now I would be shipped home a cripple, thrown on them as an extra burden for the rest of our lives.

All of us had talked a thousand times about the day when we would walk back into our homes, or the homes of our friends and loved ones. As I thought how things really would be now—I would have to be wheeled or carried home—I began to cry. My walking days were over.

I thought of the girls I had known, of the ones who attracted me the most but married someone else, of others whose faces had appeared in foxhole dreams. How could I want anyone to turn herself into a lifelong nurse? I was thirty-one years old, had lived less than half the normal span and had missed many of the normal joys that a man experiences by that age. "Now I can say good-bye to all that," I thought. "They amputated not only my legs, but all my hopes of ever having a normal personal life." I felt empty and everything I thought, saw, heard and tasted turned bitter. It was the low point in my life.

But such moods can't last forever; we adjust ourselves to even the worst misfortunes. My despair gave way to indifference. I was shifted to other hospitals, stayed a day or two for rest, and then moved on again. I reached one hospital just at dusk and was about to go to sleep when I heard music from a loud speaker system. I had not heard any music at all since coming overseas, and it was beautiful. I lay there and listened and began to glory again in the fact that I was still alive. Since then I have believed that under certain circumstances music can have a pronounced medicinal value. I never again thought I might as well be dead.

I reached the 300th General Hospital in Naples in time for a delicious Thanksgiving dinner, which I ate with pleasure. An hour later I threw it up and became violently ill. For a long time I couldn't eat anything and keep it down. They told me I had jaundice. I must have been very sick. Seven or eight days in a row I received blood transfusions. Several times five or six doctors would gather around me and discuss me in technical terms I could not understand. They came at all times, day or night, and once in a while one of them would feel my stomach.

There was a nurse here on night duty, dark-haired, with glasses. I guess she was what you would call plain looking, but I was never gladder to see anyone. As soon as she came in, she would hurry over to my bed to find out how I was. She bathed me and did everything she could to make me comfortable physically and mentally. Her mere presence always made me feel better. She was a fine person. If I hadn't been so sick, I would have found out her name and address and tried to correspond with her.

She was the first one to ease my fears about my economic status by telling me about the lifetime pension I would get from the government and showing me that it would be enough to take care of my parents as well as me. She also told me about the great progress that was being made in the field of artificial limbs, and how certain it was that some day I would be able to walk again. I remembered the words of the medic near San Pietro. I didn't really believe I would ever walk again, I feared that she was just trying to cheer me up. But she meant so well that I did not have the heart to tell her what I thought, and I pretended a confidence that I did not really have. Our talks probably did me as much good as the medical attention because they made me think about things other than myself.

I was the only amputee patient in this hospital at the time. The doctor wanted to perform another operation on me. They had taken off my left leg above the knee, and my right just below. He said the stump below my right knee was too short to be of any use and would get in the way of my using an artificial limb. But I was still too sick to go on the operating table. By the time I was able to undergo another operation, my time at the 300th was up—patients stayed there one month before being moved back to the next hospital—and the doctor said he would recommend such an operation in the medical report to be sent along with me. This made me take the whole question of artificial limbs more seriously.

Next I was evacuated by plane to the 64th General Hospital near Bizerte in North Africa. The doctor here did not think it necessary to amputate my knee. At any rate he said he wasn't going to do it, but would let them do it back in the States if they felt it had to be done. They never amputated it.

Here I came into contact for the first time with other amputees, although I was the only double case. At first I thought the hopes they had in artificial limbs, and the future generally, were misplaced and pitiful, but before I parted with them I had become infected with some of their optimism. My legs were put in traction here. A sock was glued in some fashion on each leg, and a weight of about six pounds was tied to the end of each sock and hung by a rope over the end of the bed. The weights were supposed to stretch the skin on my stumps, pulling the skin down over the open ends, after which the ends could be sewn together. The weights kept pulling me down to the foot of the bed and I was always pulling myself up again. It felt like someone pulling on your ankles all the time. The first night I kept waking up with the fantasy that the skin on my entire body, including my head, was slipping off me and that if I was not careful they would find me the next morning completely skinless, and all my skin in one piece on the floor on top of the weights.

A medical officer came into our ward one day and said, "I understand that you haven't received your Purple Heart yet." I said that was right. He then gave me one, after asking me to sign a statement, probably a receipt. The whole procedure was as unspectacular as the incident that had earned me this award.

From Bizerte I was sent by ship back to the United States. After five months in hospitals overseas, I spent two weeks at Clark General Hospital in South Carolina and proceeded to Walter Reed General Hospital in Washington, D.C., where I was to remain another eighteen months. I was still in traction when I got there, but the important thing was that now for the first time I actually saw soldiers walking successfully on artificial limbs. I knew then I could and would do it too. After pausing to kick myself for having doubted the encouraging words of that nurse, I turned all my energies and thoughts in the direction of the day when I would walk again.

Washington in the spring of 1944 was a place of hope and reunion for me. I began to get visitors from home. My parents came first. My father was now almost sixty-five years old, and he seemed to have shrunk still smaller from his illness. My mother, almost as old, also looked tired and weak. But they were so glad to see me and I to see them that the general effect remained joyful on both sides. Some of the girls I had known for a long time came too, bringing flowers and gifts and greetings from others. My best friend, George Breitman, who was drafted around the same time I was wounded, also dropped in during his last furlough before going overseas.

After a month they operated and closed up my stumps. While waiting for them to heal enough so that I could be measured for artificial limbs, I got to know several of my fellow patients quite well. It would be foolish to paint a Pollyanna picture; there was always a streak of bitterness not far below the surface. But the main lesson they taught me was one of courage and dogged determination to recover the lives of normalcy that seemingly had been blasted away. No matter how badly off you personally were, there was always someone else who seemed to have it worse. There was a lieutenant who had lost both his arms and his sight. Watching him being led or wheeled around made me feel that I could have been worse off. At any rate, I had hopes to sustain me that were forever gone for him. One of the people I became acquainted with at Walter Reed was Harold Russell, who had lost both his hands during maneuvers in the States, and who later became well known for the part he played in the movie, *The Best Years of Our Lives.*

By summer I was fitted for my first pair of artificial limbs. They stood me up between a set of parallel bars, I walked back and forth on my new legs, they made some adjustments and gave me a pair of crutches and a pair of canes. Then they took me back to my ward, where I was on my own, so to speak. Some friends were coming to visit me that day, so I decided to surprise them by coming in their direction on crutches. But after a few hesitating steps, I went flat on my face. It was the crutches that threw me more than anything else and I never used them again. Instead, the canes became like a part of my body. Little by little, I learned how to walk, first the width of the room, then the length of the ward. The first time I made it out to the corridor I felt prouder than parents watching their first-born make the transition from crawling to toddling.

At the same time I was given instruction in how to drive a car with hand controls (I had never driven any kind of car before). I also spent some time trying to learn to play the piano, but gave it up because my amputation prevented me from using the foot pedals effectively.

Eventually I became quite good at walking, relatively speaking, and had less trouble with irritation and infection of my stumps than most of the amputees I knew. When I went back to Newark the first time, on a month's furlough, I did walk into my home after all.

I was honorably discharged from the army in September 1945, a little after the end of the war in the Pacific, almost five years after I was drafted.

The joys of coming home to my family, my friends and the familiar scenes of my home town were great, but they did not last very long. Like other ex-GIs, I felt restless, I needed something to do.

I went to the library and began restudying American history. I spent a great deal of time at party headquarters, talking to comrades, catching up on what had happened during my absence. Gradually, I began to help out on clerical work for the party, addressing and mailing envelopes announcing meetings, press releases, subscription lists, etc. They knew I was looking for things to keep me occupied, and they encouraged me to keep as busy as I could in this way. They also elected me secretary of the branch, which meant I had the responsibility of taking the minutes of the weekly meetings. But the truth is that there was not much of such activity to engage in, and most of my time was free, even after I received a car from the government and diverted myself by riding around several hours a day.

They say that when a man loses his eyesight, other faculties, like hearing, are sharpened as a kind of compensation. The loss of my legs resulted in the strengthening of my arms, and made me aware of things and viewpoints that would not have occurred to me otherwise. Such items go on the plus side of the ledger, I suppose. But there was a minus side too, and that was the one that loomed largest in my mind.

I am not talking now about the obvious aspects of the minus side, like the difficulty in getting around, slipping on the ice in winter, etc. Nor about the uncomfortable feeling you get when you are stared at, or when you receive special attention in getting a seat, or when people treat you with unnecessary solicitude. You don't like such things but you know people are trying to be nice and you don't hold it against them.

The main thing I am referring to is the feeling of separateness, of differentness, that arises from all these other things. Somehow—it's hard to explain, it's not altogether rational—you feel that you don't completely belong. I never had this sensation in the hospital, but it gripped me when I got out, and I couldn't seem to shake it off. I wanted to be a whole man, to think with a whole mind, to be objective in my outlook and behavior. I didn't want to end up by seeing the world through my stumps.

In one of the hospitals overseas, some of the patients talked about what a good thing it would be if every member of Congress had to spend a year in combat. "It would be even better if every one of those politicians lost a leg in battle," somebody said. "Because then they would think it over a long time before getting us into another war." There was general agreement at this. "Yeah, they'd know what it's like then." At first I thought the idea had some merit, but I don't now. Wars are not caused by politicians' ignorance of the horrors of war, and I have not noticed the big veterans' organizations are any more pacific than other groups. Combat experience can be enlightening, but it doesn't necessarily make you smarter than somebody who had the good luck to escape it. Belief that it does results from the narrow, warped, one-sided approach to questions that I wanted to get away from at all costs.

Willard Motley's second novel, *We Fished All Night,* tells about a young veteran who lost a leg in the war and makes the most of his disability in order to promote his political career as a candidate for office. The veteran is actually able to walk without a cane but he uses one anyhow, to attract attention to his war record, and he exaggerates his limp. At the climax of the book, when he is trying to influence some strikers to go back to work, he even takes off his artificial leg, uses a crutch to get up on the platform, and has his trousers so arranged that the empty leg will flap in the breeze.

My problem was not that I felt any temptation to exploit my disability—"commercialize" might be a better word than exploit. That was the last thing in the world I would do. The problem was rather that I was oversensitive to the whole question; I was always asking myself if such-and-such a person thought I might be taking advantage of my disability when my sole desire was to work out a relationship of equality with the rest of the world.

There was something morbid about my preoccupation with this question, I know that. But I couldn't help it; it stuck with me. And it was proof that I had not succeeded in "rehabilitating" myself merely by learning how to walk.

One day I realized that there were only two times when I felt wholly comfortable: in the darkness of a movie, and when I was alone in my car, driving around like everyone else. Then at last I was driven to come face-to-face with the problem I had tried to avoid—getting a job.

In the hospital the boys talked a lot about the jobs they would get when they got out. Some said they had jobs waiting for them at home, but most did not expect to return to former jobs because of their disability. What they had their eyes on was a civil service job, which they said they would have no trouble getting because of the special preference for veterans. In fact, some didn't go home at all, but got a job with the government in Washington and settled down there for good.

I never participated in these discussions. I guess I was inhibited by my eight-year hunt for a steady job before the war and didn't want to build up any more hopes to be disappointed again.

But now I had to face it. Studying at the library, sending out mailings at party headquarters, driving aimlessly around the streets was not enough to keep me busy. More important, these things had not helped me overcome that horrible feeling of differentness that clouded everything I tried to do. There were other factors too. At first my pension of $235 a month had looked like the height of security. But with the prices rising steadily it was not going as far as I had expected, and my parents' social security pension was only $33 a month. If I could get a job, I could solve all my problems, psychological and economic, at one stroke; I would then be able to stand on my own, like everyone else.

I got the job with ridiculous ease, and cursed myself for having wasted almost a year with idle fears of failure. A representative of the Veterans Administration came to my home once and questioned me about what I intended to do. I asked him if I could get a job with the VA. He said he thought so, but suggested I would be better off going to school and learning an occupation that would lead to a good job. I said I didn't feel like going to school and would prefer a job now even if it wasn't too good. He told me I was making a mistake.

Two months later, without any help from him or anyone else, I took and passed a civil service exam. A few weeks more and I was appointed in August 1946 to a job in the Loan Guarantee Division of the Veterans Administration in Newark.

As jobs go, I guess it was nothing to brag about. My pay started at $38 a week, rising to $39 a year later. Veterans who wanted to get a loan under the GI Bill to buy a house or start a business had to come to the Loan Guarantee Division for a certificate of eligibility. I entered their claims in a register, stamped their discharge paper and issued the certificate, which was typed up by one of the girls in our office. My efficiency rating in this job was "excellent."

After more than a year, I was transferred to the Vocational and Rehabilitation Division where I handled contracts made between employers and veterans getting on-the-job training. I recorded information about the amount and frequency of wage increases due the veterans, checking to make sure the wage progressions were correct. My rating in this job was "very good." Toward the end of my second year Congress passed a bill granting pay increases of about $6 a week to all civil service employees.

Nothing to brag about, routine, even dull—but not to me. No corporation president was more content with his job. If what I have written up to now does not explain why I felt this way, there is not much I can add here. For the first time in my life, I had a sense of security. For the first time I had a real job. I was filling it satisfactorily, and although I did not magnify its importance, I was making a slight contribution to the welfare of other veterans. But above all was the realization that I was not socially useless after all, that despite my disability I could hold a job like other people, that in certain ways I was even better off than before I was drafted!

All in all, this was the happiest time of my life since my schooldays. My mother commented once that I was singing and humming again, something she had not heard me do since high school. I remained a member of the party, interested as before in social and political developments, but not as active; I still took minutes at meetings, but had no time now to help in the clerical work. I became a member of the American Veterans Committee and the Disabled American Veterans. I did not go to the movies so often. I seemed to have found a permanent niche—maybe others would call it a rut—and I liked it.

And then on August 16, 1948, came a bombshell more stunning than any I ever experienced in the war. The manager of the Veterans Administration in Newark called me into his private office and handed me a letter telling me I was scheduled to be fired within thirty days on the ground that I was "disloyal" to the government of the United States.

5

The 'loyalty' program

That night I went to see my friend, George Breitman. I must have looked despondent, because when he finished reading the letter, he said, "Well, that was a crummy job anyhow, and this is one way of getting rid of it." I didn't think it was much of a joke. "You must have read about the government's 'loyalty' program," he continued. "If you haven't, you're going to learn about it now, because you're part of it." I admitted knowing something about it, but not much. He said the best thing to do before taking any other steps was to get more information. He promised to go to the library the next day and to consult some people in New York who might be able to advise us. We arranged to meet the next night. I took the letter home with me, but said nothing about it to my parents. I read it over and over again. Marked "Personal and Confidential," it was from the Veterans Administration Branch Office in Philadelphia, and this is what it said:

1. In conformance with Executive Order No. 9835 of March 21, 1947, Public Law 419, 79th Congress, Sec. 206, Act of June 26, 1943, and Sec. 14 of the Veterans' Preference Act of 1944, charges are herewith presented for your proposed removal from employ-

ment with the Veterans Administration to become effective thirty (30) calendar days from receipt of this notice. The charges of record are as follows:

a. Evidence of record of membership in the Newark Branch, Socialist Workers Party. The Socialist Workers Party is contained in the list of organizations named by the Attorney General on November 24, 1947, as within the purview of Executive Order No. 9835.

b. Evidence of record of your employment in the Newark Branch Headquarters, Socialist Workers Party. The Socialist Workers Party is contained in the list of organizations named by the Attorney General on November 24, 1947, as within the purview of Executive Order No. 9835.

c. Evidence of record of your financial pledge to *The Militant* Fund Drive. *The Militant* is the official newspaper of the Socialist Workers Party.

d. Evidence of record of your association and activity with persons, associations, movements and groups designated by the Attorney General as subversive in nature.

2. In connection with your proposed removal, regulation entitles you to the following rights and privileges:

a. You have the right to reply to the above charges in writing, under oath or affirmation, within ten (10) calendar days following receipt of this notice.

b. You have the right to an administrative hearing on these charges before the Branch Loyalty Board, upon your written request within ten (10) calendar days following receipt of this notice.

c. You have the right to appear personally before the Branch Loyalty Board, to be represented by counsel or other person of your own choosing, to produce witnesses, and to present evidence in your behalf.

d. If you so desire, but for any reason are unable to obtain a representative, you may request the Branch Loyalty Board, or any responsible Veterans Administration official or officials to assist you in getting one.

e. You have the right, upon request made by you at any stage in the adjudication of your case, to examine a copy of Technical Bulletin 5-85 dated June 29, 1948, Executive Order 9835, and such other directives and regulations of the Commission Loyalty Review Board as may have been made available to the Veterans Administration.

3. During the course of the advance notice period of thirty (30) calendar days prior to proposed removal, you will be carried in an active duty and pay status.

Benjamin E. Hinden
Chairman, Branch Loyalty Board
R.T. O'Brien
Director of Personnel

George had a stack of newspaper clippings and notes beside him when we met the next evening. "I hope you've gotten over the surprise of this thing, and that your head is clear," he said. "Because you've got to read this stuff, and it isn't too easy to follow. After that you've got a big decision to make."

Reading a little, I protested. "But some of this I already know and some of it has nothing to do with me—it's about international politics." "Better read it all if you want to get the whole picture," he answered. "You may as well get it straight from the start. You were a casualty in the last war, and now you are a casualty in the cold war. If you don't understand that, the whole thing makes no sense." I read on, asking questions now and then. At the end of two hours, I could see the background of the letter I had received.

Things were in a mess after World War II. Like many allies in the past, the United States and the Soviet Union began to have sharp differences after their common victory. The people were looking forward to peace, but instead they got tension and talk about the possibility of another world war, even more horrible than the one just ended. Prices began to shoot up like skyrockets, but unlike skyrockets they did not come down again. The housing shortage was still acute. Workers struck in many basic industries. There was general dissatisfaction with the state of affairs, and the Republicans did everything they could to turn this dissatisfaction against the party that was in power.

They charged that the Truman administration was responsible for all the postwar evils. They accused it of being "soft on communism," of "harboring spies" and of "coddling subversives." This was for many years the theme of the House Committee on Un-American Activities, controlled by southern Democrats and Republicans. But it was not until after the war, when newspaper headlines almost daily were blaring warnings against the menace of communism at home and abroad, that the House Committee's demand for a purge of government employees really began to come into its own. The Republicans found "communism" to be an effective anti-administration issue, and they used it for all it was worth in the 1946 congressional elections.

Partly because of this propaganda, partly because of the spreading discontent with inflation, the Republicans made substantial gains in that election, and took over control of both houses of Congress for the first time in sixteen years. The Truman administration, with one eye on the 1948 election and the other on the international situation, decided the best way to deprive the Republicans of the potent "communists in Washington" argument was to outdo them in anticommunist statements and acts. This was in line with the old saying: If you can't lick 'em, join 'em.

And join 'em is just what President Truman set out to do in 1947. In March, he took two important steps partly motivated by the desire to prevent the Republicans from making any more hay on the communist issue at the expense of the Democrats. The first was the proclamation on March 12 of the Truman Doctrine on Greece and Turkey—a warning to the Soviet Union that Washington was ready to go to war rather than let those countries come under the control of any pro-Soviet government. The other was the issuance on March 21 of Executive Order 9835, setting up a "loyalty" program for all government employees.

The "loyalty" program got a friendly reception from the Republican opponents of the Truman administration. Carroll Reece, chairman of the Republican National Committee, said: "I am glad the president, however belatedly, has adopted this important part of the program supported by the Republican Party and its candidates in the 1946 campaign." Republican House Speaker Joseph W. Martin, Jr., said that "it is good to see that he has finally awakened to the truth of what we have been telling him for the last few years." Republican Representative (now Senator) Karl Mundt said: "The president's program is almost precisely that which the House Committee on Un-American Activities has been advocating for at least four years." (*New York Times*, March 23, 1947.)

The executive order directed all government departments to set up loyalty boards to pass on the loyalty of all employees, and instructed the U.S. Civil Service Commission to create an overall Loyalty Review Board to hear appeals from the decisions of the departmental loyalty boards. It set forth the procedure to be followed in investigating employees, including use of the files of the House Committee on Un-American Activities and the FBI among others. The standard set for discharging or refusing to hire prospective employees "shall be that, on all the evidence, reasonable grounds exist for belief that the person involved is disloyal to the government of the United States." The boards were told that in determining loyalty they should consider one or more of the following activities and associations:

Sabotage, espionage, or knowing association with spies or saboteurs; treason or sedition or advocacy thereof; "advocacy of revolution or force or violence to alter the constitutional form of the government"; intentional, unauthorized disclosure of confidential government documents or information; acting in such a way "as to serve the interests of another government in preference to the interests of the United States"; "membership in, affiliation with or sympathetic association with any foreign or domestic organization, association, movement, group or combination of persons, designated by the attorney general as totalitarian, fascist, communist or subversive, or as having adopted a policy of advocating or approving the commission of acts of force or violence to deny other persons their rights under the Constitution of the United States, or as seeking to alter the form of government of the United States by unconstitutional means."

Eight months later, on November 24, 1947, Attorney General Tom Clark set the program into operation by issuing a "subversive" list as guidance for the loyalty boards. On this list were several political and nonpolitical organizations, including the Socialist Workers Party.

"I remember that," I told George. "I asked about it at party headquarters, and they said it was a bad development, but there was nothing to do then but wait and see what came of it. Nothing did, so I forgot about it." And then I remembered another thing. "A couple of months after that they passed out a form down at the VA, asking us to list the organizations we belonged to. But it specifically said 'nonpolitical' organizations, and there was no trouble about it at all. I filled it out and nobody ever discussed it with me again."

"Before we go further," he said, "I want to be sure that you understand what this 'loyalty' program is really aimed at. On the surface, it is supposed to rid the government of spies, saboteurs, disloyal employees, etc. When you talk about it, people will say, 'You can't expect the government to keep such people on its payroll, can you?' Of course you can't expect that, and nobody does. But that isn't the point of the 'loyalty' program at all.

"The government never knowingly hires spies or saboteurs in the first place, and it has plenty of ways of guarding against them. Espionage and sabotage are crimes, punishable by many laws that were on the statute books long before this 'loyalty' program was ever dreamed of. So they obviously don't need this program to punish spies and saboteurs.

"Next, take the question of 'disloyalty.' That's a very loose term. What does it mean? The answer depends on the one who is answering it. Take yourself. Do you recall that when you were appointed to your job you swore an oath of allegiance to the Constitution, pledg-

Carl Gray, Jr.

H.V. Higley

Attorney General Tom Clark being congratulated by President Harry Truman.
Left to right: Clark, Dean Acheson, Alben Barkley, John Snyder, Sam Rayburn,
Louis Johnson, Fred Vinson.

ing to defend and protect it against its enemies?"

"I remember swearing something like that, but not the details," I replied.

"All government employees swear that when they get their job," George explained. "There's a law that requires it of all appointed or elected government employees. I would have to take that oath myself if I was elected in November." (George was the Socialist Workers Party candidate for United States senator from New Jersey in 1948.)

"Now follow me closely," he continued. "That oath you took was not just a mere formality; it was a sworn affirmation of your loyalty. Do you know what they can do to you if you lied when you took that oath? They can indict you for perjury and if they can prove you lied they can send you to prison for a good number of years."

"You mean that under this program I can be sent to prison as well as lose my job?" This was really new to me.

"No, you can't be sent to prison under the 'loyalty' program; the only punishment there is loss of your job. For committing perjury when you take an oath, you can be convicted and imprisoned—if they can prove their case to a jury. Do you get the point now?"

I admitted I didn't.

"Don't you see, long before they started the 'loyalty' purge, they had a law which gave them full power to get rid of so-called disloyal employees. They didn't use that law against you, and they aren't using it against other victims of the purge. Instead, by executive order, they started something else. Why? You've got to ask yourself why. And the answer lies in the nature of the 'loyalty' program itself. They don't have to *prove* that you're disloyal under this new procedure; they don't have to give you a trial; they just haul you up before some board and heave you out. They don't have to follow legal procedure; they don't have to prove that you are disloyal. On the contrary, you have to prove that you're not disloyal. Instead of being considered innocent, you are considered guilty unless you can prove otherwise. That's why I say this new program is not designed to weed out actually disloyal elements. It is designed to give the government arbitrary power to fire anybody whose ideas it doesn't like."

George's analysis made sense to me.

"The next question is: What can you do to clear yourself if you are accused of disloyalty? And here the cards are stacked against you in the following ways:

"You've read the executive order. Did you notice how vague much of it is? That opens the door to all kinds of abuses, to interpretations and enforcement of the order in arbitrary ways. Take the reference to 'sedition.' Just what is sedition? I repeat that it depends on your interpretation. Some members of the House Un-American Activities Committee think it is seditious to advocate the abolition of Jim Crow segregation laws in the South. Many conservatives think it is seditious to advocate a change in our economic system. When you read some newspapers, you get the impression they consider it seditious to question the correctness of any aspects of the administration's foreign policy.

"Or take the reference to 'revolution,' which the order puts in the same category as advocating 'force and violence to alter the constitutional form of the government.' You know that our party stands for a socialist revolution but you also know that we don't advocate violence to achieve it. Two different things are lumped together here. Who decides what is a revolution then, or what you and I mean when we talk about a revolution? Some Republicans never get tired of denouncing Roosevelt's reform program as the 'New Deal revolution.' If they come to power it is conceivable that they could use this 'loyalty' program to fire all government employees who had a hand in the so-called Roosevelt revolution."

"But what about this 'subversive' list?" I asked. "I know that we're not subversive, but how did we come to get on it?" (I was a little ashamed to ask this question because it showed I had not been following political developments or our party's press very closely.)

"The blacklist, of course, is the worst part of the whole thing," he said. "It forbids government employees to have membership or sympathetic association with any group that the attorney general designates as subversive. That's a new thing in this country: guilt by association. Here we have always insisted that a man should be judged on his own merits and not on the basis of those he associates with. In the Soviet Union the Kremlin punishes and persecutes the families and friends of those who are condemned as enemies of the state, and we denounce them for that. But under Executive Order 9835 men and women in this country too can now be punished and persecuted because of their associations.

"The attorney general is given a power that I don't think any American ever held before. He can designate any group in this country as subversive. How does he decide? Nobody knows. The designated organization doesn't even know that it is being considered. It is not given a hearing. It does not know what the charges against it are, or what evidence they are based on. It does not have a chance to confront its accusers or to present its answers to their accusations. Bang!—the attorney general comes out from behind closed doors and suddenly announces that such-and-such an organization is subversive. What can the organization do about it? Nothing, so far as the executive order provides.

"That's what happened with our party, like a bolt out of the blue. No hearing, no evidence, no chance of defense—Clark just put us on his list. You know what happened then. We protested, and demanded that we be removed from the list. No answer. We consulted with the American Civil Liberties Union, which also was alarmed by this whole business. They took the matter up with Clark himself and then told us that he had agreed to hold a hearing for any organization that challenged its inclusion on the list."

"Yes, I remember that," I said.

"So we asked for a hearing. Here's a clipping about it. It was just about three weeks ago that Dobbs wrote Clark a letter about it. [Farrell Dobbs was the presidential candidate of the Socialist Workers Party in 1948.] On July 28 he asked Clark to 'grant such a hearing to the Socialist Workers Party without undue delay.' He asked for an open hearing and to be provided in advance 'with a detailed statement of all charges against our party . . . so that our representatives can properly prepare their refutation.' Just today the party got an answer to Dobbs' letter. Clark has changed his mind, or he was lying in the first place when he talked to the ACLU. Anyhow, he refuses to grant us a hearing."

I let it all sink in, trying to grasp the thing as a whole, and its effect on me.

"Do you see what this thing means now, Jimmy?" George went on after a pause. "It means that you personally are going to have a tough time if you try to keep your job. It means our party has a big obstacle to overcome before it will be able once again to freely exercise its political rights. And it means that this country is facing an awful danger. A terrible precedent is being set by what they are doing to our party, and to you. It involves a threat to the political liberties of all Americans, including those who are not members of organizations now on the blacklist. Because if the party in power can arbitrarily proscribe our organization today, what can stop it from doing the same thing to other organizations tomorrow? If the precedent is allowed to stand in our case, what will stop it from being used in other cases? If this thing goes on, if it isn't challenged and checked, it will mean the end of democracy and the beginning of a police state."

Midnight had come and gone when we finished discussing the implications and dangers of the "loyalty" program. But we still were not done.

"The party has decided that it must fight this 'loyalty' purge, and that is what it is going to do and is doing in every way it can," George said. "But you've got a personal decision of your own to make, and less than ten days to do it in. I think you've got three courses of action to choose from:

"1. You can write the whole thing off as another bad break, resign before the thirty days are up, and go out and look for another job. The records will not show that you have been found disloyal but merely that you left while you were under investigation. You've proved that you can handle a clerical job, and it shouldn't be too hard to find another. I heard in New York today that many of the civil service people under investigation have been following this course during the last month or two, since the purge got into serious motion. Nobody will know why you left the VA except us, a few government officials and the FBI.

"2. You can deny the charges and hope that the Loyalty Board will give you the benefit of the doubt because of your war record. As far as we know, most of the accused employees who want to keep their jobs are following this policy. They deny membership or genuinely sympathetic association with any organization on the blacklist, or defend themselves on the ground that they dropped out of those organizations as soon as they realized they were on the 'subversive' list. As a variant, you might say, if you choose, that you used to belong to the party, but dropped out last November after its name appeared on the list. Then they would have the job of proving that you've been a member these last eight or nine months.

"3. Or, if you want to, you can make a really principled fight against this whole witch-hunt and help to strike a counterblow at those who are trying to destroy democratic traditions and procedures. That is, you could tell the Loyalty Board, yes, you are a member of the Socialist Workers Party, but you deny that you or the party are subversive and you challenge their right to fire you merely because of your socialist views and associations. If you did this, you would be the first government employee to offer a fundamental challenge to the 'loyalty' purge, whose constitutionality has never been ruled on."

I must have looked as confused as I felt. But George kept talking.

"Now the decision is entirely up to you, and you'd better think over all the angles carefully before making up your mind. Nobody will blame you if you follow the first course and just quit before you are formally ruled to be disloyal. It's the easiest way, the one that will cause you the least trouble and controversy. Maybe in the long run you will be better off not working for the government—at least you won't be as subject to thought control.

"And nobody can blame you if you decide to take the gamble of denying past or present membership. But I tell you frankly it is a long shot and you probably won't win it. Another disadvantage is that it will mean you will have to give up all political connections and activities, not only during the time you are being investigated but afterwards, for as long as you work for the government or as long as the 'loyalty' order is in effect or as long as the party is included on Clark's blacklist.

"As for the third possibility, that is the toughest. It would mean a public fight, and everything that goes along with one. There would be publicity, or notoriety, depending on how the press handles it. I know how sensitive you are about your legs, but that would become a big feature of the case, like it or not. You'd have to make speeches, statements to the press. You'd be publicly stigmatized as disloyal. You would lose some of your privacy. It might prove embarrassing to your family as well as yourself. It might turn out that you'd be unable to get another job while the case was being contested. And remember, this is a gamble too—there is no certainty that you would be upheld in the end.

"On the other hand, if you should decide to take this step, it would be a great contribution to the fight to preserve civil liberties in this country and a big help to the party in resisting efforts to persecute and even outlaw it. From the talks I had with people in New York today, I am convinced that many prominent groups and individuals would be grateful to you for a courageous example of resistance to tyranny and would do everything in their power to help you win your fight. But of course that is speculative too. Nobody can guarantee what would happen if you decided to buck the whole 'loyalty' program boldly and openly and as a matter of principle."

I agreed that I would think the whole thing over carefully. As I left, I thanked George for the trouble he had gone to, but I added, a little stubbornly: "The main thing I am interested in right now is keeping my job."

6

A hard decision

That was the truth. Keeping the job was my chief consideration. But before I fell asleep that night I had made up my mind about one thing: I definitely rejected the second of the three alternatives George had outlined. I had done nothing wrong, nothing I was ashamed of, so why should I lie or try to deny what I believed in? I thought of the men who had risked their lives, their fortunes and their sacred honor to set up a republic where men could think and act freely. I always thought their example was good, and tried to follow it. Why should I, a freeborn citizen of the United States, abandon my birthright and surrender the political liberties that blood had been shed to establish? I wanted my job, but I realized that there could be a price for it too high for me to pay.

Since then I have heard about cases in which government employees did try to hide their associations, past or present. I don't want anyone to think that I blame them for trying to keep their jobs at all costs, or that I have a holier-than-thou attitude toward them. Under different circumstances I might have done the same. I think I am as morally scrupulous as the next man, but I also think it is permissible for a man to lie when telling the truth will mean that he will be unjustly persecuted and his family will suffer. If I were in Franco Spain or the Soviet Union and the police asked me questions about an escaped political prisoner, I would not hesitate to lie to them if it would help the prisoner.

Anyhow, I was too angry to accept a situation where I would have to lie and then spend the rest of my life wondering when the lie would catch up with me. "I'll see them in hell first," I told myself.

The next few days were agony for me. I found it hard to concentrate on my work at the VA. I stayed away from my friends and party headquarters. After work I would drive to a park and sit in my car under a tree, looking at the lake and trying to make up my mind. I had made decisions before, but never anything like this. Joining the socialist movement was something I did almost spontaneously; previous events had conditioned me for it so thoroughly that it seemed inevitable at the time. Joining the army was something that happened to me rather than something I did; I never even debated the matter when I was called up in the draft. I made some vital decisions in the army, but they were made under fire and so quickly that I rarely had time to mull over them before acting. But now I had to make a choice on which my entire future might depend. In some ways that can be as hard as engaging in combat.

Self-interest, moral values and political considerations battled each other in my mind, with intense anger sometimes overcoming and sweeping them all out of view. For many years I had adjusted myself to hard knocks and to shrugging them off. But now a regular job and a feeling of contentment and security had made me less philosophical, or less passive. I had something I wanted, and the prospect of losing it gave me a physical pain in the stomach. I remember only two other times when I felt so angry. In 1938, when I saw a gang of Mayor Hague's hoodlums, imported from Jersey City, break up a meeting of the Socialist Party by throwing eggs at Norman Thomas as he tried to speak at an authorized open-air meeting in Newark's Military Park. And in 1940, when we received the tragic news that Stalin's assassins had finally succeeded in murdering Leon Trotsky in Mexico.

Anger and indignation must have played a part in my final decision, but I think I brought them under control. Anyhow, I know I weighed the pros and cons of each possible course of action dozens of times, balancing them one against the other, debating them over and over again. It reminds me now of the comic strip character trying to make up his mind about something, who is being advised and pulled by tiny figures on his shoulders, one an angel with halo and wings, the other a devil with horns and tail. Except that I couldn't tell which half of my mind represented right and which half represented wrong. This is the way the debate went.

A. Quit the job! That's the easiest solution. No fuss, no publicity. There are plenty of jobs available. You've cleared away the mental roadblock that was erected by the depression, so you should have no trouble getting another job. Maybe your new job will be an even better one.

B. But in the government's records you will be recorded as a "subversive" who ran out on an investigation. Maybe the public won't know it, but there will be a stigma on your name, and you'll never forget it.

A. What difference will that make? Your own conscience will be clear. Think of what it will mean if you make a public fight. That will guarantee that you will be stigmatized in public. Temporarily, for sure, if you should happen to win the case. But how can you be sure that you will win? You're only one man, and the whole government is on the other side. And if you lose the case, you will be stigmatized permanently. If it's your good name you're thinking about, the safest thing is just to quit.

B. It's easy enough to decide what's safe. But you'd better think about what is right too. You said your main aim was to keep your job. How can you do that by quitting? Your only chance of keeping the job is by fighting for it. And, as George said, fighting would be a public service at the same time. Your open challenge to the witch-hunt would encourage others to do the same. Even if you lost, your fight would contribute (no matter how much) to the preservation of democratic liberties at a time when they are being threatened on all sides.

A. I agree that somebody has to challenge this purge. But why you? Why should you be the one to stick your neck out? You've had your share of hard times—let someone else take the lead. Haven't you earned the right to take it easy for a while?

B. Suppose everyone thought and acted that way. No one would take the first step and the witch-hunt would proceed without hindrance. A job is important, but what good is a job without liberty? How much satisfaction will it give you when you know that you bought it at the price of acquiescing in a conspiracy to make a police state out of this country?

A. There are disadvantages no matter what you decide to do. Why look for trouble?

B. You've prided yourself on being a socialist. But real socialists never hesitate to defend their freedom of speech and thought—not if it means going to jail, not even if it means risking their lives. How can you call yourself a follower of Gene Debs and yet place personal considerations above everything else?

A. But you're not the right man for the job. You can't speak, you're shy, you won't know what to do, or how to do it. The whole thing might be a flop. How do you know anybody will be interested in what happens to you? You can decide to fight, but you can't do much by yourself, and the party does not wield much influence today. It might end up as a complete fiasco, with your losing the job you have now and the chance of getting another—all for nothing. Sure you want to help preserve democratic rights, sure you want to prevent the party from being gagged and suppressed, sure you want to have a feeling of self-respect—but none of that will be brought about by bucking your head against a stone wall.

B. If you're looking for guarantees of success, you'll never get them. You never demanded such a guarantee when you joined the socialist movement. You knew that the road would be hard, that sacrifices would have to be made, that defeats would be met along the way. You didn't ask for an ironbound guarantee then. Why do it now? If something you really believe in is at stake, you'll be willing to take risks for it. You're always saying how much you admire the Abolitionists—Wendell Phillips and William Lloyd Garrison and Frederick Douglass. You know how they bucked against a stone wall until their heads were bloody. They were a tiny group to start with, persecuted, slandered, ostracized, tarred and feathered, run out of town. But they were fighting for a just cause, and they kept fighting until a majority of the people learned through their own experience that that cause was just. What are you—a summer soldier?

A. But I repeat, you're not the right man for this job. Besides your other handicaps, there's the one that's worst of all: your sensitivity to your injury. Think carefully, man. Think what the publicity would be. George admitted that you wouldn't be able to keep your injury out of it. "Legless veteran," "disabled veteran"—that's what the headlines would say. The press would be more interested in that feature than any other. If you got sympathy, it would be because you lost your legs. People will say it's a shame to fire a war hero, he ought to get special consideration because of the great sacrifice he made, and so on. Is that what you want? Do you want people thinking that you are trying to exploit the loss of your legs?

This was a real poser. It forced me to think about my obsession, to try to understand it. I'm still not sure that I understand it, but since that time it doesn't bother me any more. Maybe there was an element of guilt in my feelings. I read the play *Home of the Brave* by Arthur Laurents, which with some alterations was later made into a movie. It is about a soldier who becomes paralyzed through a feeling of guilt that overwhelms him when his buddy is killed. Maybe I was something like that. Maybe subconsciously I felt I was partly responsible for my injury, and for Schulman's death, because it was at my suggestion to eat that we reached for our packs back there near San Pietro. Or maybe it was a feeling of shame that after all my combat experience, I had been so careless as to let myself get knocked off for a C ration. Whatever it was, the need to make a decision about my job compelled me to look my obsession in the eyes. And when I did, I saw the whole thing was childish, foolish. It was an accident pure and simple, and there was nothing I personally could do to prevent it. Because it was an accident, I had no right to exploit it, but I also had no reason to let it dominate me. Once I thought that, it didn't dominate me any longer. A heavy weight was lifted off my mind when at last I reached this conclusion, and I was almost thankful to the "loyalty" program for having helped to cure me.

B. That's right, you've got to be objective. You're not responsible for your injury, any more than you are for the war in which you got it. If it enters as an element into your case, it's not your fault but that of the people who drafted you and now are purging you. Let them worry about it; it's their responsibility. As long as you make it clear that you are fighting for a principle, and not for special privileges because you are legless, then you have no cause to be sensitive about it.

And that is the way I have felt about it ever since.

But the argument that carried the most weight with me was this one:

B. You fought and risked your life in a war you didn't believe in; are you going to run out on a fight you do believe in? Assuming, of course, that you do really believe in it?

The fight—to preserve the Bill of Rights—is one that I did and do believe in with all my heart and soul. I believed in democracy—rule by the majority and respect for the rights of the individual—long before I heard of socialism. In fact, I became a socialist because I believed that the reorganization of our economic system was the only way to preserve and extend democracy. After I became a socialist, I believed in democracy more than ever, because you cannot achieve socialism by shoving it down the throat of the people, you can achieve it only by convincing them of its necessity, by persuading them of its desirability, by winning them away from their present ideas. And none of that can be done without freedom of speech, press and assembly. Some people say, "You socialists are in favor of freedom of speech now because you need it in order to win enough converts to come into power, but after you win out you'll have a different attitude and you'll want to suppress those who differ from you." That's not so. To me, socialism is impossible unless it is freely accepted by the majority of the people, unless it has their enthusiastic support, their participation, their initiative. And you can't have these things without free discussion and democratic decision. In other words, I am a socialist because I am a democrat and I am a democrat because I am a socialist.

I knew that an unhealthy atmosphere was developing in this country when the cold war began, but I honestly did not realize its full menace until my own case arose. I've explained already that I did not expect World War II to result in the spread of democracy at home or abroad, but neither did I expect it to lead to such a rapid abridgment of democratic rights at home. As I thought about it then, I saw a threat not only to my job and security but to everything I believed in and hoped for.

In the end I decided that there was no real conflict between self-interest and my moral or political duty. I had to fight to keep both the job and the right to hold my political convictions. By doing that I would simultaneously help my personal interests and the broader struggle to preserve the democratic rights that are indispensable for social progress. I felt better when I made the decision: "I've had enough of being kicked around; from now on, I'm fighting back."

At no time in this internal debate, it should be noted, did I ever ask myself the question: "Are you absolutely sure that you are justified in challenging the 'loyalty' program? If loyalty is so hard to define, how can you be so positive that you are not 'disloyal'?" The question did not arise for me now because I had settled it long before the war. To be more exact, because Mark Twain settled it for me. There is a passage in his *A Connecticut Yankee in King Arthur's Court* that I used to know by heart. I wish every school child in this country was acquainted with it too. It goes like this:

"You see my kind of loyalty was loyalty to one's country, not to its institutions or its officeholders. The country is the real thing, the substantial thing, the eternal thing; it is the thing to watch over, and care for, and be loyal to; institutions are extraneous, they are its mere clothing, and clothing can wear out, become ragged, cease to be comfortable, cease to protect the body from winter, disease, death.

To be loyal to rags, to shout for rags, to worship rags—that is a loyalty to unreason, it is pure animal; it belongs to monarchy, was invented by monarchy; let monarchy keep it. I was from Connecticut, whose Constitution declares 'that all political power is inherent in the people, and all free governments are founded on their authority and instituted for their benefit; and that they have at all times an undeniable and undefeasible right to alter their form of government in such a manner as they may think expedient.'

"Under that gospel, the citizen who thinks he sees that the commonwealth's political clothes are worn out, and yet holds his peace and does not agitate for a new suit, is disloyal; he is a traitor. That he may be the only one who thinks he sees this decay, does not excuse him; it is his duty to agitate anyway, and it is the duty of others to vote him down if they do not see the matter as he does."

First I went to my parents, breaking the news about what had happened and what I proposed to do. They couldn't believe it. "Disloyal? There must be some mistake." That was all my father could say. "There must be some mistake; you'll see, they will find out they made a mistake, and then everything will be all right." I don't believe they fully understood what I meant when I said I was going to fight back, although I tried to explain it. My mother said, "Be careful, James, don't do anything rash."

Then I went to George Breitman again, to tell him that I had decided to fight, but that I was still doubtful that such a fight could make any headway. "Let's go to New York now," he said. "I want you to meet a man I've already talked to, George Novack. He's had long experience in the fight for civil liberties, and he wants to talk with you."

This was the beginning of one of the most stimulating associations it has been my good luck to make. George E. Novack is still in his forties, a good-looking man with graying hair and a gentle voice. His job is some kind of public relations work, but actually he is a scholar, a philosopher and a man of action. We later discovered a common interest—American history—but the thing that attracted me to him at once was the completeness of his devotion to the cause of civil liberties, to which he had given most of his adult life. He has actively participated during the last twenty-five years in defense of such people as Tom Mooney and Warren K. Billings, the Scottsboro boys, the Harlan miners, and union organizers tried for "criminal syndicalism" in the Imperial Valley of California.

He also played an important part in organizing the International Commission of Inquiry, headed by Dr. John Dewey, which exposed Stalin's Moscow Trial frame-ups of Leon Trotsky and the Old Bolsheviks. He served as secretary of the Civil Rights Defense Committee, which directed the defense in the Minneapolis labor case of 1941.

I never saw him pause once when there was a call on his talents and time, no matter how much it meant neglecting the work at which he earned his living or the studies in history and philosophy to which he would like to devote all of his time. Sometimes the actions of the human race make you feel cynical, but knowing a man like George Novack restores your belief in man's potentialities. (From now on when I write "George" I am referring to Novack, because it was with him that I worked most closely since the beginning of my case. Breitman plays no further direct part in this story, although as editor of *The Militant* he wrote what I think are the best articles anyone wrote about my case.)

After questioning me about my life and making sure that my decision to fight for my reinstatement was definitive, George Novack explained to me what a civil liberties case entails.

"We will have to set up a committee to handle your defense. If you have no objection, we will call it something like the Kutcher Civil Rights Committee, a name that clearly indicates its objective. You understand of course that this will not be a political organization; we will try to enlist the support of people of all political convictions, and most of those who will join will not share your political views. Since it will be a legal contest, among other things, we will have to get some lawyers too.

"Through the committee we will appeal to every organization we can reach in this country. We will tell them your story, we will explain the issues involved in your discharge, and we will solicit their aid and endorsement for your fight. We will seek publicity in order to make the facts in your case as widely known as we can. Our aim will be to pose this question to every American: Do you think James Kutcher got a fair deal? Where do you stand—for or against him in his fight for reinstatement? Your case is sure to attract attention because it will be the first real test of the 'loyalty' program. If we can mobilize sufficient support behind your fight, we may be able to strike a mortal blow to that unconstitutional measure."

It would be no easy job, he warned. We had no resources to begin with, and our adversary was the administration of the most powerful government on earth. It would involve a great deal of work, and we would both be kept busy for a long time. "The case may take a year or two," he said, "because our lawyers will go through the administrative channels of the Loyalty Board apparatus before going to the courts, and then all the way up to the Supreme Court, if necessary." (As this is written, the case is already in its fifth year.)

I told him that I would do whatever I could to help, but that I was inexperienced, couldn't speak in public, etc. He laughed at this and promised that I would be "making speeches with the best of them" in two months. (It was he who helped me to overcome stage fright and coached me how to speak "the same way you do when you talk to me"—so that eventually I felt no embarrassment whatever in getting up before any audience, large or small.)

"And you'll face your first audience next week," he added, "because the first thing we have to do is prepare a press conference where we will break your story to the public."

While he was working at that, he said, he wanted me to draw up a letter to the Loyalty Board answering their charges against me, and to begin thinking about the statement I would make to the press conference. Under the spell of his enthusiasm and confidence, I agreed. When we parted I was still not sure about what would happen in the future—but I knew we were going to give the would-be thought controllers a run for their money.

I spent the whole weekend composing my answer to the Loyalty

Board. I had never written anything like this before, but I had my heart in it and I managed to express my thoughts and feelings. George Novack said it was a well-written document, and proof that I was being overmodest when I said I was afraid I had little to contribute to our joint work. We sent it off so that it would reach the Loyalty Board in Philadelphia on the same day that we held our press conference in Newark. This is what it said:

In reply to your letter dated August 13, notifying me that I am to be removed from my job as a clerk in the Veterans Administration office in Newark on the grounds of my membership in the Socialist Workers Party, I hereby challenge your right to do so.

I have never denied my membership in the Socialist Workers Party; I do not deny it now; on the contrary, I proudly affirm it. What I do deny is the false accusation that the Socialist Workers Party is "subversive" or advocates the overthrow of the government by force and violence.

The Socialist Workers Party has publicly demanded that it be removed from the "subversive" blacklist compiled by Attorney General Clark; it has publicly requested a hearing for that purpose. Instead of granting such a hearing, the administration has rejected this request and is proceeding to punitive and discriminatory measures against the members of the Socialist Workers Party. This procedure violates my constitutional and civil rights, and smacks of the worst practices employed in police states.

I entered the armed forces in January 1941. My draft board did not ask me about my political views or the party to which I belonged; they drafted me. I became an infantryman, serving in the 9th and 3rd Divisions and participating in the North African, Sicilian and Italian campaigns. When I was at San Pietro, Italy, in November 1943, the German mortar crew on the other side of the lines did not ask me about my political views or the party to which I belonged; they fired at me. The army surgeons did not ask me about my political views or the party to which I belonged; they amputated both my legs, one above the knee, the other just below. The army did not ask me about my political views or the party to which I belonged when it gave me the Purple Heart.

It took me a long time to learn to use my artificial limbs, but I learned how in order to get a job because I must contribute to the support of my aged and sick parents. You can understand that it is not too easy to get a job when you have no legs. But two years ago this month I went to work for the Veterans Administration, and have filled my job satisfactorily. Now you propose to deprive me of that job, solely because of my political views and the party to which I belong. This is political persecution, and I intend to fight against it with all my vigor—because my job is at stake, because a great principle involving my own rights is affected, and because it concerns thousands of other government employees, many of them veterans, whose rights are similarly threatened by this dictatorial procedure.

I make no secret of my views or those of the Socialist Workers Party, which have been publicly expressed for many years over the radio and in the press. I believe that socialism is the only system that can bring humanity peace and freedom, and in support of that belief I propose next November, whether employed by the government or not, to vote for the Socialist Workers Party national ticket, Farrell Dobbs for president and Dr. Grace Carlson for vice president. I do not advocate force and violence to achieve socialism; the only time in my life I ever practiced force and violence was under the orders given me in the army by the U.S. government. I did not believe that the recent war was a war to eradicate fascism and to establish the "four freedoms," and everything that has happened since the end of the war strengthens me in that belief. Furthermore, I am opposed to the preparations for a new war. I am opposed to restrictive legislation against labor and minority groups. I am opposed to witch-hunts and attacks on civil rights. And I am in favor of political organization and action by the working people, who represent the great majority of the population, to put an end to these evils.

You have a right to disagree with my views, but not to deprive me of my job for holding them, or for belonging to a party and associating with people who share them, or contributing my money to support of a newspaper that defends them. I contend that I have the same right to a government job as you or any other American, and that not a single shred of real liberty will remain for anyone in this country if I and other political opponents of the administration in Washington are to be hounded out of our jobs because of the principles we believe in. I have already been deprived of both my legs and my freedom of movement. I do not propose to have any government official deprive me of my freedom of thought and expression and my right to earn a living. The methods employed against me are those of totalitarianism and not of democracy.

Please consider this as my written reply to your charges and my written request for the administrative hearing before the Branch Loyalty Board, referred to in Paragraph 2 of your letter, although like many other people I consider the entire procedure involved in these hearings as illegal and unconstitutional. I insist, however, that this hearing be open to the public and the press, since I feel that this issue concerns the American people as a whole. For the same reason, I cannot restrict the defense of my job to these channels alone, and serve notice on you that I will take such measures as I may find suitable.

I affirm that all the statements made above are true, to the best of my information and ability.

James Kutcher
August 25, 1948

7

Organizing a committee

The press conference was a success. Held at the Robert Treat Hotel in Newark, it attracted reporters and photographers from New York as well as New Jersey. George Novack did most of the talking to the press, but he was not alone. He had the able assistance and legal counsel of Mr. Arthur Burch, a New York attorney. And although only a few days had passed since my meeting with him, he had already reached a number of prominent people in New Jersey, and had interested some to the point where they attended the conference and spoke for themselves.

Outstanding among these was Carl Holderman, president of the New Jersey State CIO Council, who had recently been given the national CIO award for the best work in defense of civil rights during 1948. Mr. Holderman took a clear-cut stand on my case from the very beginning and did more than any other union leader to get the labor movement to help me. Explaining to the reporters that he did not agree with the views of my party, he said: "But I do agree that there is a great danger to democratic rights involved in the prosecution of individuals who hold such views. Regardless of politics, our state CIO and I as its president will give full support to James

Kutcher and to the rescinding of the executive order."

Ewald Sandner, CIO regional director in New Jersey and a veteran of the miners union, spoke too. Expressing approval for Mr. Holderman's remarks, he said he was certain that the national CIO would "repudiate this vicious persecution and give full support to the defense of James Kutcher."

When he finished, my last doubts were gone. To have the support of the New Jersey CIO, with a quarter of a million members, on the very day that the case was presented to the public, and to have the possibility of support from the national CIO and its five or six million members, was evidence enough for me that at the very least my voice would not fall on deaf ears. To some people, ignorant of history, the word "unions" still suggests labor bosses and other unpleasant things. To me it recalls the fact that the unions in our country were always in the forefront of the struggle for democratic rights and other benefits for the people. How many Americans realize, for example, that it was the union movement that led the fight for the public school system? I was not only grateful for their help, but proud too.

Peter Flynn, who was then secretary-treasurer of the New Jersey CIO, made a statement that was short and widely quoted: "The government did three things for Jimmy Kutcher: It gave him a pension. It gave him two artificial legs. And then it gave him his walking papers."

I had never seen any of these union leaders before. But there was one familiar face present: the Rev. John I. Daniel, a Congregational minister who was chaplain of the Newark area council of the American Veterans Committee, to which I belonged. He testified in my behalf, generously declaring that I was "the best liked man in Newark Chapter 1, a loyal member of the AVC." He praised me for climbing the three flights of stairs to attend AVC meetings regularly, and added: "I have never in my life met a person who was more of an idealist than Jimmy." He said all veterans should come to my defense.

George Novack announced that a national Kutcher Civil Rights Committee was in process of formation, a nonpartisan citizens group that would aid my fight to keep my job. Then I spoke a few words: "I am not fighting this case only for myself. This witch-hunt in government offices has gone far enough. Somebody has to stand up some time and call a halt to these persecutions. If, by my stand, I can save any veteran or government employee from persecution in the future, I will consider my fight worthwhile."

The reporters were really interested and asked a great many questions about me, my party and our differences with the Communist Party. After the conference, almost everybody crowded around to shake my hand and wish me luck. I made a pledge to myself that I would not fail these warmhearted people and that I would never do anything to make them regret the stand they had taken.

The next day's papers printed the story with pictures, excerpts from my letter to the Loyalty Board, and so on. I was still working at my job in the VA, and everybody in the place had read the story. But I did not hear a hostile comment from anyone. They were all surprised because I had never discussed politics on the job, not thinking it was much of a field for socialist activity. One employee came over, however, and said, "You really told them off good."

The publicity must have been very effective, because since that time, I keep running into people in all parts of Newark who remember those first newspaper articles and want to know how I am getting along. All my fears about how people might react proved groundless. Nobody ever said anything unpleasant to me. My uncle, now dead, had a newspaper stand in his candy store, and he told me that for several days after the story first appeared people kept asking if I was a relative of his and expressing indignation at what had happened. My address was printed in the papers too, and in a day or two I began to get letters and postcards although no one solicited them. These two were typical:

"My wife and I think socialism is utopian, and believe that a man of your common sense will realize this yourself some day. But we say God bless you for your honesty and courage! If only our public officials had some of your qualities, this would be a better country to live in."

Press conference held September 1, 1948, in Newark, New Jersey, to announce formation of the Kutcher Civil Rights Defense Committee. Left to right: George Novack, James Kutcher, Carl Holderman, Rev. John I. Daniel.

James Kutcher Civil Rights Defense Committee banquet held in Detroit, Michigan, October 22, 1949. Left to right: Dr. Orville Linck, Dr. Henry Hitt Crane, George Novack, James Kutcher, Al Barbour, August Scholle.

"I wish to say my whole family and our entire circle of friends are in sympathy with your cause. These various boards are missing the foundations of these our United States, which were the *free* choice of political party, religious beliefs, etc. Enclosed you will find $1 to help your fight for your right to believe in any philosophy. I care not what political or religious creed you hold to and preach. You should have a right to your beliefs! I wish that I could send you $1,000 or $100,000. Fight On!—An American Lutheran Protestant, Montclair, N.J."

There was an interesting incident in connection with the newspaper publicity. The *Newark Star-Ledger* is a conservative newspaper and has no use for radicals of any kind. I was pleasantly surprised, therefore, to see that its first news story about my case was prominent and on the whole quite impartial. Later I was told (third- or fourth-hand, and so I cannot vouch for it) that the editor was out of town when the story was submitted, and that he didn't like either its contents or the position it got on the top of the left-hand side of the front page.

Anyhow, an editorial on my case appeared in the *Star-Ledger* on the following Sunday. It was an obvious attempt to let its readers know that the editor had no sympathy for me, and to counteract the effects of the CIO's support. It was entitled "Question of Facts" but it contained a number of incorrect statements which could easily have been avoided by someone who read the *Star-Ledger's* own news story carefully and honestly. It claimed, for example, that I had been "discharged" because I was "found to be subversive" when the truth was that I had not yet even been suspended and I still was to face the Loyalty Board for the first time.

The editorial professed to have an open mind on the case, but it hastened to assure its readers that the members of my party are hostile to "our way of life." It pretended to be glad that the CIO was helping me, and then it sought to create the impression that the CIO did not know what it was doing because "it should not be assumed that he is being persecuted . . . [The public] will not assume an injustice has been done until some substantial proof is developed."

This warning against helping me until more "facts" were known would read better today if the *Star-Ledger* had helped to provide the public with all the facts about later developments in the case. But the truth is that after two months in which it printed a number of short items on my case, the paper curtain descended. Although the *Star-Ledger* continued to receive wire dispatches and press releases about the case, only two more small items appeared in that paper during the next three years. The editorial was apparently a delaying action. The editor of the *Star-Ledger* was not at all eager to help spread the facts that he had urged the public to study.

The *Star-Ledger* was one of the only two daily papers in this country to caution its readers against helping me. On the other hand, the *Newark Evening News,* also a conservative paper, gave me fair treatment all the way through, reporting the main facts adequately and objectively. The *News* never commented on my case editorially until four years later, but it never withheld important news on it.

When I say that the initial response to the case was on the whole friendly and encouraging, I don't want to leave a wrong impression. Many people were personally sympathetic, but at the same time reluctant to join a committee or sign their names to a letter of protest. In the first stages, especially, it proved much easier to get organizations to endorse my fight, pass resolutions or contribute money toward our legal expenses than it was to get individuals to join our committee. And yet without an imposing committee of public figures the work of approaching organizations for help would remain strictly limited.

George Novack assured me that this was generally the case in civil liberties fights, and that I must not get impatient if we had a slow start in recruiting prominent individuals. "After all," he explained, "the people we are asking to join the committee want to be sure of what they are doing; they want to be sure that they are joining a responsible group, one that will confine its activities to furthering the originally stated objectives, one that will not be used as a political football." He then related to me how the Communist Party, through its front organizations, had abused the confidence of many liberal and labor leaders by getting them to join an organization for one purpose, only to find later that it was being used for quite different purposes.

"We can't blame them for being wary after having had their fingers burned this way in the past," he continued. "In addition, you must take into account the new political atmosphere that is developing in this country since the end of the war. The doctrine of guilt by association has made alarming progress in the last two years. It is beginning to take real courage for a man to stand up for an unpopular cause, and most of all for an unpopular cause associated in any way with charges of disloyalty or subversion. The bravest men have a living to make, and we mustn't blame them in the least if they prefer to think it over two or three times before taking a step that might conceivably jeopardize the welfare of their families.

"Besides," he laughed, "in this field, as in most others, nothing comes to you on a golden platter; you have to work for what you get. People aren't going to come looking for us in large numbers. We have to go and look for them. The only difficulty is to get the ball rolling."

And work for it we did. Eventually, a large committee of some of the most prominent labor, liberal, religious and educational figures in this country was assembled to help me, and they all joined voluntarily out of devotion to a great principle. But it was not easy to reach them and find them in the first place.

To get the ball rolling we needed a small sponsoring committee to invite others to join. Carl Holderman of the New Jersey CIO was the first to volunteer his name for this purpose. We agreed that it would be a good idea to get a number of veterans as sponsors. The first one we thought of was Merle Miller, former executive editor of *Yank*, the service magazine, and author of a widely discussed novel about veterans, *That Winter*. (Later he wrote a novel about the "loyalty" program in Washington and a book about the blacklist in radio and TV that was sponsored by the American Civil Liberties Union.) George Novack reached Mr. Miller, through the ACLU, I think, and after convincing him that this would not be a front organization or a scheme for promoting anybody's political program, he signed the initiating appeal. Then somebody thought of Bill Mauldin, the great cartoonist and author of *Up Front* and *Back Home* who became the voice of the enlisted infantrymen in World War II and won the everlasting gratitude of the GIs for his defense of their rights and grievances. From his postwar cartoons it was evident that he was becoming concerned about problems of civil liberties and civil rights, and he proved quite willing to act as a sponsor.

Then I happened to think of the one well-known veteran I was personally acquainted with: Harold Russell, who had won an Oscar for his portrayal of the handless veteran in *The Best Years of Our Lives.* For the last couple of years Harold had been going around making speeches against racial, religious and other types of intolerance. I read one time that he was serving on a committee to defend a Chicago Negro worker who had shot his landlord after four of his children were killed in a fire he attributed to the landlord. Both from these facts and from my own conversations with him I knew him to be moved by sincere humanitarian impulses.

"He's a natural to be chairman of the sponsoring committee!" George cried when I suggested Harold as a possibility. "Let's find where he is at once." In short order he traced Harold's address and in a day or two managed to reach him by phone in Massachusetts.

Harold was genuinely indignant when he heard what had happened to me, and said he would be pleased to lend a hand to protest such an outrage. It was understood that he would serve as chairman of the sponsoring committee, and then as chairman of the committee itself, if the other members wanted him.

I know Harold meant what he said because I have a newspaper clipping from that time describing a speech he made in New York at the Fraternal Clubhouse under the auspices of the Anti-Defamation League, for whom he was making a lecture tour. He spent the major part of his talk discussing what had happened to "my buddy in the next bed at the Walter Reed Hospital." He said he was not a socialist and did not share my views, "but I do defend his right to think, act and do as he sees fit." He scored the undemocratic procedure followed in blacklisting my party without charges, evidence or a hearing, demanded that I should get a fair deal, and read the audience large parts of a personal letter I had written him.

But something was wrong. A copy of the sponsoring letter was sent to him for his signature, but he failed to return it signed. Somebody—his agent or his advisers—was putting pressure on him, warning him not to get mixed up in anything that might bring him a bad reputation, and he did not know what to do. George would reach him by phone, and he would be friendly and express his eagerness to help just as strongly as at the start. Then someone else would talk to him, and he would again fail to send the letter. This vacillation went on for several weeks, delaying the issuance of the letter.

I felt miserable about the whole thing because I didn't want to put anybody on the spot, least of all someone I liked as much as Harold, and I didn't want him to be talked into doing something he was not sure of. But George had told the press about Harold's acceptance of the sponsoring committee chairmanship, and he said it would look funny if the letter went out without his name. So he kept phoning to Harold whenever he could reach him, and finally Harold signed. George himself was the fifth sponsor, and the letter went out at last.

At the same time Harold sent George a letter making so many reservations about his connections with the committee that it was plain he wanted to call it quits. The other sponsors all joined the committee, but not Harold. I don't hold any grudges against him for that. On the contrary, I will always think warmly of him for going as far as he did. His impulses were all on the right side; it was just outside conditions he couldn't cope with. This incident was proof to me of how correct George was when he said nothing came on a golden platter, and everything had to be worked for.

But that was the low point in the process of forming the committee. The sponsoring letter produced wonderful results. I have never met most of the men and women who joined our national committee, and I would like to express my gratitude to them here by listing their names. The most heartening thing about their help was that most of them gave it to one whose political ideas are quite different from their own. That, after all, is the real test of civil liberties. It takes no special vision or courage to defend somebody whose ideas you agree with; the real test comes when you are confronted with the question of helping someone whose ideas you reject or even detest. The members of the committee passed this test with flying colors. May their example become the standard for the whole American people in all civil liberties cases!

I will begin by paying my respects to three of our committee members whom I will never meet, because they have died. Foremost was Dr. John Dewey, the philosopher and educator who never hesitated to step out of his study to take part in public controversy, and who associated himself with the Mooney and Sacco-Vanzetti defense movements, to name only two out of dozens. Dr. Dewey was an opponent of Marxism but that did not stop him from becoming chairman of the International Commission of Inquiry into the Charges Made Against Leon Trotsky in the Moscow Trials, whose findings did so much to expose and discredit those frame-ups. Nor did it stop him later, at the age of eighty-nine, from accepting George's invitation to join our national committee.

Also dead now are John Sloan, the distinguished artist, and Louis Adamic, the writer who incurred the hatred of Stalinists and pro-fascists by becoming a supporter of Tito and who was found shot to death under mysterious circumstances in 1951.

I can only list the others:

Irving Abramson, the eastern regional director of the CIO; Warren K. Billings, codefendant with Tom Mooney in the famous California case; Algernon D. Black of the Society for Ethical Culture; Prof. Paul Brissenden of Columbia University; Arthur Burch, New York attorney; Rabbi Jonah E. Caplan of Congregation Beth-El in Long Island City; Dr. Abraham Cronbach of Hebrew Union College in Cincinnati; Farrell Dobbs, national chairman, Socialist Workers Party;

Kutcher Civil Rights Defense Committee National Committee included: Left to right (top) Warren K. Billings, John Dewey, Bill Mauldin, Alexander Meiklejohn; (bottom) Merle Miller, C. Wright Mills, A.J. Muste, Paul O'Dwyer.

Prof. Thomas I. Emerson of Yale Law School; Duncan Ferguson, sculptor; Clement Greenberg, art critic; Arthur Garfield Hays, noted civil liberties attorney; Carl Holderman; Oscar Jager, editor of the CIO telephone union paper; Rev. John Paul Jones of the Union Church of Bay Ridge, Brooklyn;

Dr. Horace M. Kallen of the New School for Social Research and member of the President's Commission on Higher Education; Alfred Kazin, author and critic; Norman Mailer, novelist; Margaret Marshall, critic; Carey McWilliams, author of many books on civil rights; Merle Miller; Prof. Alexander Meiklejohn of Leland Stanford University; Prof. C. Wright Mills of Columbia University; Lewis Mumford, author and critic;

Rev. A.J. Muste, secretary, Fellowship of Reconciliation; Walter M. Nelson, civil liberties attorney in Detroit; Paul O'Dwyer, New York attorney; Lyman Paine, architect; Prof. Selig Perlman of the University of Wisconsin; William Phillips and Philip Rahv, coeditors of *Partisan Review;*

Prof. Meyer Schapiro of Columbia University; Vida Scudder, professor emeritus of Wellesley College; Max Shachtman, national chairman, Independent Socialist League; Willard A. Smith of Toledo; Mark Starr, educational director of the International Ladies Garment Workers Union, AFL; I.F. Stone, columnist; Dr. Willard Uphaus of the Labor and Religious Foundation; Edmund Wilson, critic; A.L. Wirin, civil liberties attorney in Los Angeles. (Organizations are listed for purposes of identification only.)

In addition, there were hundreds of others who served on local and campus branches of our committee.

Meanwhile, the VA Branch Loyalty Board in Philadelphia notified me that it would hold an administrative hearing on my case on September 10, 1948, and that I should be present with legal counsel and witnesses, if I so chose. I accepted the invitation and repeated my request that the hearing be open to the public and the press. George Novack had a personal interview with Mr. Benjamin Hinden, chairman of the Loyalty Board, on this matter. Mr. Hinden told him that the president's executive order provided only for hearings behind closed doors so as to "protect the individual from adverse publicity." George explained that "this individual considers his only protection is the greatest possible publicity." The ban remained, however, when we went to Philadelphia to open the first legal stage in the case.

8

A fair hearing?

Lawyers are still debating whether or not I got a fair and full hearing in Philadelphia—in fact, whether in the proper sense of the word, I got a hearing at all. Lack of space prevents me from reprinting the entire transcript of the Philadelphia proceedings, but I will summarize them here, as fairly as I can. The reader can judge for himself if it was a fair hearing, in accord with democratic practices and traditions—the kind he would want if his job and reputation were at stake—or if it was a kangaroo court.

The members of the Loyalty Board of Branch Office No. 3, Veterans Administration, who heard my case, were Benjamin E. Hinden, chairman; Dr. William A. Jacques; and John P. Elzroth. They were all supervisory employees of the VA. George H. Merker acted as Management Representative (or prosecutor).

On the other side were I and my two attorneys, M.J. Myer of Chicago and Arthur P. Burch of New York. At our request George Novack, as secretary of our committee, was also allowed to sit in. Witnesses were not admitted until they were ready to testify. Everything took place behind closed doors. I felt I had nothing to hide, but had to abide by their rules.

Mr. Hinden announced the procedure that would be followed and then gave the floor to Mr. Merker to present his case. He read the charges contained in the letter that had been sent to me, relating to my membership in the Socialist Workers Party; my "employment" in the party; my financial contributions to *The Militant;* and my association with persons and groups designated as subversive. Then:

> Mr. Merker: The charges are based upon investigation, reports of which are in the possession of the Board, and no witnesses will be presented on behalf of the government. I wish to call the Board's attention to the reply of the employee by letter dated August 25, 1948, wherein it was stated in paragraph 2, "I have never denied my membership in the Socialist Workers Party; I do not deny it now; on the contrary, I proudly affirm it." I have nothing further to present at this time.

And that was his full case!

Mr. Myer then took the floor. He fully confirmed Novack's estimate of him as one of the finest civil liberties lawyers available, and he did a magnificent job. But he had all the cards stacked against him. For it became clear after he had spoken a few minutes that he was to be barred from going into the central issue of the case.

That issue, as I saw it, was whether or not the attorney general had the right to place any organization on a blacklist on his own say-so—without a hearing, without a chance to see evidence against it, without a chance to rebut the evidence. I had not concealed my membership in the Socialist Workers Party, but I denied that the party was subversive. I contended that the attorney general had not proved it was subversive—he merely said it was—and that therefore his action was unconstitutional. In other words, in line with the accepted tradition that you are considered innocent until proved guilty, the burden of proof—of establishing the alleged subversiveness of my party—still rested on the attorney general.

But no—discussion of that issue was out of order, Mr. Hinden ruled. The Board, he said, was operating under the rules set forth in

Veterans Administration Technical Bulletin 5-85, dated June 29, 1948, paragraph 4g of which said:

"Therefore loyalty boards will not enter upon any evidentiary investigation of the nature of any of the organizations identified in the attorney general's list for the purpose of attacking, contradicting or modifying the controlling conclusion reached by the attorney general in such list. Any and all questions proposed with respect to the merits or appropriateness of the inclusion of a particular organization in such list would, therefore, be for the attorney general to decide and not for the board and the board should permit no evidence or argument before it on the point."

From that moment on I knew that it would be impossible to get justice from this Board. Even if its members had wanted to hear the main issue presented, they were barred from doing so. How could it help being a mockery of decent judicial procedure?

Mr. Myer made a number of attempts to get around this ruling—which put him in the position of a fighter having to operate with one arm strapped behind his back—but with no success. So he went ahead, reserving the right in future proceedings to attack the charges and the constitutionality of the whole business. He made a motion to dismiss the proceeding on the ground that my constitutional rights of free speech, press and assemblage were being violated and that I was being subjected to victimization under the abhorrent doctrine of guilt by association. He charged that Executive Order 9835 was too vague and indefinite in certain parts to be enforced in a fair and impartial manner. He showed how the attorney general's method of listing organizations as subversive violated due process of law. This motion was denied.

Mr. Myer then made another motion to dismiss on the ground that none of the four charges against me proved that I was personally disloyal to the government. It was not enough to determine that I was or wasn't a member of a listed organization, he explained, because the executive order said the standard for removing a person was that "on all the evidence, reasonable grounds exist to believe" that he is disloyal. This motion was in line with the accepted tradition that guilt is a personal matter.

Mr. Merker's reply was one that came to his lips like a parrot throughout the whole affair: the attorney general had ruled that my party was subversive, and the Board would have to abide by that. Mr. Hinden denied this motion too.

Then Mr. Myer made a motion with regard to the last of the four specific charges—which claimed that there was evidence of record of my association and activities with persons, groups, etc., designated as subversive by the attorney general. He asked that I be provided with "a bill of particulars as to what association, what persons, what groups, etc., [so] that he will have something specific to meet, or else . . . that paragraph be stricken from the charges."

> Mr. Merker: I wish to state that in view of the peculiar nature of these proceedings and the sources of information upon which they are based, Technical Bulletin 5-85 is explicit, inasmuch as it states that information concerning sources of information are not to be divulged. Consequently, a certain generality of terms is frequently necessary . . .
>
> Mr. Hinden: The information upon which these charges were predicated was based upon a complete investigation conducted by the Federal Bureau of Investigation, and for security reasons the information contained in those reports as to sources cannot be disclosed, and I would like to reiterate the statement made by Mr. Merker within the Technical Bulletin that this statement is made . . . Consequently, the Board must deny your motion.

My lawyer had not asked for the *sources* of the alleged information about me, he had requested only a concrete bill of particulars. But even that was too much for them to give us. Mr. Merker was not exaggerating when he spoke of "the peculiar nature of these proceedings."

By now I felt that we might just as well pack up and go home, for all the good that would come out of this "hearing." Instead, Mr. Myer called on me to testify. I took an oath to tell the truth, and in response to his questions I told the story of my life, much as it has been related in the early chapters of this book. It was rather long, and there was only one interruption, during questions about the nature of my work at the VA:

> Mr. Merker: We will admit that the job of the employee is not sensitive for the purposes of the record if that is what you are establishing.

Mr. Myer questioned me at length about my political and social beliefs, especially with relation to the question of force and violence.

> Mr. Myer: What are your social views with respect to the form of government in the United States?
>
> Mr. Kutcher: Well, I don't think it serves the best interests of all the people.
>
> Mr. Myer: What form of society do you believe in?
>
> Mr. Kutcher: A socialist society which is based upon the principle of production for use rather than profit.
>
> Mr. Myer: In your opinion how will such a society be achieved?
>
> Mr. Kutcher: Well, you have to convince the majority of the people that such a society is necessary and that it should be established by constitutional amendments.
>
> Mr. Myer: Do you advocate the violent overthrow of the present form of the government in order to achieve a socialist society?
>
> Mr. Kutcher: No.
>
> Mr. Myer: Have you at any time heard any of the leaders of the Socialist Workers Party advocate violence as a means of achieving socialism?
>
> Mr. Kutcher: No.

And so on, with Mr. Myer attempting to present not only my views but those of my party, although he could do so only by asking my opinion of them. Under his questioning, I described how my branch of the Socialist Workers Party had engaged in numerous election campaigns to promote socialist ideas and try to elect socialist candidates. I volunteered the information that in 1947 we ran candidates for delegates to a constitutional convention to revise the New Jersey Constitution.

It was also brought out that I had heard about my party being put on the blacklist, but that I regarded this designation as incorrect and unjust, and that I knew my party was taking steps to be removed from the list. Mr. Myer said this last point was important because it explained why I had made no move to leave either my party or my job after the list was published.

Mr. Myer's questions covered a great variety of matters, including my attitude to the Soviet Union and the Communist Party, and I was tired by the end of them. Testifying was something new for me, and I felt uncomfortable and dissatisfied because the main issue was ruled out of order. But as soon as Mr. Myer was finished, Mr. Merker began his cross-examination. Among his first questions was this:

> Mr. Merker: Are you in "full agreement" with the statements contained in *The Militant?*

It was a pretty broad question. I knew that if I wanted to I could hedge on the question, in all honesty. I found myself in agreement with the general policies of *The Militant,* but not fully with everything that was written in it. Sometimes I had a different analysis of some current event. But I was too sore to want to appear to be making any concessions to a proceeding that I had already decided was rigged against me.

> Mr. Kutcher: Yes, sir.

I gave the same reply when he asked if I was in "full agreement" with the writings of Leon Trotsky. At this point Mr. Myer objected, and the chairman suggested that the question be changed to "general accord."

Mr. Merker also was curious to know if I intended to vote for the presidential ticket of the Socialist Workers Party in that year's election. I felt like saying it was none of his business. Instead, I said, "Yes, sir." Later I regretted that I had not added: "and that proves, of course, that I want to overthrow the government by force and violence."

He questioned me about the dispute that had taken place in the Socialist Party over the Spanish Civil War in 1937, but his questions were so idiotic and uninformed that no one could possibly have learned anything from the exchange. His final question on this point was: "In other words, you agreed with the situation, but not as to the methods. Is that correct?" Whatever that meant.

Finally, he came to the end:

> Mr. Merker: Now you testified in direct testimony that you advocated a change in the governmental form of government in the United States, but not by force. Is that correct?
>
> Mr. Kutcher: Yes, sir.
>
> Mr. Merker: What methods do you personally advocate to achieve the purposes of the party to which you are a member?
>
> Mr. Kutcher: Well, education, political campaigning and so on, in order to educate the people for the necessity of the change.
>
> Mr. Merker: You advocate the convincing of them of the propriety and wisdom of your beliefs? Or do you believe in using coercion in any form?
>
> Mr. Kutcher: No coercion.
>
> Mr. Merker: I have no further questions.

Instead of recessing, the chairman asked the members of the Board if they would care to ask me any questions. The first was Dr. Jacques. He had irritated me very much by smirking at many of the statements made by me and Mr. Myer. In general he made faces and mugged like a clown at a party. Here is a sample of his contributions into the inquiry on my "disloyalty":

> Dr. Jacques: At the present time, according to your statement, your total income from the government is $5,486 per year [wages plus pension]. What is the most you ever earned before you went into the army?

Mr. Kutcher: I didn't earn half that much.

Dr. Jacques: In your beliefs of the operations and the policy of the Socialist Workers Party, do you believe that under socialism you could get $5,486 per year yourself personally?

Mr. Kutcher: I think it would be possible for a majority of mankind to live that way, yes, sir.

Dr. Jacques: You believe that. [The transcript does not show the offensive expression on his face.]

He asked me to define fascism and totalitarianism. When I did, he asked me for my definition of democracy.

Mr. Kutcher: Rule by majority.

Dr. Jacques: Rule by majority. A moment ago you wanted rule by minority, now you want rule by majority.

Mr. Kutcher: What did I say to make you think that?

Dr. Jacques: You mentioned something to give the minority of workers a chance to do this or . . .

Mr. Kutcher: I didn't say that.

Dr. Jacques: Sorry, I misunderstood you . . .

I still don't know if he was trying to bait me and get me to lose my temper, or if he was as stupid as he seemed. But I was losing my temper.

The other Board members soon took over. I will proceed directly to the crucial question:

Mr. Hinden: Another question that I have, Mr. Kutcher. Do you believe that the aims and policies of Leon Trotsky—which you state the Socialist Workers Party is in general agreement with—that that form of government could be brought about within the framework of the Constitution of the United States?

I hesitated for a moment. I could in all truth say "Yes" to this question, as I had done to similar questions previously. But I had been nettled by Dr. Jacques and annoyed by the whole "hearing." Here they were grilling me about my views on constitutional procedure, and at the same time they were collaborating in the denial of my constitutional rights. So I didn't answer just "Yes."

> Mr. Kutcher: It would depend on the willingness of the minority of the capitalists to accede to the change. We have no example in history of the minority group in power consenting to a change that was necessitated by the development of social conditions. For instance, in our own history we have the story of our own Civil War where a minority of slaveholders in the South tried to overturn the decision of the majority when they elected Abraham Lincoln president of the United States, and we believe that the minority for the second time will use violence in order to prevent this social change. We tell the working class that although we don't advocate violence, it's not wrong to protect yourself against violence if it is used by the minority to prevent the carrying out of the majority decision.
>
> Mr. Hinden: In the history of this country we've had Federalists, Republicans, Democrats, Whigs, all of which parties came into power or elected representatives within the framework of the Constitution. I would like to repeat my question: Do you believe that the Socialist Workers Party could come into power within the framework of the Constitution, or in order for them to come into power would they have to throw out the Constitution of the United States?
>
> Mr. Kutcher: They can come into power.

They evidently had been waiting and hoping for the explanation I had volunteered about conditions that might make it necessary for the majority of the people to use force to resist a minority's use of force to thwart the will of the majority, as in our Civil War and in the Spanish Civil War. George Novack told me later that I could just as well have dispensed with these fine points in the exposition of my ideas. Maybe he was right, but at that time I felt I might as well get the satisfaction of entering into the record a full account of my beliefs, whether the Board members liked it or not. I don't think it made any difference as far as they were concerned anyhow.

They kept after me on this point, hammer and tongs, until the recess, firing questions designed to confuse me and make me contradict myself. From the transcript I can see that they did succeed in making me say things that didn't properly express my ideas. But they were no longer making a pretense of finding out what I believed and advocated; they were just trying to trip me up.

Then came an exchange which the authorities considered so damning that it later was reprinted (out of its context) in the government brief to the federal courts:

> Mr. Elzroth: You stated in your response to an answer a while ago that you believed all this could be accomplished through open and free elections. Your answer now seems to imply that you do not so believe.
>
> Mr. Kutcher: It could be accomplished if the minority of the capitalists consent to it. If they don't consent to it, then the majority must use force to enforce its will.
>
> Mr. Elzroth: Do you believe then that unless the commissions, so to speak, of this minority who now holds control through a conspiracy does not adhere to the doctrines that you espouse, that force then will be necessary and justifiable?

This was rather a confusing question. It was later explained that Mr. Elzroth said or meant to say "wishes" rather than "commissions." But that change doesn't improve the question much so far as clarity goes. I took it to be an amplification of his previous question, however, and answered it accordingly.

> Mr. Kutcher: Yes, sir.
>
> Mr. Elzroth: Even though you do not meet with success in the elections, you believe that that ultimately may become necessary?
>
> Mr. Kutcher: It may be necessary.

Mr. Merker then began again. His clever aim was to try to get me to say that I thought force would be necessary when my party "assumed" it had become a majority. I denied this angrily, and he wanted to know: "By what method would you determine whether you were in a majority or a minority?" I replied that we would know by the way election results turn out. Here is how he tried to twist that:

> Mr. Merker: You state, Mr. Kutcher, when you have two or three representatives elected you would consider yourself a majority?

I had stated nothing of the kind. But they must have thought I was a simpleton because I had volunteered information which they regarded as "damaging" to me. The government didn't reprint that exchange in its brief, but it did include (also out of context) the following, which came just before the recess:

> Mr. Elzroth: You have definitely stated that at some point along this escalator of progress you are discussing, revolution would be justified because there would be an apparent majority. At what point would that occur?
>
> Mr. Kutcher: Nobody can make any exact predictions like that.
>
> Mr. Elzroth: Somewhere around that time, when you are convinced in your own mind that the majority of the people believe as you do that they are somehow prevented from expressing their opinion through the ballot box, then you would consider revolution justified? When the majority would be prevented from expressing their opinions through the normal electoral processes—do you believe that this will be so?
>
> Mr. Kutcher: It has happened in instances of successful election the socialist delegates [I meant candidates] were not permitted to take their seats.

There were two witnesses for me. The Board plainly showed it was not interested in hearing them. When the Rev. John I. Daniel appeared as a character witness to testify to my reputation and moral character, they didn't even bother to ask him one question. I felt sorry he had gone to the trouble of coming to Philadelphia to talk to people who were totally indifferent to everything he said.

My second witness was George Clarke, national campaign manager of the Socialist Workers Party. But he wasn't permitted to give more than his name and address before Mr. Merker started objecting that Clarke's testimony would violate paragraph 4g of Technical Bulletin 5-85. "Consequently," Mr. Hinden ruled, "the Board is not in a position to hear that type of testimony."

Mr. Myer then made a brilliant summation—within the framework of what he was allowed to say. In passing, he cleared up some possible misunderstandings of what I was trying to say about force and violence; he also took a rap or two at Dr. Jacques' contemptible implication that I had no right to be talking about socialism when I was being paid so handsomely by the present government for my disability and my job with the VA. I'm sorry I can't reprint his entire summation, but here is how he ended:

> Mr. Myer: I want to say . . . you have to decide this case on all of the evidence and I say that his membership in the party is only one bit. There is no evidence here that he was guilty of any sabotage, any treason, or that he was in a position where he did or could give aid to the enemy or give them information. This isn't that kind of case at all. If there ever was a case in my humble opinion where a person is being prosecuted—yes, and even persecuted—for his thoughts, that's all, for his thoughts and beliefs, I say this is one. That has always been contrary to the very best traditions and best constitutional principles of this government and I think they should still be carried on. I think that, weighing all the evidence, this Board cannot determine that this man has been disloyal and should therefore be retained in the service.

But the Board was not weighing all the evidence—the most important issue was completely excluded to begin with—and the

Management Representative, in a summation that was almost as brief as the "case" he presented against me at the beginning, demanded that I be found guilty.

> Mr. Merker: With full cognizance that the organization of which he was a member was upon the attorney general's list, yet the employee did not forego his membership but continued active therein. Consequently, it is the opinion of myself that he has intentionally avoided the requirements pertaining to employment and consequently I submit to the Board the employee should be found guilty of disloyalty to the government of the United States.

Mr. Hinden then closed the proceeding by assuring us that "this Board is not—and I repeat not—a callous, unsympathetic Board," that it would take into consideration my war record and injury, and that it would soon reach a conclusion "based upon all the facts in evidence of record."

Personally, I would have preferred an admittedly callous and unsympathetic Board, but one which allowed all the evidence to go into the record.

9

I write President Truman

Disgusted by the Philadelphia "hearing," I asked George Novack how much longer it would be before we finished with such pointless proceedings and were able to get our appeal before a body where the real issues could be discussed. He explained that the "channels" through which we had to go were the following: in case of an adverse decision from the Branch Loyalty Board, we would go to the VA Loyalty Board of Appeals in Washington; then to the VA Administrator, Carl Gray, Jr.; then to the top Loyalty Review Board of the U.S. Civil Service Commission. That would exhaust all of the administrative procedures, and after that we could go to the U.S. Federal District Court; then the U.S. Circuit Court of Appeals; and finally, the U.S. Supreme Court.

I had not yet learned that the chief quality you must exercise under such circumstances is patience. I felt restless. The case was a month old, and everything seemed to be dragging. So I suggested to George, "What do you think of the idea of trying to shortcut this business, by making a direct appeal to the people who have the authority to do something, maybe to President Truman himself?"

He said he honestly had not thought of such a thing. After considering it, he told me, "Maybe you've got a good idea. I don't see what harm it can do. The president has been making a great many speeches lately about the need to defend civil liberties. Let's wait until he makes another, and then make a direct bid to him for action on your case." But he cautioned me, "However, don't build up too many hopes on the outcome. It's all right to try, but don't be too disappointed if nothing comes of it."

President Truman was making numerous statements against the witch-hunt at that time, especially since the House Committee on Un-American Activities was staging hearings designed to embarrass his administration. He accused the Committee members of using a "red herring," infringing upon the Bill of Rights and doing irreparable harm to certain persons. He also spoke strongly against guilt by association.

He was on his famous "whistle stop" campaign tour when I began to follow his statements more closely. It so happened, however, that I did not wait until he made his next statement on civil liberties.

On September 20, 1948, the president, taking time out from his regular campaign speeches, visited the Army Fitzsimmons General Hospital near Denver. The press reported the next morning that he chatted with a number of amputees and declared, as he left the hospital, "Nothing is too good for these men."

As soon as I read this report, I sat down and composed a letter to the president.

"This is a fine sentiment, Mr. President, and I would like to call your attention to my own case, in the hope that you will take appropriate action." I related the essential facts, emphasizing that "I am as proud of my membership in [my] party as you are of yours in the Democratic Party." Then I continued:

> So this is the situation I am in at the present time: I belong to a party that is legal, and appears on the ballot and runs candidates for office. The attorney general says it is subversive, but he has never attempted to prove it, and he even denies us the elementary democratic right to defend ourselves against this charge at a hearing.

I ask you, Mr. President, is that the democratic way? Would you like to be charged with a crime, and not told exactly what the crime is, or when you committed it, or where, and not permitted to face your accuser, or examine the evidence, or have a lawyer or a trial—and then be told you are guilty? What is the difference between such a procedure and the one followed behind the iron curtain?

Although I regard the entire Loyalty Board procedure as unconstitutional, I have followed this procedure and made my appeal through its channels. But at the Loyalty Board hearing in Philadelphia on September 10, my attempts to discuss the main issue—is my party subversive or not—were ruled out of order as irrelevant and immaterial, and the questioning was confined to something I had already publicly admitted: am I or am I not a member of the Socialist Workers Party. I see no reason to expect justice from such a set-up, and I ask you, Mr. President, to intervene in this case.

Specifically, I request you to halt the dismissal proceedings against me until such time as you have called a public hearing at which my party can defend itself and me against the subversive charges. Surely, this is a modest request to make of a public figure like yourself, who has endorsed the widely publicized recommendations of your Committee on Civil Rights.

I would be glad to meet with you, Mr. President, to discuss this case further. If not, I would be pleased to hear from you as to the action you intend to take in this case.

As one of those about whom you said, "Nothing is too good for these men," I think I am speaking for most of them when I say that we don't want special privileges, we just want a square deal.

Mr. Truman went on making speeches about civil liberties and other important issues, and they helped to win his election that fall. But neither he nor any of his secretaries ever answered my letter.

Some of the labor leaders active in helping our committee told me not to feel too bad because they were sure that once the election was out of the way, the Fair Deal administration would see that justice was done to me. I.F. Stone, the columnist who had joined our committee, gave an expression to some of these hopes in the now defunct *New York Star* on January 19, 1949, a day before Mr. Truman's inauguration. Entitled "An Imaginary Press Conference," his column described a scene at the executive mansion on Inaugural Day, where the president introduces me to a press conference as "a friend of mine," tells my history and says:

"I've decided to start the next four years by reinstating Jim. I called you fellows in to tell you why." Then he explains that his administration has made the mistake of becoming a "government-by-panic" but now is determined to "change all that." He is restoring me to my job, he says, in order to express two things in a "human and dramatic" fashion: "One was, 'Look, we're not going to be scared of bogeymen any more.' The other was, 'Look, this is the kind of silly meanness being scared gets us into.'"

The column was an effective journalistic device to publicize the discrimination in my case, but unfortunately the scene it half-wishfully pictured did not have the slightest basis in reality. The only change that President Truman made in the "loyalty" program during his entire second administration was a concession to the witchhunters that they applauded as enthusiastically as they had the initiation of the "loyalty" program itself.

Originally, Executive Order 9835 provided that an employee could be discharged only when "on all the evidence, reasonable grounds exist for belief that the person involved is disloyal . . ." On April 28, 1951, President Truman amended this section so that an employee could be removed from his job when "on all the evidence, there is a reasonable doubt as to the loyalty of the person involved . . ." Previously, the Loyalty Boards were supposed to have something positive to point to (reasonable grounds) before firing an employee. After the amendment all they had to express was uncertainty (reasonable doubt) and he got the axe. As a result, hundreds of people who were cleared under the original version of the executive order had to face new investigations, with much less chance than before of winning their cases.

If the Truman administration thought it could appease the witch-hunters into calling off their smear attacks against the administration, it made a bad mistake. The more concessions the witch-hunters got, the bolder they grew. McCarthyism became a powerful factor in American life in 1950, but it could thank the administration's policies since 1947 for creating the atmosphere in which McCarthyism could flourish.

Senator McCarthy's charges about Owen Lattimore and "Communists in the State Department" and his demand for Secretary Acheson's head led to a Senate hearing which made a big stir and had the White House visibly worried. In the midst of it, on April 24, 1950, President Truman went out of his way to make a speech before the Federal Bar Association sharply denouncing guilt by association smears and promising to continue "operating within the framework of the democratic liberties we cherish." I just couldn't resist writing him a second letter after hearing that speech on the radio.

I reminded the president about my case, and said that while I remained opposed to the policies of his party, I was "just as unalterably opposed to subjecting the members of any party [including his party] to witch-hunts." I also tried to show him the connection between my case and the McCarthyite treatment he and his administration were getting:

> I think you have now gotten a small taste of how I and the Socialist Workers Party felt when you put the SWP on your "subversive" blacklist and fired me . . . From the tone you used [over the radio], it was clear that you don't like the taste of the smear medicine which your administration has dispensed rather freely to people like myself who advocate socialism as the alternative to capitalism and Stalinism. I use the word "taste" because what is being done to you and other targets of McCarthy is by no means as bad as what you did to me and my party.
>
> Whether or not the charges against Owen Lattimore have any substance, at least he was told what they were, and what the al-

leged evidence was for those charges. At least he was given the right to attend an open hearing where he could defend himself against those charges.

I then reminded him about what happened to me and my party, noting that "We were put in the position of being 'convicted' without having had a trial, fair or otherwise."

> Has it occurred to you, Mr. President, that the arbitrary methods you used against me and my party encouraged and emboldened McCarthy to imitate you and use similar methods against your administration? He probably figures that if you can smear your opponents without being required to submit proof, why can't he do the same?
>
> Last night you also said: "We're going to keep the Bill of Rights on the books." It would also be helpful if, in addition to keeping it on the books, your administration would begin to observe it in practice. As a first step toward again making the Bill of Rights a reality for all, the unconstitutional "loyalty" purge order should be revoked [and] the "subversive" blacklist should be rescinded . . .

This time, of course, I didn't expect an answer to my letter. A man learns from experience.

10

Encounters with Mr. Clark

But in 1948, while I was waiting for the decision of the Loyalty Board in Philadelphia, I still had certain hopes (or illusions) about the possibility of getting results from direct negotiations with top administration officials. I therefore jumped at the first opportunity that came along for a conference with the attorney general, Mr. Tom C. Clark.

The Nation, weekly liberal magazine, commenting on mine as an "almost perfect test case," said I was receiving "strong support," among others, from Eleanor Roosevelt. This was an inaccuracy, which I would like to clear up here, in all fairness to Mrs. Roosevelt. She did not give me any direct support at all, although it was through her intervention that the chance to meet Mr. Clark arose. What happened was that she learned about my case somehow, I think through a letter from my attorney, Mr. Burch.

A few days after the Philadelphia "hearing," a letter arrived for me at the Newark VA, where I was still working. It was from Mrs. Roosevelt at Hyde Park, written just before she sailed to attend sessions of the General Assembly of the United Nations in Paris. Her letter revealed that she had written about me to Mr. Clark, and contained his reply to her:

"The recourse of the individual in such cases is by appeal under the procedure set up by the Loyalty Review Board. As to the organization, I will be glad to arrange for an appointment of one of its representatives to present to this department any material which it may wish to submit relative to its designation under the order."

My party had asked for a hearing, and knowledge of what it was accused of so it could answer it. Instead of granting this reasonable request, Mr. Clark would do no more than let us present "material" to one of his assistants. You're guilty, and I won't tell you of what, but I will let you submit material relevant to the charge whose nature you are ignorant of—that was what his stand amounted to.

But, in handwriting, at the end of Mr. Clark's note was the following: "P.S. I would be happy to talk with Mr. Kutcher if he desires . . ." My optimism flared up again; here at least was a crack in the door, and I saw no reason for not grabbing and trying to widen it. After consulting with George Novack, I wrote to Mr. Clark requesting an appointment for myself and George. He agreed to meet us in Washington on September 30.

I think George was somewhat surprised by this development. But he cautioned me again not to become too hopeful about the consequences: "The protests of the labor movement against your proposed discharge must have the administration worried a little, and they are evidently trying to show that they are acting in a humane manner, and hoping to stall things off until after the election in November."

A few days before our conference, Mr. Clark published an expanded list of "subversive" organizations which convinced me that his readiness to meet me did not signify any change in his policy. For his new list included the Socialist Workers Party not once, but three times—once, under the heading "communist" where we were lumped together with the Communist Party, which had been fighting us viciously ever since our party was formed; a second time, under the heading "subversive"; and a third time, under the heading of groups "seeking to alter the form of government of the United States by unconstitutional means."

Reading this new list, I couldn't figure out what Mr. Clark was up to. After some thought, I decided to draw up a formal petition to present to him, so I would have a written document to give the press either before or after the interview. After some preliminary recitation of the facts, my petition went on:

> Why won't you permit my party to have the hearing it requests, Mr. Clark?
>
> When Mrs. Eleanor Roosevelt wrote to you about my case, you answered her (as you answered the Socialist Workers Party when you denied its request for a hearing) that you would be glad to arrange for one of its representatives to present to the Department of Justice "any material which it may wish to submit relative to its designation under the order."
>
> Such an offer cannot be considered as a substitute for a hearing, for the good and simple reason that you have never offered this party any bill of particulars on which you base your charge. I do not pretend to be a student of law, but your offer seems to me like asking a man to defend himself against a charge of murder, without letting him know whom he is charged with murdering, or when, or under what circumstances.
>
> That is why I insist that only a public hearing can rectify a horrible miscarriage of justice in the case of my party.
>
> And only a public hearing, leading to the removal of my party from the blacklist, can enable me to save the job to which I believe myself as much entitled as you are entitled to yours.
>
> You informed Mrs. Roosevelt that my only recourse was "by appeal under the procedure set up by the Loyalty Board." Although I hold this procedure to be unconstitutional, I am following it as you have suggested. But I do not believe I will ever get a fair deal in this way. [I then described what happened at the Philadelphia "hearing."] How can I hope for justice from a board that will not or cannot even deal with the real issue?
>
> For these reasons, I ask you to halt the dismissal proceedings against me and to immediately call a public hearing at which my

party can defend itself, and me, against this false "subversive" charge.

The Trenton (N.J.) *Evening Times,* in an editorial on September 24 supporting my request for a public hearing, stated:

"Surely, there is nothing unreasonable in his demand and he has also earned, it seems, exceptional consideration regardless of his membership in an organization of questionable character."

I want you to know, however, that I am not asking for "exceptional consideration." All I am asking for is justice to myself and my party.

Mr. Clark was quite courteous. His office was in the Department of Justice building and, after waiting a while and signing a card stating our business, George and I were ushered into a tremendously big room, almost as large and high as an auditorium. We stood there, with portraits of former attorney generals looking down at us from the walls, until Mr. Clark was fetched by an assistant. He entered from the rear out of his private back room, shook our hands, and helped me to a chair. He himself sat on a bench against the wall during our interview, which lasted about half an hour.

He began by claiming that he could not provide a public hearing for the Socialist Workers Party because such a thing was not provided for in the president's executive order. We objected that the order did not prohibit hearings even though it did not require them, and that therefore he had the power to provide them. He at once dropped his first line of argument and said that he had held a couple of hearings for organizations he did not name, but they became so "boisterous" that it was considered "impractical" to hold any more.

I was a little flabbergasted to see the man change his story so radically in less than five minutes.

He then asked me if I didn't think I had received a "fair hearing" in Philadelphia. I told him I couldn't get a fair hearing there because the Board had been bound in advance not to consider the chief issue.

Evading this, he told us that hundreds of government employees had been discharged under the "loyalty" program, but that I was the first to protest directly to him. I didn't quite catch the significance of this, but he went on to say that this was "proof" that the procedure was "fair." I challenged him on that: "The reason most discharged employees wouldn't come to you or take any other action is that they have been intimidated. They accept their dismissal because they do not want to be publicly stigmatized as having been branded 'disloyal.'"

Mr. Clark then said that his list was "essentially the same" as a secret list prepared by the Department of Justice in the early 1940s, when the attorney general in the Roosevelt administration was Francis Biddle. What he hoped to convey by that revelation, I do not know. Maybe he thought we would be so impressed by the fact that the original list was drawn up under an official with a liberal reputation that we would think, "Oh, that changes everything."

The present list, he asserted, was intended to eliminate "undesirables" from public employment, and not to harass any political party. "Whatever the intention may be," I replied, "the net effect is grave injury to any party on the list. When people hear that somebody can lose his job for belonging to a certain party, are they going to join such a party or attend its meetings or associate with its members? Not many will do that, so that the result of your list is definitely discrimination against any organization on the list, especially since it has not had a chance to answer the charges at a hearing."

But he refused to discuss this central question. "Unlike others," he declared, "the Department of Justice does not conduct its hearings under kleig lights and amid great fanfare." This, no doubt, was supposed to indicate the superiority of the Department of Justice over the headline-hunting House Committee on Un-American Activities. But it did not change the fact that Mr. Clark's behind-closed-doors blacklist could and did work just as much havoc as the activities of the House Committee.

"Don't worry," he told me, "the Loyalty Review Board can be depended on to give an impartial decision in your case." He did not explain how he could guarantee this when the Board was supposed to be an agency entirely independent of the Justice Department which conducted all its work in secrecy, presumably even from that department.

He promised that he would personally "study the record" in my case (which meant he had not studied it yet) and would talk the matter over with Mr. Carl Gray, the head of the Veterans Administration, whom he called a just and kindly man. This was a polite way of denying every single one of the requests I had made to him. When I hinted as much, he said:

"I don't see what good all this publicity in this case is doing you. If you're just trying to make a political issue out of it, I won't have anything to do with it. It seems to me that you're acting too much under the influence of a political group. If that's your aim, I won't do anything for you."

I knew what he meant, even though he didn't say it out loud. He wanted me to quit talking about my party, its rights and the crime that was being done against them. He wanted me to confine my remarks and activities to pleas about my personal plight, to appeals for special treatment. He wanted me to say I was sorry I had got mixed up with "a political group" and one that he had labeled "subversive" at that, and throw myself on his mercy.

That was just what I refused to do. And that was just what I was trying to prevent in the petition I gave him, which stressed that I could get justice only if my party got it because I had no intention of seeking "special treatment" because of my war injury. All I said was, "After all, Mr. Clark, it was for political reasons that I was fired."

George related what the Loyalty Board had said about taking my war record into account, and asked Mr. Clark if he thought it would have any bearing on the final decision in my case.

"Why, that's just the purpose of this loyalty program," Mr. Clark assured us. Turning to me, he put his arm around my shoulder and said: "What we're trying to do with it is protect all the things you boys fought for." (As George told the press later, "Kutcher doesn't think taking his job away from him constitutes such protection.")

Before we left, I asked one final question in an effort to show him how arbitrary it was for organizations to be proscribed on the say-so of one man:

"Suppose that you are not in this office as attorney general next year, Mr. Clark. Suppose someone else has your job. What guarantee has anyone that that man will have the same ideas that you have about who is subversive and who is not subversive?"

He must have thought that I was needling him about the possibility that the Democratic administration might be thrown out of office in the coming election—which was not the reason why I asked this question at all. Anyhow, his face got red and it was obvious that he did not like what I had said. "I'll have you know that the Loyalty Board includes a number of Republicans as well as Democrats," he replied. The implication was that what he considered subversive a Republican attorney general would consider subversive too. The election must have been weighing on his mind so heavily that he completely missed the point I was trying to make. He had been doing that all along, only in this case I think it was unintentional.

If Mr. Clark talked to Mr. Gray, it did not have much effect. Twelve days after our conference, I was handed another "personal and confidential" letter from the Branch Office of the VA in Philadelphia:

"You are hereby notified that decision has been made to remove you from employment with the Veterans Administration. All evidence of record, including the testimony presented at your hearing, has been fully considered and reasonable grounds exist for belief that you are disloyal to the Government of the United States. . . ." I was suspended without pay and told that if I did not appeal I would be discharged within two weeks. I was given ten days in which to appeal to the VA Loyalty Board of Appeals in Washington.

Reading the newspaper clippings about the press conference we called the next day, I am afraid that I became over-emotional now that the awaited axe had fallen. I find that I said, "I intend to spend the rest of my life proving the falsity of the charges against myself and my party. I intend to prove that we are not subverting the democratic process, but that they are persecuting us in an unconstitutional manner . . . If anyone knows of a job for a slightly used veteran, rewarded for the loss of his legs with a stigma of 'disloyalty,' I wish you would refer him to me as I am now in the market for a job that will help me support my parents." I had resolved to abstain from all pathos and appeals to pity, but the excitement of the moment must have overcome me. It never happened again, so far as I remember.

But what I want to do here is follow up the story of my relations with Mr. Clark, rather than continue with a chronological recital of the developments in my case.

On October 21, 1948, about two weeks before election day, Mr. Clark set off from Washington to Toledo to address law students on "Combatting Subversive Activities in a Democracy." He changed planes at Newark Airport, where an alert reporter for the *Newark Evening News* interviewed him and asked some questions about my case. He said he had seen my appeal and it was in the hands of Mr. Gray. Then he said:

"I felt from my talk with Kutcher that his activities must have been motivated by a political standpoint and that he had been prompted by persons with political interests."

This was along the lines of the remarks he made to me. Mr. Clark, who had been very active in that year's election campaign, was himself motivated by a political standpoint and prompted by persons with political interests. But he didn't seem to regard that as a crime or something that might justify dismissal from his government job. He apparently had a double standard on this matter of politics.

"However," he continued, "his war record is very much in his favor as far as I am concerned. If it can be shown he was not actually subversive I'm sure he won't be moved."

Reassuring news! Mr. Clark was sure I wouldn't be "moved"—more than a week after I had been suspended from my job. But that was not the most revealing part of his statement.

"If it can be shown he was not actually subversive"—this was certainly a new concept in American legal procedure, and all the more sinister because it was enunciated by the top law-enforcement officer in the land. It was something that used to be called "un-American" because it is one of the most reactionary concepts of dictators. Instead of considering me innocent until proved guilty, Mr. Clark had reversed matters, leaving it up to me to prove my innocence if I did not want to be held guilty.

But how could I prove that I was not subversive? I had said I was not, and no evidence was ever offered to show that I had done or said anything subversive. How else could I prove it—except through a public hearing where Mr. Clark would be able to say why he considered me and my party subversive, and where I and my party would have an opportunity to try to show that his evidence did not support his finding that we were subversive? Yet Mr. Clark refused to grant us such a hearing.

"Prove you're innocent," he was saying in effect. "All right, just give me the chance to prove it," I was replying. "No," was his answer. Who was better qualified to tell students how to combat "subversive activities in a democracy"?

I had only one more exchange with Mr. Clark. That was a couple of months later, when he was chosen to be the principal speaker at the Jefferson-Jackson Day Victory Dinner held in Newark on February 24, 1949, under the sponsorship of the State Democratic Committee. Mr. Clark accepted the invitation from another great Democratic leader, Frank Hague, who had retired as mayor of Jersey City after passing on the scepter to his nephew but was still boss of the party in New Jersey.

At that time I had just returned from the hospital where an inch and a half of bone and some tissue were trimmed from my left stump in an attempt to make it more adaptable to the use of my artificial limb. I would have preferred to confront Mr. Clark in person, but the stump had not fully healed and I was immobilized. So I sent him a letter, repeating the facts and repeating the demand for a public hearing and urging him again to restore me to my job. In an effort to prod him into discussing my case in his speech, I released copies of the letter to the press. Unfortunately, most of them did not quote its final paragraph, which I thought was particularly timely:

"I should like to remind you that Thomas Jefferson, whom you are celebrating tonight, was a firm defender of free speech and free political activity. I cannot believe that the author of the Declaration of Independence, who also had revolutionary views, would have approved any resort to thought-control and police-state methods. He firmly opposed the Alien and Sedition Laws from which your political blacklist was copied and he pardoned those who had been unjustly victimized by the previous U.S. Attorney General through these instruments of oppression."

Mr. Clark had been willing enough to discuss my case before the elections and to make hints that I might get my job back if I stopped fighting for it. But he declined my invitation to discuss it in relation to the ideas of Jefferson. That disappointed but did not surprise me. However, I was a little surprised to find that, at least as far as the news reports of the dinner went, neither he nor his fellow-speakers had anything to say about Jefferson.

Instead, Mr. Clark devoted the major part of his address to—Boss Hague. What brought this on, I cannot say. Maybe Mr. Clark was informed only that he was to speak at a New Jersey dinner in honor of the heroes of the Democratic Party and he took it for granted that naturally this meant it was a Hague Day celebration. (This dinner took place just a few months before the voters of Jersey City kicked the Hague machine, nephew and all, out of office.)

Mr. Clark paid his respects to Mr. Hague by calling him "one of the great political organizers in the country." I think what he meant was "one of the great political *machine* organizers." Mr. Hague certainly merited all the superlatives in this field. The people of Jersey City could testify that few compared with Mr. Hague in building and maintaining a corrupt political dictatorship, suppressing opponents, fleecing taxpayers and feathering his own nest. But I don't think anyone should question the sincerity of Mr. Clark's tribute to his fellow-Democrat.

Since Mr. Hague was the subject of some criticism at that time, Mr. Clark sprang to his defense. Those who criticize Mr. Hague, he thundered, "do so only because he is not on their side." I can't be sure whom he was referring to, but I know it wasn't me or my party, who had fought Hagueism actively for more than a decade. Could it be, I wondered, that our lack of appreciation for the talents of such "great" political organizers contributed to Mr. Clark's decision to put us on his blacklist? The question is worth speculating on, since Mr. Clark never did divulge the reasons.

It goes without saying that I was glad to see Mr. Clark leave the post of attorney general, but my pleasure vanished when I heard that he was leaving it for a seat on the U.S. Supreme Court, the body that may some day rule on the constitutionality of my discharge. I am told that it is customary, although not mandatory, for Supreme Court justices to abstain from participation in cases in which they themselves were once involved, and that Mr. Justice Clark will in all likelihood adhere to this custom when and if my appeal comes before that tribunal. I hope so. He has judged me before, and I was not impressed by his impartiality or his devotion to elementary democratic principles, such as the rule that a man must be considered innocent until proved guilty. I hope he will abstain. I also hope I will be forgiven for saying, on the basis of my past experience with him, that when the time comes for him to announce if he will participate or abstain, I will have my fingers crossed.

11

The news spreads

It should not be assumed, because of the last two chapters, that we spent most of our time chasing around after interviews with high government officials. Actually, that consumed less than one percent of our thought and energy. George Novack explained to me at the start that we would do everything humanly possible to get a favorable decision from the Loyalty Boards or the courts, but that above all we would concern ourselves with bringing the facts and issues involved in the case to the widest circles of the American people. "The best way to get a favorable verdict from the courts," he said, "is to show the courts that public opinion is on your side, and that there will be great resentment and indignation over an unfavorable verdict."

Newspaper publicity, press conferences, publication and distribution of literature, interviews over the radio—we looked for and grabbed every opportunity to reach the public ear with the facts. But the main part of such a job consists of leg work. You have to get out and around to people where they are; you can't just open up an office and wait for them to come to you. You can't go knocking on the doors of people's homes, either; you must concentrate your energies by going where people are in groups—that is, you must search out organizations and prevail upon them to listen to you.

It is not an easy job, especially where the element of alleged "disloyalty" enters, and sometimes you get ignored, or get put off with phony excuses, or get rebuffed altogether. Sometimes you know that if you can get before a certain organization and tell your story, the members will listen to you with attention and sympathy, but the officers or executive committee are afraid or hostile for one reason or another and they bar your way. And even when you succeed in getting the floor, it is still no picnic. Unless you are a trained speaker with leather lungs it is pretty tiring to make four or five speeches a night, as I often had to do.

The case was best known in my home town, and in the weeks following the first press conference I spent most of my time in and around Newark, taking my case to as many organizations as would listen to me. Unless I am mistaken, the first local group, after the State CIO, to act on my case was my own chapter of the American Veterans Committee. They branded my discharge as "a cruel abuse of official power" and "a flagrant violation of civil rights." They opposed my prospective discharge, condemned the practice of blacklisting organizations without a hearing, and took a collection toward the expenses in the case. Since they knew all about me, after the newspaper publicity, it was not necessary for me to make a speech asking their endorsement.

A couple of weeks later, however, I did not have as good luck with the other ex-servicemen's organization I belonged to, the Disabled American Veterans. A motion was made by someone at a meeting of my chapter (composed of amputees) to support me in a mild sort of way. Then someone else suggested that the motion be made stronger. That got the majority of the meeting frightened, and a motion was passed to table the whole matter. Most of them worked for the Veterans Administration, and they did not want to jeopardize their jobs. I wasn't given the floor to tell my side of the story.

By coincidence, the first organization I spoke to on the case was the Newark Teachers Union, Local 481 of the American Federation of

Teachers, AFL. All the time I was talking to them, I half wanted to say: "If things had gone differently, if I had done what I wanted to do, I would be sitting down there in one of the seats among you as a member of your local and your profession instead of standing up here defending myself against the charge of disloyalty." But I refrained. They unanimously passed a resolution to be sent to President Truman and the press, asking the VA not to turn me out of my job and the president "to grant Kutcher's request for a public hearing at which his party can defend itself against the subversive charges." Later, the New Jersey Federation of Teachers, AFL, took a similar stand.

Next I appeared before the Baptist Ministers' Conference of Newark and Vicinity, representing congregations of about 100,000 Negroes. They listened to me politely, questioned me closely and then endorsed my case vigorously. Through them I obtained access to a great many churches where I told my story to their congregations.

The Newark Branch of the National Association for the Advancement of Colored People applauded after I finished, took a collection for me and referred the question of endorsement to their executive board. At first I was afraid that this was a nice way of avoiding action, but that showed how inexperienced I was. The executive board turned it over to the branch's legal committee, which studied the whole question carefully and then brought in a resolution of whole-hearted support which was adopted by the executive board.

I appeared before a committee or group of officers of the Commission on Social Work, New Jersey Conference, Methodist Church. I couldn't tell from their expressions, questions or comments whether or not they were sympathetic to what I was saying, although they were polite enough. They said we would be notified about their decision. Weeks went by, and we heard nothing from them. I thought the least they might have done was send me a letter stating they did not intend to act. Then George Novack told me on the phone one day that the New York office of our committee had received a resolution of endorsement from the Commission some time before. It was evidently the only address they had. I began to learn the virtue, and even the necessity of patience.

By the middle of October 1948 when the Loyalty Board in Phila-delphia handed down the first unfavorable ruling, we had quite an imposing array of community and religious support, in addition to endorsements from an ever-growing list of CIO and AFL locals. Despite my initial doubts and impatience, I can report that none of the organizations I spoke to, with a tiny proportion of exceptions to be discussed later, ever denied me help in one form or another.

But we did not intend to confine our efforts to New Jersey. We felt that public pressure on a national scale was needed to create the necessary impact on the originators and executors of the "loyalty" program. We began to get some good breaks. The Philadelphia rul-ing became the occasion for comment and protest by a number of people who had been waiting to see if the government would really fire me.

The first editorial in a daily newspaper outside my state appeared in the *Brooklyn Eagle* on October 18, 1948: ". . . No one has been more vigilant or critical of the Communist movement in America than we have. Yet, we deplore this incident and believe an injustice has been done."

The next day I was summoned to New York City where James B. Carey, secretary-treasurer of the CIO, was scheduled to deliver a speech on civil liberties. To illustrate his theme, he mentioned five different cases, most of them involving trade unionists who had been removed from their jobs as "security risks." In each instance he asked the person involved to stand up. When I arose, he said I had been dismissed "because he was an admitted member of an organiza-tion . . . gratuitously termed subversive in the personal opinion of the attorney general."

One day later the writer Gerald W. Johnson had a long article about me in the *New York Star*. Sarcastically, he commented: "James Kutcher has been discovered, exposed, and driven from his job. . . . So we can once more sleep easy at night; the country is saved."

In the same paper, two days later, appeared the first of the many columns on my case by I.F. Stone. This one bore the title by which the case became most widely known, and which I have borrowed as the title of this book. It began by saying: "The Case of the Legless Veteran is beginning to haunt the men in charge of the loyalty program." It ended by stating: "Basic political liberties and basic procedural safeguards are threatened by the standards of judgment and procedure applied in The Case of the Legless Veteran. These in turn are not the handiwork of the 80th Congress, but were established by the loyalty order. The order was Harry Truman's and Harry Truman claims to be a friend of civil rights. More pitiable than a man without legs is a president without firm principles."

That same day the *Reading* (Pa.) *Times* printed an editorial entitled "Borders on Ridiculous." It said: "It is no exhibition of vigilance when a man is fired from a federal job simply because he does not believe in a democratic republican form of government and a profit system of economy. Theoretically, unless he was a good Democrat or a Republican stalwart, he should not have been able to get the job in the first place. His discharge now is an exhibition of shortsightedness, insecurity, and a fear unwarranted by the very virtues of our form of government. And since, in this case, the Trotskyite-Stalinite hostility is a matter of historical record, the whole performance becomes downright silly." This was a syndicated editorial and appeared in many papers throughout the country.

There was a good deal in some of these comments that I did not like. I didn't think there was anything "silly" about what had happened to me. I discussed this with George Novack and asked him if I should write to the publications involved, expressing my differences with them. He persuaded me not to.

"You aren't responsible for what people say or write about you," he said. "Holding different political ideas, they naturally are going to approach the question from a different standpoint than you would. We would be in a very poor position if we had to rely on those who analyze the case the way you do. It's true, as you say, that some of the people deploring your discharge are using you to grind their own axes. Many of them are not against the 'loyalty' program on principle, as you are, but are using your case as a jumping-off point for their contention that the 'loyalty' program isn't being executed wisely or energetically enough. Look—" and he showed me a statement by the National Americanism Commission of the American Legion declaring, "The Kutcher case is therefore an almost perfect example of bureaucratic bungling in how not to handle a doubtful loyalty case."

"The American Legion," he went on, "is one of the most rabid advocates of a purge of government employees. Here they mention your case, not out of sympathy for you, but to belabor the Administration for not carrying out the purge in such a way as to enlist public support for it. All right—that's their angle. You don't have to assume responsibility for what they say—you can speak for yourself and make your own position clear. Our job is to fight for your reinstatement, not to get involved in polemics with everybody who happens to use you as a vehicle for promoting his own ideas.

"Some of the publicity may not be good, some of it will surely not be helpful to you in the long run," he agreed. "But that is secondary right now. The government tried to bottle your case up, to keep the whole story concealed from the public, they wanted to lop you off the rolls quietly. Well, our job is to see that the public gets the facts because this case can be won in the final analysis only when they do get the facts. The important thing about the publicity, no matter what editorial line is attached to it, is that it is getting the basic facts about the case widely known."

And so it was. Dorothy Fuldheim, a radio commentator sponsored by the Brotherhood of Railroad Trainmen, discussed the case over the American Broadcasting Company network on October 23, finishing with the question: "How many legs does a young American have to sacrifice to prove that he is a loyal American?" The Ohio CIO State Executive Board passed a resolution supporting me and urging all affiliates to do likewise. The National Planning Committee of the American Veterans Committee wrote from Washington to tell us it had unanimously adopted a resolution stating: "The case of James Kutcher dramatically symbolizes the present dangers to the democratic rights of the American people. The American Veterans

James Kutcher at national CIO convention November 1949, Cleveland, Ohio.

Committee calls upon all liberal organizations and upon all individuals who believe in our Bill of Rights to come to his defense." George L-P Weaver, director of the National CIO Committee to Abolish Discrimination, sent a letter congratulating our committee on its "very firm and forthright position in defense of civil rights as it has been expressed in the case of Mr. James Kutcher."

The case was beginning to attract national attention. In November the *Minnesota Daily,* published at the University of Minnesota, reported that the campus Civil Liberties Club had discussed it. The *Daily Bruin,* published at the University of California, printed an article warning, "An extremely dangerous precedent is being set. Remember, those of you who love your freedom, this is only the beginning." Students at Roosevelt College in Chicago held a meeting on the case. George began to receive requests for information, literature and speakers from all parts of the country. Local branches of our committee were formed in several big cities.

But the biggest developments that month, following the elections, were the national AFL and CIO conventions. As I reported earlier, the conservative Republicans greeted President Truman's Executive Order 9835 with joy in March 1947. But many of his political supporters took an opposite position and expressed it firmly after his election, in an attempt to convince him to change the policy.

The American Federation of Labor, at its national convention in Cincinnati, unanimously adopted a resolution which said in part:

". . . This [loyalty] program has been conducted in violation of lawful and constitutional rights. . . . The effect of this program is to create fear and insecurity among government employees. . . . This atmosphere has been detrimental to the pursuit of regular trade union activity. . . . We have no objection to the theory of removing employees who are really disloyal to the government from Federal jobs, where proper steps are taken to maintain the constitutional guarantees of rights. . . . RESOLVED, That this convention of the American Federation of Labor go on record favoring the rescinding of the Loyalty Executive Order, and that all employees suspected of disloyalty be charged and tried in accordance with Civil Service and legal procedure as provided by the Constitution of the United States."

The Congress of Industrial Organizations, holding its national convention in Portland, Oregon, also in November 1948, took a similar stand, calling for:

"The establishment of guarantees to protect the freedom of thought and the freedom of political views of government workers and the revocation of Executive Order 9835."

The resolutions did not mention me by name, but that didn't matter much, because mine was the chief "loyalty" case in the public eye. These resolutions opened many a door for me, and not only the doors of labor halls. Nothing is more handy for someone in my position than a couple of resolutions like these from the highest bodies of the labor movement.

"Pack your bags," George phoned me. "We've just received an invitation to speak at our first national gathering—the Third National Convention of the American Veterans Committee. It will be held in Cleveland on November 26."

"But that's such a long trip," I protested. "Couldn't you go?"

"Of course not—it's you they want to hear, not me. You can go by plane."

There was no way out, so I went. When it was over, I knew I would never again be afraid to speak anywhere.

I sat on the platform with other guests in the Cleveland Public Music Hall, but I did not get the floor until evening because the convention was chiefly occupied with skirmishes between pro- and anti-Stalinist groups fighting for control of the organization. There was a lot of noise and disorder all day as fighting went on over seating of contested delegations, with groups meeting and buzzing all over the hall. Then I was introduced as an AVC member "leading a fight on behalf of civil liberties" and absolute silence fell over the whole place. But as I told my story, they began to interrupt me with applause.

Word had got around that I was an opponent of Stalinism, but in passing I took care to show that I was not soliciting their support on that ground: "My party's differences with the Communist Party are fundamental and irreconcilable. Nevertheless we believe that they too have constitutional rights which must be guarded and defended." This statement was not applauded, neither by the Stalinists nor their opponents. I didn't know it when I spoke but John Gates, editor of the Stalinist *Daily Worker*, facing expulsion from the AVC at that time, had been questioned by a trial committee about his attitude to my party and had answered that he did not consider it a party but a band of "assassins." I was told later that the contrast between his attitude toward my party and my attitude toward civil rights for his had made a favorable impression on even the most determined anticommunists at the convention.

When I finished, the fifteen hundred delegates gave me a stormy ovation. A resolution protesting my dismissal and demanding my reinstatement was read and adopted by a unanimous standing vote, followed by more applause.

I made many friends in Cleveland, and not only among veterans. The local press ran stories and pictures. The influential AFL paper, the *Cleveland Citizen*, ran an editorial on my case criticizing the blacklist system and saying: "Now all the Justice Department has to do is put the Democratic Party on the subversive blacklist and we will have an entirely new administration." The editor of this paper, A.I. Davey, Jr., spent most of a broadcast in his weekly radio program discussing my case. The Cleveland chapter of Americans for Democratic Action adopted a sympathetic resolution. I met with members of our local committee, and they introduced me to some educators, religious and labor leaders who later joined.

When I got home, I found a copy of an article by Matt Weinstock in the *Los Angeles Daily News*. "Kutcher has now become a national symbol for those protesting the wave of witch-hunting," he wrote, adding: "Two quiet young men, one with a steel hook where his hand used to be, came in to tell us they're setting up a local committee. As they explained it, the only time they figure Kutcher used force and violence was against the Germans." A little later, we heard from Secretary-Treasurer Emil Mazey that the International Executive

Board of the CIO United Auto Workers, the most dynamic union in the country, had voted to "work with the National CIO in bringing about a satisfactory solution to the Kutcher case."

Everything was coming along most encouragingly in our efforts to inform and arouse the public. In fact, the case was starting to get international publicity too. I have clippings from papers in France, England, Germany and Italy. A magazine in Denmark printed an article linking my case, as a symbol of World War II, with the Unknown Soldier who symbolized the casualties of World War I. Someone in Buenos Aires sent a donation to help the work of our committee.

But the other side of the fight—with the Loyalty Board machinery—was not so heartening. I had appealed to the Veterans Administration Board of Appeals in Washington. In November, O.W. Clark, executive assistant administrator of the VA, suggested by letter that we bypass a hearing before that body and turn the appeal over directly to Mr. Carl Gray, the VA Administrator. Feeling that this would save us time, because the Board of Appeals would be bound by the same restrictions as the Philadelphia Branch Board, we agreed.

We then waited for Mr. Gray's decision, hoping for the best but not expecting it. But even the most pessimistic of our supporters were surprised by what actually happened.

12

Memorandum 32

Before the November 1948 elections, when the case was only three months old, there was a tendency among some of our supporters to regard my discharge as a "blunder" or "hysterical excess" which would surely be corrected sooner or later if the Democrats won the election and were relieved of the necessity of competing for anti-communist votes. I think Mr. Clark, among others, encouraged this belief for a while by the readiness with which he met with me, his promise to talk things over with Mr. Gray, and his statement at the Newark Airport that my "war record" was very much in my favor. I think the administration must have been surprised at the scope of the protest that broke out—right in the middle of the election campaign. They must have noticed that a large part of this protest came from their own closest political supporters, including a section of the labor leadership. I guess they decided to stall until after the election, to create the impression there was still a chance that I might get my job back. If they won the election, they would decide definitely then; if they lost, it would no longer be a headache of theirs.

Some friendly labor leaders urged me not to worry. "I've heard on good authority that the thing is in the bag," one told me. "Because of your special circumstances, you will get your job back after election day." Another told me he had heard the same rumor, and believed it. "It would look funny if they rehired you now, so they are going to wait and let the appeal go a little higher, and then have a routine decision clearing you." During the first ten days after the election, two reporters phoned my home to ask if I knew anything about a rumor that I was to be reinstated.

I was suspicious about these assurances and rumors because I thought they had been started by friends of the administration as a clever trick to make me shut up voluntarily. "How can that be?" I asked. "How can they reinstate me so long as I admitted my party membership—unless they grant our demand for a hearing or take my party off the 'subversive' list?" And the answer I got was this:

"You forget that the loyalty order, discriminatory as it is, provides that decisions shall be based 'on *all* the evidence.' Didn't the Loyalty Board in Philadelphia promise to consider the *entire* case, including such factors as your war record? That means that your party membership is only one piece of evidence in the whole picture. That is what your own lawyer told them. And that is why you can still win the case even within the framework of the loyalty order."

I had to admit that it sounded possible, especially after I reread Mr. Myer's arguments in Philadelphia. But I decided to wait and see.

The answers to such speculation and to my appeal to Mr. Gray both came at the same time—in a letter dated December 29, 1948, and written by Mr. O.W. Clark, VA Executive Assistant Administrator, acting "for and in the absence of the Administrator." The pertinent sections read:

> Careful analysis of this case leads me to the conclusion that there is no choice but to affirm the action of the [Philadelphia] deputy administrator in suspending you from duty and pay. You have admitted and therefore it must be concluded to be a fact that you are a member of the Socialist Workers Party. You admitted such membership in your letter of August 25, 1948, addressed to the chairman of the Branch Office Loyalty Board and you again

admitted it during the hearing held by that loyalty board.

The attorney general has determined that the Socialist Workers Party is an organization that seeks to alter the form of government in the United States by unconstitutional means. *The Veterans Administration is bound by that determination of the attorney general.* The chairman of the Loyalty Review Board in a memorandum dated *December 17, 1948,* copy of which is enclosed, states that Section 9A of the Hatch Act makes it *mandatory* to remove from the service any employee found to be a member of that organization. (My emphasis.)

I was also given twenty calendar days in which to lodge my appeal with the Loyalty Review Board.

This business about the Hatch Act was new to me, but the enclosed letter quoted the pertinent Section 9A, which says: "It shall be unlawful for any person employed in any capacity by any agency of the federal government, whose compensation, or any part thereof, is paid from funds authorized or appropriated by any Act of Congress, to have membership in any political party or organization which advocates the overthrow of our constitutional form of government in the United States." This law was passed by Congress in 1939. But the thing to notice about it is that it did not provide any method for determining which organizations do or don't advocate the overthrow of the constitutional form of government.

Another thing to be noted is that the VA Administrator did not find, as the Branch Loyalty Board had found, that "reasonable grounds exist for belief that you are disloyal to the government of the United States, in accordance with standards set forth in Executive Order No. 9835." In fact, his letter did not even mention the executive order as his authority for ruling against me. On the contrary, he based his decision on Section 9A of the Hatch Act, as interpreted by the chairman of the Loyalty Review Board.

This discrepancy between the decisions and authorities quoted by the Branch Loyalty Board, on the one hand, and Mr. Gray, on the other, became an important legal point in later proceedings. (For example: if you are arrested and fined for speeding and you appeal the case to a higher court, it is not considered legally proper for the higher court to uphold the fine without regard to the speeding charge you were arrested for, but on another ground, say, because you resisted arrest by an officer.) But I leave this technicality aside for the time being.

Attached to the VA letter, and cited as authority for its decision on my appeal, was a copy of a new document, Memorandum No. 32, signed by Mr. Seth Richardson, chairman of the Loyalty Review Board, on December 17, 1948. It said, in part:

"The attorney general has furnished the Loyalty Review Board with a classified list of organizations heretofore characterized by him according to Section 3, Part III, of Executive Order 9835 . . . In this classified list the attorney general designated the Communist Party, U.S.A., the Communist Political Association, the Socialist Workers Party, the Workers Party, and the Young Communist League as organizations which 'seek to alter the form of government of the United States by unconstitutional means.'" (This was the "expanded" list Mr. Clark issued just before my conference with him, in which the Socialist Workers Party was listed three times, instead of once, as it had been originally. Now at last the mystery of the triple listing was cleared up.)

Memorandum 32 then reported the fact that the Loyalty Review Board had decided to "construe" the Hatch Act and Executive Order 9835 as having "a common meaning," and:

"Therefore, in accord with the designations of the attorney general, *present* membership in any one or more of the organizations listed above, or in any organization which may in the future be designated by the attorney general as in the same classification, for the purposes of adjudicating cases under Executive Order 9835, should be considered as bringing the case within the purview of the [Hatch Act]; and, if in the consideration of a case a Loyalty Board finds as a fact that an employee or an applicant is a member of one of the foregoing organizations, or that he advocates the overthrow of the government of the United States by force or violence, then the removal of the employee, or the refusal of employment to the applicant, is mandatory." (Mr. Richardson's emphasis.)

In other words, the rules had been changed in the middle of the game. When I was brought up on charges, membership in any organization on Mr. Clark's list was supposed to be one factor in determining an employee's eligibility to keep his job, but not necessarily the sole factor, according to the rules. It was still theoretically possible that a member of such organizations might be retained "on all the evidence," that he might be found not to be personally "subversive" despite his membership. But three months later, while my appeal was pending, the Loyalty Review Board, acting under the guidance of Mr. Clark, threw out the old rules, selected five out of the hundreds of organizations on his list, and established the new rule that membership in these five organizations was sufficient ground to make discharge of their members *mandatory.*

This put an end, once and for all, to any pretense that my case was to be judged solely on its own merits. Mr. Gray now admitted that he was "bound" by the attorney general's designation of my party. He, like the Philadelphia Board, was prohibited from considering the central issue. (Mr. Clark evidently kept his promise to talk to Mr. Gray; the joke was that he had not committed himself on what he would tell him.) I was told that I could appeal to the Loyalty Review Board, but what good would that do so long as they were going to hear my appeal along the lines of Memorandum 32?

There was only one consolation that I could derive from this development. I had been saying that my discharge was not only a matter of individual injustice, but of political discrimination against my party and its members. I had been telling everyone that it was impossible to separate the individual from the greater injustice. Now the government, in its own way and from its own standpoint, was saying the same thing through Memorandum 32. Not much consolation, it is true, but sometimes you can't be picky.

In March 1949 we were notified that the Loyalty Review Board would hear my appeal in New York at the end of the month. While we were waiting, the Phi Beta Kappa Association of Essex County held a dinner in Newark on March 3, at which Mr. Thurman Arnold delivered a strong denunciation of the "loyalty" program. Among other things, he called it "a reign of terror," in which jobs and reputations are destroyed "by an unconstitutional process, through secret evidence, association and hearsay."

Mr. Arnold is a former U.S. assistant attorney general (like Mr. Tom Clark), and for a long time it was thought that he, rather than Mr. Clark, would succeed Francis Biddle as attorney general. Yet his attitude to the government purge was the opposite of Mr. Clark's, although they are both Democrats. It seemed to me that this was a good illustration of how arbitrary the "loyalty" program really is.

There was another and even better illustration at the same dinner. After Mr. Arnold sat down, another man at the dinner got up to answer him. His name was John Kirkland Clark, and he was not only a national Phi Beta Kappa official but a member of the Loyalty Review Board. He said: "I don't think there is any consideration fairer than that these [loyalty] boards give these cases. Whether or not it is desirable to have people working in our government who are against the government is a matter of opinion." (By people "who are against the government" he meant those who favor a form of government different from that advocated by Democrats or Republicans.)

I thought it was astonishing that he should admit it is "a matter of opinion" if such people should be retained in their jobs or purged. If it is a matter of opinion, then it is not a matter of law, and therefore there is no legal sanction for the purge in general or my discharge in particular! By what legal right, then, did the Loyalty Review Board issue its Memorandum 32?

I am a great believer in freedom of opinion and expression. I am in favor of letting Mr. Tom Clark and Mr. John Kirkland Clark and Mr. O.W. Clark have their opinions about what is and what is not subversive. But I am decidedly not in favor of letting their opinions become a substitute for law while at the same time they deny me and other government employees the right to have our opinions.

I hoped that Mr. John Kirkland Clark would be at my hearing in New York, and that he would repeat there what he said at the dinner in Newark, and that he would try to square this statement with the contention of the party in power that it has the right to blacklist opponent parties and fire their members out of government employ. He was there, in fact he was a member of the three-man panel that "heard" my case, but he did not repeat his after-dinner remarks.

The other two members of the panel, which conducted its proceedings behind closed doors at the Federal Building in New York on March 31, 1949, were John Harlan Amen, a New York lawyer, and Henry Parkman, a Boston lawyer. I was represented again by Mr. Myer of Chicago. Also present was Sol D. Kapelsohn, attorney for the New Jersey State CIO Council.

The members of this panel were more sophisticated than the Dr. Jacques type. But it wasn't their manners we were interested in. Mr. Myer began at once by asking if they were going to restrict themselves to my membership in a party on the attorney general's list. Mr. Amen's answer was: ". . . anything which is within our jurisdiction we are willing to consider for what it may be worth." Exactly what that meant can be seen by what followed, for it became clear that like the others before them, these three were "bound" by Memorandum 32. Consequently, this proceeding was as cut and dried, in essence, as the one in Philadelphia.

However, they permitted us to enter testimony from an authorized representative of the Socialist Workers Party, something which the Philadelphia Board had said was prohibited by the regulations. The witness was Farrell Dobbs, who was my party's candidate for president in 1948, and is now its national secretary.

Under direct questioning by Mr. Myer, Dobbs explained the principles of the Socialist Workers Party, and the educational and electoral activity it conducts in order to persuade the American people of the need to make a change from a capitalist to a socialist form of society. He flatly denied that our party advocated the use of violence or unconstitutional means in order to achieve its aims. If there was any violence in the course of the changeover from capitalism to socialism, he emphasized, it would be because the minority of people who wanted to hang on to their capitalist privileges would forcibly resist and use violence in order to thwart the will of the majority. In that case, he said, the majority would defend their rights by force, if necessary, and the Socialist Workers Party would support the majority.

The members of the panel then put him through a rigorous cross-examination, centered mainly on the question of advocacy of force and violence. Dobbs answered all their questions calmly and clearly— much too clearly for their satisfaction. They then peppered him with dozens of hypothetical questions in an attempt to get him to admit, directly or indirectly, what he had not said and did not believe. But Farrell Dobbs is not the kind of man to let anyone fluster him or put words into his mouth, and he set the record straight every time.

I was sworn in next. They questioned me for about five minutes on my record, but I could see they did not have much interest in their own questions.

The rest of the session, which only lasted about two and one-half hours altogether, was devoted to argument on constitutional aspects of the case by Mr. Myer, interrupted by questions or objections from the panel members. Part of it duplicated what he had said in Philadelphia, and part of it was a little too technical for me to follow, although toward the end Mr. Clark told Mr. Myer: "You have done a very good job and much clearer job than other people who raised the same points in other hearings." But it was plain that they did not agree with what he said, and that Memorandum 32 was their chief consideration.

> Mr. Clark: Somebody has to decide whether or not an organization is subversive, disloyal, and that has to be deputed to an officer of the government. He has made a finding on it. Is there any way you have to suggest that will enable this Board to say we will not follow the directive given to us?

Mr. Myer then suggested that the Board could and should "decide whether Kutcher is a member of an organization which advocates force and violence."

Mr. Clark: . . . We are called upon to take advice from the chief law officer [the attorney general] of the government we are a part of. That being so, and he having on such investigation as he made rendered a decision that this is such an organization, what possible course is there [other than to abide by his finding]?

When the proceedings ended, Mr. Kapelsohn gave the press a statement in the name of New Jersey CIO President Carl Holderman:

". . . These are the decisive questions in [the] case:

"Have public workers the same rights as other American citizens, including the right to their political beliefs, as guaranteed by the Constitution? Or can they be demoted to second-class citizens?

"Do representatives of the party in office have the right to proscribe other parties by decree and penalize their members? Or shall the principle of free political activity be preserved so that the American people can have full and free expression for their political ideas and affiliations?

"To support Kutcher is to defend the best traditions of American democracy. To aid the persecution of the legless veteran is to help clear a path for thought-control practices belonging to police states."

This was substantially what Mr. Myer had been telling the panel. As we left the Federal Building I thought: For all the good it did the members of the panel, he might just as well have confined himself to giving a statement to the press, like Mr. Kapelsohn.

On April 25, 1949, Mr. Seth Richardson, chairman of the Loyalty Review Board, sent a letter which said:

You are advised that the panel of members of the Loyalty Review Board which met in New York City on March 31, 1949, to consider the case found that Mr. Kutcher had been and continues to be a member of the Socialist Workers Party and it, therefore, affirmed the decision of the administrator of the Veterans Administration.

In accordance with the Regulations and Directives of the Loyalty Review Board, the Socialist Workers Party is an organization within the purview of Section 9A of the Hatch Act and Mr. Kutcher's removal is mandatory.

The Veterans Administration has been advised of the decision and has been requested to remove Mr. Kutcher's name from its rolls.

That ended the final stage of the administrative appeal machinery. The Kutcher Civil Rights Committee met and voted to take the case into the federal courts, and up to the Supreme Court if necessary. My consolation this time was that the courts, at least, would be able to consider the chief issues in the case which had been arbitrarily waved aside until then.

13

My national tour

While getting these setbacks from the Loyalty Boards, we were winning victories in the battle for public opinion. Each administrative defeat, stripping away illusions about the intentions of the witch-hunters, seemed to create new areas of interest and to open new avenues of support for us. By the end of 1948 the facts in my case were fairly well known in liberal and labor circles.

Around that time I went to Connecticut as a guest speaker at the State CIO Convention, and was invited to give a talk over a radio station in Hartford. When I finished, George Novack told me I had handled myself more than adequately and should soon be ready to undertake a national speaking tour under the auspices of our committee.

"Our local committees have been clamoring for it," he explained. "Your presence will stimulate and strengthen their work, not to mention the fact that it will be a shot in the arm to our finances. We can try to arrange the tour in such a way that it will not be too big a tax on you physically. I think you'll find it a very stimulating experience."

But I had been having some trouble with my artificial legs, and I soon had to go to the hospital for the operation on my left stump already mentioned. The demand of the local committees for a speaker continued, however, and George decided he would have to take time off from his job for at least a tour to the Midwest. Arrangements were made for a six-week tour, starting early in March 1949 in Pittsburgh, then through Ohio, Michigan, Illinois, Wisconsin, Minnesota and ending in Buffalo.

George had great success from Pittsburgh on. In fact, there was more work for him than he could take care of. He spoke morning, noon and night—to unions, religious groups, women's organizations, veterans, at colleges, over the radio—and still he couldn't comply with all the requests. Wherever he went, a stream of resolutions, letters and financial contributions began to move to our office in New York. A new local committee was formed while he was in Akron. He apologized that he was not able to take care of all the work in Youngstown in the two days he spent there. He introduced the case to CIO and AFL leaders in Canton. He was exhausted by the time he got to Cleveland, but he went through the strenuous first half of his four-day stay there, and then collapsed, stricken with influenza. We phoned him to cancel the rest of the tour and come home to recuperate. He agreed to skip some of the smaller cities but insisted on going to Detroit and Chicago to fill his major engagements. Then even he had to admit he didn't have the strength to continue, and he returned to New York.

I visited him at once, to chide him for acting in such disregard of his health. "That's not my usual practice," he confessed. "But, Jimmy, I have never seen anything like what I saw these last few weeks. I've made several tours on other cases in my time, with more or less success. But nothing compared to the reception and interest that met me this time. Next to the fear of war, I believe civil rights is the number one issue in the minds of thinking Americans today.

"And your case symbolizes the issues in dispute for everyone who hears about it. Students shot questions at me for an hour and a half at a sociology class I spoke to in Youngstown. A number of professors joined our committee. Others who hesitated to do so expressed admiration for the forthright stand we were taking and hoped we would win our fight. There is a great deal of alarm in the universities I visited about the effects of the witch-hunt on academic freedom, and these people sympathize with us not only because they feel shocked at what happened to you but because they see the connection between their own situation and the general state of civil liberties.

"There was one young man who didn't see any connection at first, but he learned quickly. He is an ex-GI, student editor of an Akron university paper. When he was asked to give my tour and your case some publicity and support, he replied that he thought you got a raw deal but he personally could not see how the inclusion of the Socialist Workers Party on the 'subversive' list concerned him, since he believes in World Federalism and is opposed to socialism. A day or two later the press reported that a Veterans of Foreign Wars convention had passed a resolution demanding that World Federalism be outlawed as 'subversive.' The next issue of the university paper had an editorial denouncing this extension of the witch-hunt to the World Federalist movement, as well as an article captioned 'Men of Principle Take Up Cry for James Kutcher.' You see, there is a growing identification between your case and the general defense of civil liberties. That was why I was reluctant to cut the tour short."

While I was waiting for my stump to heal so that we could make definite plans for my tour, additional support reached us from some of the most distinguished academic and scientific figures in America. On March 1, 1949, five members of the University of Chicago faculty sponsored a letter to their colleagues on the campus, asking them to sign a statement in my behalf. The five were Prof. Anton J. Carlson, former president of the American Association for the Advancement of Science; Prof. Richard P. McKeon, former chairman of the American Council of Learned Societies and dean of the Division of Humanities; Prof. Malcolm P. Sharp of the University Law School; Prof. Harold C. Urey, director of the War Research Atomic Bomb Project and Nobel Prize winner in chemistry; and Prof. Louis Wirth, former president of the Sociological Society and of the American Council on Race Relations.

The letter of the five professors said that the issue in my case "goes beyond sect or party; that it involves every type of man and group concerned with civil liberties and freedom of conscience." The statement they circulated said: "We think that doctrines of 'guilt by association' are inconsistent with genuine freedom of association and thought. Because we are concerned with both these freedoms, we protest their denial in the case of James Kutcher."

The response of the University of Chicago faculty gave a great moral stimulus to our work. By April 27, 1949, 105 of the faculty had signed the statement! These two documents were widely circulated at universities and colleges all over the nation and were endorsed by hundreds of educators. A similar statement was issued a year later by 60 members of the Harvard faculty, including Pulitzer Prize winner Arthur M. Schlesinger, Jr.; Kirtley F. Mather, then president-elect of the American Association for the Advancement of Science; and F.O. Matthiessen, the noted literary critic. (This was one of Mr. Matthiessen's last public acts. Partly from despair over the cold war and its effects on civil liberties he committed suicide a few days after the Harvard statement was issued on March 28, 1950.)

Encouraged by the University of Chicago faculty support, we laid out plans for my tour, beginning early in June 1949 in Minnesota, and then heading for the West Coast. We made the schedule loose so that I could stay in the main centers longer than George had done and so that I would not overexert myself. But the tour had as stimulating and exciting an effect on me as George's had on him. I never was conscious of being tired until it was finished, nine months later. I cannot hope to tell the whole story of the tour here because it would take a book by itself. All I can do is touch on some of the high spots of an experience that was truly the time of my life. I made hundreds of friends, scores of whom still correspond with me. I helped to educate tens of thousands of people to what is happening in this country, and in turn I was educated by them and given a new hope for the future that will sustain me whatever happens in the end to the fight for my job. I kept notes on what happened, and I want to quote from some of them to indicate what the tour was like.

Minneapolis: "A balding, cheerful little man who is the central figure in one of America's most controversial civil liberties cases was in Minneapolis Tuesday to carry on his fight for political freedom." That was how the *Minneapolis Morning Tribune* began its story today. And I used to think people would stop calling me little after my artificial legs increased my height from 5 ft. 2 in. to 5 ft. 4 in. . . .

One of our first local committees was formed here, and it has done a bang-up job. Waldo Byrne, our secretary, showed me a list of sixty Minnesota labor leaders, ministers, educators and liberals who have signed a statement pledging to help me get a fair hearing. There will be a broad participation in our big meeting at the CIO Hall Friday night. Among the speakers will be the president of the Hennepin County CIO Council, the president of the NAACP branch, the field representative of the CIO Packinghouse Workers, a clergyman, a leader of the Fellowship of Reconciliation and Waldo . . .

The Rev. Claypool, still a young man, escorted and introduced me at the Hennepin County CIO Council and the AFL Central Labor Union tonight. On the way from the first to the second hall, he suddenly said he'd forgotten something at the CIO meeting. I asked what. "I neglected to denounce your party." I laughed and told him not to forget at the AFL if that is what he wants to do, but warned that I wasn't going to remind him . . .

Society Slovene, No. 110, and Lily of the Valley Lodge, Society Slovan, of Chisholm, have endorsed my case. One thing about this tour is that I will learn about a lot of organizations I never heard of before . . .

"Attorney General Clark is the greatest subversive in the United States and ought to be deported back to Texas." That's what Dr. Irving E. Putnam, pastor emeritus of the Methodist Church, told them at our well-attended meeting tonight. And I used to think of clergymen as meek types, good only for turning the other cheek. "Most of the revolutionary fathers of this country would be considered subversive by Clark and the House Un-American Activities Committee," Dr. Putnam noted. Amen! NAACP President Albert Allen warned the audience: "When the time comes that thought and association are controlled, then all freedom is gone." A collection of $150 was taken by the audience to help our fight. Packinghouse Local 4 announced their endorsement and gave a $25 check. . . .

I appeared before the Minnesota CIO Executive Board today. I hear they spent over an hour debating before they agreed to support my fight for a fair hearing and reinstatement. . . .

They had a social affair in St. Paul tonight so I could get to know committee members and friends personally. They presented me with a leather billfold and a card: "To James Kutcher—a brave fighter in the vanguard of the struggle for civil liberties—we offer this token of appreciation. Minnesota Friends." Funny feeling, being thanked by people who are doing so much to help you. . . .

Seattle: Spoke to Machinists Lodge 79, very good reception; first local of the International Association of Machinists I've attended, although some have endorsed. That was right after I arrived two days ago. An AVC luncheon the next afternoon, then an interview with the press at the CIO office, attended by CIO regional director, president of AVC university chapter, president of Seattle Americans for Democratic Action, secretary of American Civil Liberties Union, vice president of National Lawyers Guild student chapter, and Frank Krasnowsky, secretary of our local committee. . . .

I was scheduled to participate in a forum on civil rights sponsored by the American Civil Liberties Union tomorrow. They tried to get someone to defend the "loyalty" program. All three members of the regional Loyalty Review Board were invited, also the Civil Service Commission, also the FBI. None was willing, so the ACLU called it off and urged its members to attend our committee's public meeting. I guess it was a moral victory for us, but I would have preferred to meet one of these people in a public debate under conditions where they did not set the rules. . . .

Drove out to Everett and spoke at meetings of AFL Boilermakers Local 104 and the AFL Lumber and Sawmill Workers. One fellow suggested I come up to Canada to talk to some groups there, but our schedule doesn't permit. . . .

The example of the 105 Chicago faculty has made a big impression here. Max Savelle, professor of history, and Ivan C. Rutledge, assistant professor of law at the University of Washington, sent a statement to their colleagues asking them to join the protest: "We believe this is an important test case of the validity of one of the most precious principles of American democracy . . . and will strengthen the hands of the Kutcher Civil Rights Committee by showing that there is an alert public opinion behind it." Fifteen professors have signed already. Prof. Rutledge was fellow-speaker at university AVC meeting. . . .

What I took to be Minnesota hospitality and warmness isn't peculiar to Minnesota. . . .

At our big meeting at Swedish Hall tonight, Franke Grande, pastor of the Church of the People, said he was behind me because his church may be next on the list if thought-control persecutions aren't stopped. A young woman, still a college student, told me she has changed her mind about seeking a civil service job since learning the truth about the "loyalty" program.

San Francisco: There's a hot fight going on here now [June 1949] over a "loyalty" oath at UC. Five hundred out of seven hundred faculty members on the Berkeley campus adopted a resolution against the oath. I'm going to speak there next Tuesday at a meeting jointly sponsored by Americans for Democratic Action and Students for Democratic Action. A lot of the protesting professors are expected to attend. Twelve professors at San Francisco State College sent the press a statement denouncing my discharge. UC professors are circulating a similar statement. . . .

The press has clammed up on us, but that doesn't stop me from getting around to organizations. I just made a half-hour recording at a Berkeley radio station, to be broadcast later this week. Have engagements with Alameda County AFL Central Labor Union and Santa Cruz County AFL Central Labor Council. Also at Local 10 of CIO Longshoremen; that's Harry Bridges' local. Going to Stalinist-dominated "Conference Against Thought Control" tomorrow; wonder what they'll do. [See next chapter.] Our committee has a picnic later in the day. . . .

Fine meeting at Univ. of California. Look forward to meeting Warren Billings. When I joined the YPSL fourteen years ago, we used to adopt resolutions demanding freedom for him and Tom Mooney. Never thought the day would come when he would join a committee in my defense. Another committee member I want to see here is Prof. Alexander Meiklejohn. I've never read a more stirring and logical defense of civil liberties than his little book, *Free Speech and Its Relation to Self-Government.* He's to be chairman at our public meeting.

The leading newspaper in Copenhagen, Denmark, has devoted a full page to my fight but the daily papers here and in Seattle do not consider it newsworthy enough for a few paragraphs.

Los Angeles: Large delegation met me at the airport. Then to reception at house party where more than one hundred people attended. Committee is working here busily at new fund-raising method (new for us, that is)—getting out a souvenir journal with greetings from sympathetic organizations and individuals, to be issued at a banquet.

Newspaper publicity is better here. *L.A. Sentinel,* Negro weekly, has editorial on case. Samuel B. Gach, columnist for the *California Jewish Voice,* ran item entitled "No Legs, But Plenty to Stand On," beginning, "A distinguished visitor is in town today." *Crossroads,* the Nisei weekly, has long editorial, "Who Is 'Subversive'?" tying up my case with the treatment of West Coast Japanese as "subversives" during the war. . . .

Next to the labor movement, most of our support here is coming from the minority groups: Negro, Jewish, Japanese-American, and now I've been invited to talk to the Community Services Organization (Mexican-American).

I've also been invited to explain my case to the national convention of the National Association for the Advancement of Colored

People which will open here next week. Understand I will be the only speaker who won't be either an NAACP official or a government spokesman. . . .

I begin to understand the point that George made to me after his tour: These minority groups identify their fight for their rights with my fight. When they support me, it is one way for them to say: We want our rights just as we want everyone else to have his rights. That *Crossroads* editorial really drove the point home to me.

Too much work to be done in the two weeks I was supposed to be here. So my stay in L.A. has been extended indefinitely. George agrees I can stay here two months if necessary, and will make adjustments in midwest tour dates. Prof. Linus Pauling of California Institute of Technology, president of American Chemical Society and winner of many awards in chemical research, has come out in my behalf. . . .

The banquet was really something: 325 present, and an enthusiasm I've never seen surpassed. Loren Miller, NAACP attorney, said: "I think it is to Mr. Kutcher's eternal credit that he is not one of those who has taken refuge in denial of his views." Masamori Kojima, editor of *Crossroads,* stressed that, like me, "A public hearing is what we Japanese-Americans demanded to decide our case [during the war]—but we didn't get it." A.L. Wirin of the American Civil Liberties Union charged that it is not a loyalty program but "obviously merely a conformative program"—to make people conform to the ideas of Tom Clark. Labor attorney Leo Gallagher made a militant speech against Taft-Hartleyism and the "subversive" list as attempts to intimidate the people so that they will be afraid to fight for any social change. . . .

The Ford Local of the CIO United Auto Workers in Long Beach is having trouble with the company and talking about strike. But they took time out from consideration of this pressing matter to hear me talk, then voted to endorse and send our committee $25 to help in the court fight. . . .

The case is one year old today. It certainly has changed the course of my life as definitely as the depression and the war. . . .

After one of the meetings tonight, an old Negro couple came up to shake my hand. The wife said, "I am going to pray for you." Her husband said, "Maybe the ones you ought to pray for are those people in Washington"...

My first success with one of the old-time veterans groups. Spoke to Veterans of Foreign Wars Post 1556 Wednesday night; they passed a strong resolution and sent a wire to their national convention, now meeting in Miami, urging it to do the same. Tonight I spoke to the L.A. County Council of the VFW, representing 153 posts. After I left, a motion was made to table the matter, that is, kill it. Then they decided to reconsider the thing, maybe at the next meeting. A number of delegates came outside to talk to me. One said he'd resign as delegate to the council if it fails to assist me. I told him not to resign for such a reason, but to stay inside and fight for his views, even if he was temporarily in a minority. . . .

George Novack writes that demands for speakers are so great in the midwest that he is going to join me in Chicago to help out. I've been in L.A. over ten weeks now.

Chicago: Prof. Anton J. Carlson, chairman of our local committee, was present at the reception dinner at the Central YMCA tonight. Good to see George and Mr. Myer again. Will have a day off from my Chicago schedule next Sunday, but must go to Milwaukee that day. . . .

Spoke at forum of the Chicago City Club, made up of professional and business men. My remarks touched off quite a lively discussion of the "loyalty" program. Theopholous Mann, a noted Negro attorney, told about an employee with the Department of Agriculture for thirty years who was accused of "sympathetic association" with "subversives." He was finally cleared of the charge but his wife was prostrated and his own health broken by the ordeal and he lost his job anyhow. Labor attorney Francis Heisler told about a federal employee in Chicago who was simply investigated by the FBI. As a result his whole family was boycotted by their neighbors in his apartment house; they wouldn't even let their children speak with his.

He can't get a transfer to another city and remains subject to daily humiliation. Leon Despres, counsel for the American Civil Liberties Union, told of a postal employee charged with "disloyalty" because he associated with colored people. Seems he invited some of his fellow workers who happen to be Negro to attend his daughter's wedding. He was grilled on whether he ever held meetings in his home, held radical ideas, etc. Thanks to help from the ACLU, he was cleared and restored to his job. But it shows that the purge is an instrument of racial as well as political discrimination.

Walter F. Dodd, chairman of the Regional Loyalty Board, was also present, and was invited to comment on my case. He declined, saying he hadn't read the whole record, and defended the "loyalty" program as giving accused workers the chance for a hearing. Prof. Carlson asked him if he thought I had obtained justice from the Loyalty Board, but he refused to voice his opinion. . . .

The pattern of the tour is to have a public meeting or banquet under our own auspices at least once in each city, in addition to speaking before as many organizations as possible. We don't get to talk to as many people as by appearing at other meetings, but our own gatherings consolidate our work and lay the basis for continued activity after I leave. I liked the remark at our meeting by Sidney Lens of the AFL United Service Employees Local 329, and author of *Left, Right and Center,* an interesting book on American labor: "The Kutcher case is like a hole in the dike holding back the flood waters of reaction and thought control. Unless we take action here and now to stop that leak, the witch-hunt can submerge all the rights of labor."

A heartening feature of this meeting was telegrams from the leaders of the two packinghouse unions, AFL and CIO. Patrick Gorman, secretary-treasurer of the AFL Amalgamated Meat Cutters and Butcher Workmen, said: "We believe his fight is entitled to support by everyone concerned with civil liberties today." Ralph Helstein, president of the CIO United Packinghouse Workers, said, "I view the Kutcher case as part of our overall battle to preserve our traditional civil liberties and to extend to every citizen the right to dissent from majority views. . . . He has the support of all people who are committed to the preservation of the democratic ideal."

Flint: This used to be a General Motors town; now it is a United Auto Workers town too. I spoke to the three large GM locals—Chevrolet, Fisher Body and AC. Publicity in the union papers made up for lack of it in the daily press.

A waitress at one of the hotels had heard about my case somehow. "I can hardly believe it," she said. "This isn't Russia; this is the USA. They can't do that sort of thing in a free country."

Detroit: They used to call this the arsenal of democracy; I can testify that its organizations represent one of the great strongholds of democracy in this country. I've never seen anything like this. I thought they kept me busy in Los Angeles, and they did; but we've got more speaking engagements here than we can possibly handle, and only two weeks to cover them in. Right now we have more than seventy invitations from organizations, and more coming in all the time. Since many take place at the same time, George, Ernest Mazey and others will have to speak at some instead of me. We've been averaging six to eight meetings a day so far. Al Barbour, Wayne County CIO secretary, is chairman of our committee, which includes leaders of dozens of organizations, clergymen of many denominations, two judges, a city councilman, professors, etc., too numerous to list. The State and County CIO Councils asked all affiliates to help us, and that is just what they are doing. . . .

Spoke to the executive board of the big West Side Local 174 of the UAW this afternoon. They had postponed action on my case, the president said, because "some members couldn't believe Kutcher was discharged solely because of his membership in the Socialist Workers Party." They applauded spontaneously when I finished.

The Joint Board of the CIO Amalgamated Clothing Workers passed a recommendation to their international executive board that I be made an honorary member of the union and be clothed free for life. It was a very emotional scene. They also voted a donation to the committee and then took me down to the Labor Cooperative Clothing Store and gave me, "as a token of our affection," two new suits, a topcoat and other clothing. . . .

Today I was the guest of Ford Local 600, the biggest in the world, in an inspection of the River Rouge plant. Almost fifty organizations have sent greetings to our souvenir journal. . . .

When George Novack was here in March, he was denied permission to discuss my case at open meetings at Wayne University. When the Student League for Industrial Democracy applied for me to speak, we were turned down at first. But so many protests came from students that there has been a change of heart (or policy) and I will speak at a public meeting there after all. Also will speak under AVC auspices at University of Michigan in Ann Arbor. An article in *The Voice of Branch 1,* published by the National Association of Letter Carriers, has a good one on the "subversive" list they call it "Tom Clark's 'S.B.' list." . . .

The Baptist Ministers Conference discussed the case for at least half an hour after I spoke. The chairman praised me as "one man who comes to us for help who tells us right off what party he belongs to." They voted to take offerings for me in their churches. . . .

Our banquet was a big success. It was held at the Central Methodist Church, whose minister, Dr. Henry Hitt Crane, a member of our committee, repeated the sermon on "Loyalty by Mandate" that he gave the church last Sunday. "Loyalty must be voluntary, not coercive; it must be deserved and earned, not commanded and extorted. . . . James Kutcher had the courage to dramatize the validity of the principle of free speech. We are fighting whether we are to think as we please and we are fighting for the right of assembly. I am proud to salute this man and hope the end he seeks is attained."

Michigan CIO President August Scholle said: "Speaking for the CIO, we are going to fight to the last ditch with you."

Prof. Orville Linck of Wayne University said: "I am here because it is a question of survival for me as a citizen and as a teacher. If he can be fired from a minor post in the government because of his ideas and because he believes in the ideas of a party which is listed as subversive but which has not been tried, I too can be fired. This is star chamber justice. We must battle strongly to get back to real law. Kutcher's fight is everybody's fight."

The Rev. Robert Bradby, president of the Detroit NAACP, said the Kutcher Committee "will have our full and complete support."

Rabbi Joshua Sperka of Congregation B'nai David said freedom of conscience was being violated in my case.

Toledo: Two interesting talks at our public meeting. City Councilman J.B. Simmons, Jr., likened my case to the persecution of the Negro people. He made some scathing remarks about liberals who privately deplore what is going on in this country but "won't stick their necks out in public." Walter C. Guntrup, editor of the AFL *Toledo Union Leader,* seventy-nine years old and a union man for sixty-three of them, called for a sustained fight to help me regain my job. He told how the government had tried to remove him from a mail carrier's job because of his Social Democratic activities many years ago.

Among the unions helping me here is the Toledo AFL Building and Construction Trades Council. Together with a $25 check was a message: "The unanimous support given this motion is significant in that it conveys to the Kutcher cause the support of laboring people to whom the rights denied Mr. Kutcher are so sacred. We pray that Mr. Kutcher will soon benefit by those rights for which he paid the inestimable price of two legs." . . .

The Socialist Workers Party branch in Detroit presented me with a handsome travelling bag; here the comrades gave me a gold tie clasp and cuff links engraved with my initials. I don't wear such things, but I'll always treasure them.

Cleveland: It's only a few weeks less than a year since I came here to the AVC convention for the first time. The committee, developing splendidly then, has become an important force now.

I've spoken here to twenty-five labor, fraternal and student groups, as well as a radio broadcast, three press interviews, etc., and I'm still not done. One was the Jones and Laughlin IWW Local [Industrial Workers of the World]. This was once a thriving movement, but this is the first local I have run into. They gave me a $50 check, and after the meeting took up an additional collection of $22. They're especially sensitive to my case because they have the distinction of being the first union to be put on the attorney general's "S.B." list. . . .

Spending quite a bit of time at the national CIO convention, held here this week, where we have a special display table among the various CIO exhibits in the convention hall lobby. I sit at the table whenever I can get away from other meetings, pass out literature and talk to the delegates. Many of them know about the case, and congratulated me on my fight. Others promised to bring it to the attention of their locals when they get home. . . .

Had a personal interview today with Dr. F.E. Townsend, the leader of the Townsend Old Age Insurance Plan that grew so strong during the 1930s. Hope I look as vigorous as he does when I reach his age. He said he agreed with what our committee was trying to do, would publish the facts in the *Townsend National Weekly,* and would support my fight through the American Civil Liberties Union.

Akron: Three busy days: union meetings, a class on constitutional law at the University, the Jewish Community Council, a committee luncheon. The CIO Council not only made a contribution but paid my hotel bill. My comrades gave me a belt with an initialed silver buckle. Just before leaving, I got a phone call at the hotel from one of the men in Company K overseas. He wished me good luck but doesn't want to join the committee because he works for one of the nearby towns.

Youngstown: The tour schedule is too rigid. I could profitably spend much more time in this steel center. Had three interviews over three different radio stations in a single day, which sets a record for me. The main paper, the *Youngstown Vindicator,* ignored me, but all the smaller and weekly papers, including the labor press, gave me a fair play. The secretary of our committee, Merlin Luce, a steel worker, is a veteran of the Italian campaign too. The highlight of our banquet was a speech by Innocenzo Vagnozzi, former city councilman and water commissioner, a defender of Sacco and Vanzetti many years ago, and a prominent Democrat. "I am compelled to attack the party with which I am affiliated," he said in discussing the "loyalty" program.

Buffalo: Another rousing meeting at the Statler Hotel last night. Today, after I spoke to IUE-CIO Westinghouse Local 1581, a spontaneous collection of funds was started at the rear of the hall. As I left the building, they cheered and yelled: "Atta boy, Jim" and "Keep up the fight!"

Pittsburgh: Two student groups at Pennsylvania State College for Women, a radio broadcast, and a talk to union stewards at a meeting specially called to meet me—that's what I've done so far today, and it's still daylight. Tomorrow I talk to the Women's International League for Peace and Freedom, which I think has already endorsed my case. One of the union stewards told me I ought to run for Congress because "you're the kind of man we need in office." If I did, I wouldn't be the first man to sit in Congress because he couldn't hold a job somewhere else.

Asbury Park, N.J.: Back home at last [December 1949] though the tour will last for another two or three months in the East. Attended the State CIO convention here to thank them personally for having helped to start the ball rolling in my case. They passed a strong resolution promising support until the fight is done. George Novack tells me a group of professors at New York University has protested my dismissal. He and I have an invitation to speak at Queens College in New York.

I didn't keep notes after that, although my clippings show I spent much time speaking in New York, New Jersey, Pennsylvania and Massachusetts. However, I want to report on one more meeting and to quote somewhat more extensively from the speeches made there, because in many ways it was the most representative and because of the occasion on which it was held. That was the meeting held at the Capitol Hotel in New York on December 15, 1949—the 158th Anniversary of the Bill of Rights. It was most representative because it included prominent spokesmen not only of the CIO and AFL but also of the Liberal Party, Americans for Democratic Action, the Progressive Party and the Socialist Party.

The mood of the rally was well expressed by Arthur Chapin, civil rights director of the New Jersey CIO, who said that the same forces engaged in promoting the witch-hunt today are those who sought fourteen years earlier to prevent the formation of the CIO. He warned that "the CIO itself could well have been put on that 'subversive' list if it were not six million strong today." He promised that the CIO would continue support of my fight because the freedom of labor is at stake too.

Benjamin F. McLaurin, representing the Brotherhood of Sleeping Car Porters, AFL, reported that his union's international executive board had just endorsed the case. He said the Negro people have been constant victims of hysteria in the past, and fully understood the need to defend all minorities against oppression. "The constitutional rights to life, liberty and the pursuit of happiness become empty words if thought control exists."

Prof. Thomas I. Emerson of Yale Law School, co-author of the most penetrating study ever made of the "loyalty" program (*Loyalty Among Government Employees*, Yale Law School, 1948), said our meeting was "in the finest tradition of American democracy." Tracing the long struggle for civil liberties through U.S. history, he added: "In part, we have been victorious. The past oppressions, the Alien and Sedition Laws and the Palmer Raids are today considered a disgrace. I am confident that the time will come when we will consider the Kutcher case equally disgraceful. . . . But we cannot rest upon past laurels. We are living in a period of profound change and it is fear of change that induces this wave of hysteria. . . . The inevitable outcome of the loyalty program is the establishment of a professional political police which can destroy all constitutional freedoms."

Roger Baldwin, director of the American Civil Liberties Union for three decades, commended the Kutcher Committee for its work, which he called a contribution to the defense of the Bill of Rights. "Protest meetings do good. In this business when you and all of us stick to the fundamentals and make common cause in doing so, we are building on a sound basis for the future of civil rights in America."

Norman Thomas, who had not joined our committee but had protested my discharge, struck a somewhat different note from the other speakers. He again denounced what had happened to me but he spent most of his time explaining why the government had to protect itself against the "Julian Wadleighs who give state secrets to a foreign power" and had to have some kind of loyalty measure against the Stalinists. The trouble with the present "subversive" list, he said, is that "it is ridiculous intellectually and tyrannical in effect."

I.F. Stone, the journalist, took issue with Mr. Thomas:

"The purge is not intended to get an occasional Julian Wadleigh," he contended. "It is to prevent liberals and radicals from being staffed in Washington. The government didn't worry about the 'loyalty' of forty Big Business tycoons known to have ties with the Nazis during the war. No one smeared them. . . . That there are real problems connected with the Communist Party I will not deny. But either you have a Bill of Rights for all, or you have no Bill of Rights. And when it comes to selecting who shall have these rights or not, you don't get Norman Thomas, you get a J. Parnell Thomas. . . . Jimmy Kutcher has done a very great job in the fight for civil liberties. I think that with Kutcher we have an opportunity to strike a decisive blow against the Loyalty Board and its entire procedure."

In my own talk I attempted, as usual, to set the record straight on the meaning of my case. The following is an extract from a transcription of what I said:

"There are some people who have offered me their aid primarily because of the fact that a mortar shell and my legs happened to meet in the same place in Italy in 1943. I have said it before and I will say it again: I don't want any special sympathy or pity because I lost my legs; all I want are the rights that belong to any man or woman. The significant thing about my case is not that I lost my legs but that I lost my rights, which are infinitely dearer and more precious to me. Please remember that there are thousands of men and women who didn't lose their legs whose plight is just as bad as mine because they have been stigmatized and blacklisted for daring to hold or express ideas different from those of the ruling class. . . ."

But most of my talk was taken up with the main impressions and ideas I had received from my tour:

"The first thing that struck me is that there is a rising resistance to witch-hunts and thought control and purges throughout the country. I can testify to this from my own experiences. In fact, it was this which encouraged and inspired me to go through a schedule that was sometimes grueling. . . .

"The greatest source of my support has come from the organized labor movement. That began with the New Jersey CIO a day or two after I received notice of my pending discharge and has since extended all over the country to include AFL and independent unions. If I did not know it before, I would know it now—that the labor movement is the greatest bulwark of our democratic liberties and that it has the ability as well as the duty to assume the leadership of the entire nation. [*]

"Of course, it wasn't only the unions that helped me, although they took the lead. In addition there were scores, hundreds, of liberal, civil liberties, veterans, civic, religious, student, old-age, Negro, Jewish, Japanese-American, Mexican-American, Slavic-American, fraternal, academic, political and social groups and organizations

---

[*] This was in 1949. In the four years that followed, the leaders of many unions became more cautious, timid and conservative. Some of them completely abandoned the defense of the Bill of Rights for all, while others paid it only lip service, and a number seized on the witch-hunt as a pretext for purging the unions of their opponents. Nevertheless, it remains a fact that the labor movement has the *power* to put the McCarthys and McCarrans in their place, and I am sure that this power will eventually be used.

who came to my aid morally and financially, although the overwhelming majority of their members disagree—and sometimes violently—with the social and political views for which I was purged from my job.

"Some people are not only alarmed but discouraged and demoralized by the trends in Washington and the advances that have been made toward transforming this country into a police state. Alarm is certainly in order; in fact, there ought to be more of it. But there is no good reason for discouragement or demoralization. The overwhelming majority of the people are on our side. And if we redouble our efforts and reach them with the truth, they will come to our aid and guarantee that the liberties won in the Bill of Rights will never be destroyed in this country.

"That was demonstrated to me beyond question by the way in which all tendencies in the labor and liberal movements responded to my plea for support. Not only Democrats but even workers who vote Republican showed that they want to defend the civil rights of all victims of the witch-hunt. Negroes and other minorities showed that they understand no one's rights can be won or preserved so long as the rights of any are in danger. Protestants, Jews and Catholics, including members of the Association of Catholic Trade Unionists, and atheists as well, showed that they are ready to join in common defense of their own liberties which they realize are threatened by the precedent set in the 'loyalty' purge. . . ."

14

The role of the Communist Party

I said in that New York speech that "all tendencies" in the labor and liberal movements helped me, but this was not strictly accurate, and I corrected it at once. This brings me to a sordid chapter in my case, without which its history is not complete. I report it because of its educational value: it teaches a lesson on how *not* to fight for civil liberties that ought to be absorbed by every opponent of witch-hunting. What I refer to is the role of the Communist Party. That affected me because I was on Stalin's blacklist as well as Truman's.

It is hard to decide where to begin, because the origins of the role they played in my case go back to a period many years before I became a socialist.

The Socialist Workers Party was formed by people who were expelled or resigned from two parties: from the Socialist Party in 1937, an event I participated in; and from the Communist Party in 1928. The latter expulsions took place when a number of Communist Party leaders and members in this country refused to give slavish obedience to the policies of Stalin and sided with Leon Trotsky in his struggle against the rise of anti-working class, nationalist and totalitarian trends in the Soviet Union and its repercussions in Communist Parties all over the world. Stalin eventually murdered most of his opponents whom his assassins could reach, and the Stalinist movement carried on a relentless campaign of character assassination against those whom it called "Trotskyists."

From the day the Socialist Workers Party was organized, the Stalinists were out to get us in one way or another. They lied about us, beat up our literature salesmen, and expelled our members from unions under their control. (I myself had to fight them once on the main street of Newark in behalf of my right to pass out literature, and I personally know two socialists who were expelled by them from a local of the Fur and Leather Workers Union, and therefore from their jobs, on the most outrageous frame-up charges.) They hated us more than anyone else because we attacked them in their sorest spot—proving that they were perverters of Marxist socialism, interested only in promoting the foreign policy of Stalin (whatever that policy might be at any given moment) and willing to break strikes or prevent revolutions if that fitted into Stalin's scheme.

Even the lies of the Communist Party were altered to suit the needs of Stalin's foreign policy. In 1938, when Stalin was trying to get an alliance with the United States, they called us agents of Hitler and Franco. In 1939, after Stalin had himself made a deal with Hitler, they switched not only their general policy but their slanders against us. Now, they said, we were agents of American imperialism. In 1941, when Hitler abruptly cancelled his pact with Stalin by invading the Soviet Union, their line changed again. Overnight, they became supporters of Roosevelt again, voting both for him and Truman in 1944, and calling us Hitlerite spies and agents once more. After the war they returned to denouncing us as agents of Wall Street imperialism.

There was, therefore, little political love lost between their party and mine.

But our mutual political hostility did not automatically dictate what course they would follow in my case. To understand that, one must be acquainted with the tradition of labor and liberal solidarity in civil liberties cases that has existed in this country since at least the 1880s (the famous Haymarket "anarchist" case in Chicago).

This was one of America's most glorious traditions. Its underlying principle was that when anyone was persecuted or victimized by the forces of reaction, everyone should rally to his defense and help him secure justice, no matter how opposed they were to his political ideas. Thus, for example, when Tom Mooney was imprisoned on frame-up charges, most of the labor movement protested and demanded his liberation even though they did not agree with his socialist ideas. And, for another example, when the anarchists Sacco and Vanzetti were convicted for a crime few people believed they had committed, it was not only anarchists but liberals, communists and socialists who came to their defense.

I am a firm supporter of this tradition of solidarity, and so is my party. When someone is persecuted because of his labor activities or his political beliefs, we support them to the hilt and urge everyone else to do so, despite political differences. That is the attitude we take to the civil liberties of all our opponents, including the Stalinists. That is the attitude that used to be common in the labor, liberal and radical movements until the Communist Party began to violate and besmirch this fine tradition.

The first big case was the Minneapolis trial of 1941, while I was in the army, when eighteen members of my party and the truck drivers union in Minneapolis became the first defendants convicted under the Smith Act. Convinced that the eighteen were being prosecuted for their ideas and not for any illegal acts, the labor and liberal movements rallied to their support in large numbers, despite their political disagreements with the defendants. The Stalinists, on the other hand, applauded the convictions, complaining only that the sentences were not harsher, and carried on a virulent campaign to isolate and discredit the supporters of the defendants and to prevent the unions from giving contributions to help pay the legal expenses of their trial and appeal.

This earned the Stalinists a foul reputation, one which they have not lived down to this day. And when, seven years later, their own leaders were indicted under the same Smith Act, their rotten record toward the civil liberties of their opponents was thrown in their faces by many organizations they went to for help in fighting the indictments.

Despite the scab-like behavior of the Stalinists in the Minneapolis case, my party condemned the indictment of the Communist Party leaders in 1948 as a threat to the liberties of all, and offered to help them fight it. This was not out of love for the Stalinists, but out of concern for civil liberties and the tradition of labor solidarity. We said that the Smith Act was unconstitutional, and that indictments under it menace the right of free speech and set a precedent that can be used against all groups.

In line with this general principle, I myself told the first press conference on my case in August 1948 that while I oppose the policies of the Stalinists, "I would stand ready to defend any Communist Party member in the same position as I am at present." (*Newark Star Ledger,* August 26, 1948). And I have already told how, at the first national gathering I ever addressed, the American Veterans Committee convention in Cleveland, I spoke in defense of the Stalinists' constitutional rights.

During the first few weeks after the news about my case became public, the Stalinist press said nothing about me, one way or another. Rodney Gilbert, who wrote a column for the *New York Herald Tribune* entitled "Feathers from the Left Wing," called attention to the strange silence of the *Daily Worker* on a case that had been reported "with some sympathy" by "practically all 'Leftist' papers, and many that are not."

But the Stalinists would not be provoked, and I began to assume that they would lay low all the way through. I watched the American Veterans Committee convention closely to see how they would behave, but their conduct on my case was no different from that of the other delegates.

The first signs of a change appeared shortly after Mr. Gray ruled against me.

Union Progress, the official publication of Local 14 of the CIO United Auto Workers in Toledo, ran a column called "Vets-N-Views," signed by Irv (Meatball) Linver. On January 17, 1949, Mr. Linver devoted most of his column to my case. "The Socialist Workers Party," he explained, "is a fancy name for the Trotzkyites, and a Trotzkyite is an excuse for a human being who believes in force and violence as the first and last step in attaining a socialist state. . . . Trotzkyites are often confused with Communists although they are completely different in their ideologies."

Then he listed some of the groups and individuals supporting me who were known for their hostility to the Communist Party (he falsely included the American Legion among my "sponsors") and continued:

"It is not hard to explain why some of these sponsors will fight for the rights of Trotzkyites and not for the rights of Communists. An organization such as the Trotzkyites which openly stands on soap boxes and advocates bomb throwing offers no threat to the existing economy. And these other organizations which represent opinions of social democracy, or appeasement to the bosses, are all in the same boat as agents of Wall Street."

However, he did not end by opposing my defense openly. Instead, he said: "My argument in this whole matter is that we fight for the rights of Kutcher and Burkart [a member of our local committee who belonged to the auto union] and at the same time that we fight for the rights of Foster and Dennis [Communist Party leaders]."

I was not taken in by this pretense of "impartiality" at the end. If Mr. Linver wanted to defend me, he wouldn't go at it by lying about what I stood for. As George Novack wrote in a letter of protest to *Union Progress:* "Mr. Linver has a right to disagree with James Kutcher's political views, but he has no right to misrepresent them so crudely, especially since his falsifications coincide with those of the witch-hunters responsible for Kutcher's discharge. When Mr. Linver writes: 'A Trotzkyite . . . believes in force and violence as the first and last step in attaining a socialist state' and 'advocates bomb throwing,' he not only repeats the false accusations of Kutcher's prosecutors but goes far beyond them. . . ."

What surprised and angered me about this article was its double-barrelled use of guilt by association. I was damned for being defended by people who disagreed with my belief that the civil rights of Stalinists should be protected, and they were damned for defending somebody who allegedly "believes in force and violence" and "advocates bomb throwing." A more vicious hatchet job it would be hard to conceive. It deliberately undermined the foundation of the civil liberties tradition, which rests on collaboration between groups of *different* political opinions. The Communist Party does not demand political agreement from the groups it asks to defend its civil rights; why then should it attack me because my defenders did not share my politics?

I asked George if he thought the Linver article represented the Communist Party attitude to my case. He said it might. He also suggested it might be an example of "local initiative." That is, the author might not be a Stalinist himself but one who was under their influence and simply spouted, maybe even in distorted fashion, what the Stalinists had told him about me in private. "Don't worry," he said. "If it is their line, it will appear sooner or later in their official press and not merely in a local union paper with limited circulation. As support for your case grows, they are going to be under pressure from their members to let them know what to say. I wouldn't worry about it anyhow, Jimmy. If they attack you, it will do them more harm than it will do you."

But I didn't see it that way. I was interested mainly in getting as much support as I could behind my fight for reinstatement, and I felt I had enough trouble without having to defend myself against the Stalinists too. The feeling that there are snipers behind you is just as irritating in peacetime as in war.

A month went by, and then on February 18, 1949, came a poisonous attack in the West Coast Stalinist paper, *Daily People's World*, written by its associate editor, Adam Lapin. Under the title, "Diversion," Mr. Lapin pretended to examine the question of why it was that I was being defended by "right-wing CIO leaders who have long since abandoned any real fight to preserve civil liberties."

After citing their failure to defend Irving Potash, one of the indicted Stalinist leaders in New York who was an official of a union then still in the CIO, he went on:

"But the case of James Kutcher is apparently in a separate and favored category. . . . Needless to say, Kutcher is not a Communist. He is rather a member of a group called the Socialist Workers Party which was aptly described by Carey McWilliams as 'a sort of international conspiracy for the assassination of Joseph Stalin.'"

This was a typical Stalinist "quotation." Mr. McWilliams, a noted liberal author, was a member of the Kutcher Civil Rights Committee, and had just finished a lecture tour where in every speech he protested against my dismissal. It was ridiculous to think that he would lend his support to a member of what he considered an international assassination conspiracy. We had heard that in a speech he had used an expression something like the one quoted by Mr. Lapin, but he explicitly stated—and this Mr. Lapin knew and "aptly" concealed—that the remark was facetious. What he was trying to say, as many other civil libertarians have done, was that I could not possibly be regarded as an "agent of a foreign power" because my party is such a bitter foe of Stalinism, and that this fact showed how far-reaching the current witch-hunt was.

My party, Mr. Lapin continued, "has not cavilled to cooperate with the most reactionary and antilabor forces. . . . It has been praised by the Chamber of Commerce, and has been useful to the FBI. As McWilliams indicated, it is an oddity that he should lose his job."

An oddity? It would be the eighth wonder of the world if the Truman Administration would fire a member of a party that cooperates with antilabor forces, is praised by the Chamber of Commerce and is useful to the FBI! Such a man would get promoted and rewarded instead of fired and stigmatized.

In an effort to explain this contradiction, Mr. Lapin proved himself to be a true master of the poison pen: "Perhaps Kutcher's dismissal was a product of overenthusiasm or of sheer ignorance on the part of hard-working FBI officials. If those who espouse his case seek merely to get him his job back, a friendly hint to the Department of Justice that it committed a boner would no doubt be sufficient."

He knew, of course, that the Department of Justice was not in need of a hint, gentle or otherwise, to learn the facts in my case; that Mr. Tom Clark had heard about it in far-from-gentle terms from scores of organizations; and that the Department of Justice did not think the case was a "boner." He knew that the overenthusiastic, ignorant, hard-working FBI officials had not initiated the case, but were simply executing the policy of the administration. He knew that the protests on my case had led to the issuance of Memorandum 32, making my dismissal mandatory. Knowledge of facts has never given pause to a graduate of the Stalin school of falsification.

"But in any event," he continued, "it [my dismissal] was outside the mainstream of the current attack on civil liberties. And by the same token the defense of Kutcher is outside the mainstream of the defense of civil liberties."

The administration seemed to think differently. They thought a victory for me would discredit the whole purge setup. That was why they stubbornly refused to listen to "hints" and stuck by their dismissal of me despite protests from many of their political supporters.

The ones who were really "outside the mainstream of the defense of civil liberties" were those who dismissed me—and those who were seeking to deny the significance of my case or prevent the mobilization of support for me—notably, the Stalinists.

There were people in the labor and liberal movements who did not support me, whatever the reason. But the Communist Party was the only group in the country that went out of its way to try to influence others not to support me. They weren't merely indifferent to my case, but actively hostile. If their influence had prevailed, I would have received no support whatever—to the satisfaction and benefit of those who had fired me and were firing Stalinists too. Talk about cooperation "with the most reactionary and antilabor forces"—I was confronted with a genuine though informal united front of Stalinist and Trumanite witch-hunters!

On June 24, 1949, when I had already reached the West Coast on my tour, the *Daily People's World* greeted me with an editorial entitled "Look out for this booby trap." It made Mr. Lapin's article look mild by comparison:

"Let it be stated that everything connected with this sorry affair reeks of fraud and deceit. What is being touted as the 'case of the legless vet' and a 'test case' for civil liberties hasn't the remotest connection with the defense of civil rights." (This of course was not original; the Loyalty Board said it first.)

Proof? "On the record," I belonged to a movement whose members were or are agents of Hitler, the Japanese militarists, Chiang Kai-shek, the Dutch imperialists in Indonesia, Franco and Tito. Furthermore:

"Indeed, the Trotskyites themselves give the show away by blandly presenting the American Legion as one of the organizations defending Kutcher. This big brass military outfit, which has brazenly added book burning to its long list of blows at the fundamental rights of all citizens, has the gall to say that the firing of the Trotskyite is a 'doubtful' loyalty case.

"In other words, the so-called fight to restore Kutcher to his job is in reality a fight to establish the 'right kind' of police state thought control."

Now the authors of this editorial knew that we had never, anywhere or at any time, presented the American Legion as my defender. We couldn't, for the simple reason that the Legion had never come to my defense.

What happened was this: The Kutcher Committee had put out a leaflet containing extracts of various statements on my case. Under the heading, "Here Are Some Comments," was included this extract from an American Legion publication: "Kutcher, the legless vet, lost both legs in Italy. His job in the VA was definitely nonconfidential or sensitive. . . . The Kutcher case is therefore an almost perfect example of bureaucratic bungling in how not to handle a doubtful loyalty case." Notice well, our leaflet did not say "Here Are Some Comments by Supporters of Kutcher" or anything of the sort. So there was nothing improper about the use of this item as publicity.

Now, what was the sense of the Legion comment, which amounted to one paragraph altogether? The opening sentence of the paragraph, printed in the September 1948 issue of the Legion's National Americanism Commission bulletin, *Summary of Trends and Developments,* makes it perfectly clear: "An extremely suspicious and provocative little job was recently pulled off in New Jersey which may very well result in the whole loyalty program being badly compromised in controversy and confusion."

In other words, the Legion bulletin was interested in my case solely because it feared that its "mishandling" would discredit the purge as a whole—and not, as the Stalinists tried to intimate, because the Legion wanted members of my party kept in government jobs while Stalinists were purged. The Legion didn't care about me. That was why no Legion post ever helped me in any way. What worried it was the fear that my case, among the first to receive any publicity, would serve to "badly compromise" the purge system before it received public acceptance.

The Stalinists knew all this—and what they didn't know about it in detail, they could easily have learned before printing their editorial. But they tried to cover it up and distort it for the purpose of weakening support for a case that even the Legionnaire backers of the purge admitted could deal a blow to the "loyalty" program. What is more, they even borrowed one of the most notorious features of the purge—guilt by association—to link my position up with that of the Legion.

If there is anyone anywhere who is still influenced by this Stalinist distortion, let me add the following: George Novack originally obtained a copy of the Legion comment by writing to W.C. "Tom" Sawyer, director of the National Americanism Commission. Mr. Sawyer explained that that issue of the bulletin was exhausted, but sent a typed copy of the pertinent paragraph. In a subsequent letter to our committee, Mr. Sawyer's aide, K. Huggins, wrote on March 30, 1949: "The use of the item mentioning Mr. Kutcher, by the Kutcher Civil Rights Committee, has been brought to our attention, and you are advised that at the time, material from our monthly 'Summary of Trends and Developments' was not for general publication and was restricted to key Legionnaires then receiving it. It does not reflect the official policy of the national organization of The American Legion."

In short, the Legion never supported me and never had any intention of giving the impression that it did. Even if it had, the Stalinists were guilty of the most brazen dishonesty when they tried to make it appear that my attitude to the purge had anything in common with that of the Legion.

The *Daily People's World* articles were understood as a call for all Stalinist members and sympathizers to oppose any aid to my defense. Here is one example out of many:

The April 1949 issue of *Shop News,* official organ of Local 450, United Electrical Workers (this was before that international union was expelled from the CIO), reported that a meeting of that local, whose members work at the Sperry Gyroscope plant in Long Island, had listened to a representative of our committee and passed a motion to support me and contribute financially to the expenses of my case. It concluded by noting:

"A strange and rather ironic note at the meeting was the opposition of the Communist Party members to the motion. Unfortunately they are so blinded by their hatred of the Socialist Workers Party, that they refuse to recognize that the question being voted upon was not one of a political nature, but a pure and simple issue of civil rights."

In June 1949 the Stalinists, alarmed by the current trial of their leaders under the Smith Act in New York, decided to build a new national organization to enlist support against the prosecutions. On June 2 the Stalinist-dominated Civil Rights Congress invited all organizations in the New York area to a "Conference on Civil and Human Rights." My party sent representatives and succeeded in getting the floor during a panel discussion to call for support of my case and of a pardon for the eighteen victims of the Smith Act in the Minneapolis trial. This proposal was made in the form of an amendment to an official motion calling for the defense of the civil liberties of the Stalinists. A number of non-Stalinist delegates, sincerely wanting to defend the civil liberties of all victims of the witch-hunt, voted for the amendment. But the Stalinist majority steamrollered the original motion, minus amendments, through the conference.

This created quite a scandal, and gave a handy weapon to opponents of the Stalinists. *The New York Post* in an editorial entitled "With Justice and Liberty—for Some," wrote: "The proposal offered a true test of the Congress' devotion to the cause of unpopular minorities. . . . But Communists hate Trotskyites more than any other form of contemporary humanity and Communists do not believe in civil liberties for those whom they dislike. So the delegates to the Civil Rights assemblage voted to reject the proposed resolution. Their deliberations ended with fiery denunciations of all curbs on civil rights of Communists and stolid silence on the subject of Trotskyite freedom."

The conference's stand was also condemned by people like I.F. Stone, *Daily Compass* columnist, who forthrightly opposes persecution of the Stalinists. Defeat of the amendment, he wrote, "meant the Congress could not help people who were on the outs with the Communist Party. . . . They taint the issue [of civil liberties] by talking one way when their own rights are at stake and screaming for police action against the rights of their opponents, as they did in the Minneapolis case. The crisis now developing is serious enough to call for joint action by everyone, right or left, who believes in liberty—but this can only be brought about on a basis which provides for aid to everybody, irrespective of political views."

Similar conferences were going on throughout the country at that time. I was in San Francisco on June 26 when a "Conference Against Thought Control" was held. I decided to go there and present my case to their attention. They denied my request for fifteen minutes in the morning session on the ground there was "no time on the agenda" for me. All the speakers followed the general Stalinist line. In the afternoon session I made a second request, again denied. Finally, after several hours of "official" speeches, they allowed twenty minutes for discussion from the floor, and I was able to get five minutes. I spoke briefly about my case and the need for all organizations to work together in defense of their common rights.

As soon as I was done, the chairman recognized a young man who delivered one of the most vicious attacks I have ever heard. After the usual prize assortment of Stalinist lies and slanders, he concluded by saying it was not possible to have "a united front with stool pigeons." A number of people were taken aback at this performance and asked for the floor to answer him or discuss what I had said, but the chairman refused to give it to them. I was told afterwards that some rank-and-file Stalinists were discontented with what had happened. It certainly seemed to me like a strange kind of "conference against thought control."

A week later I had a chance to meet these people again, under different circumstances. It was at a meeting of Local 10 of the CIO International Longshoremen's and Warehousemen's Union. The local had endorsed my case previously, but the Stalinist said nothing at that time. Since then the *People's World* had laid down the line, and we heard in advance that the Stalinist bosses were whipping up their members to come out in the open against me.

I presented my case as usual, trying to show how it affected the rights of all workers. As usual, I declared I was against the persecution of anyone for his beliefs, including members of the Communist Party. I also spoke against the many efforts to deport Harry Bridges, president of their international union. This was Bridges' own local, and he sat on the platform from which I spoke.

There was applause when I got done. As I started to leave the platform by way of a set of narrow steps that were a little difficult for me to negotiate, several men in the front row jumped up and motioned me back to the front of the platform, from which they picked me up bodily and set me on the floor.

A motion was made to contribute some money to help my fight. At this point a committeeman, known for his unswerving adherence to the Stalinist line, took the mike and launched into a violent attack against me and my party, along the lines of the one made at the "Conference Against Thought Control." As he called us stool pigeons, agents of the bosses, etc., I wondered if I would be granted permission to answer him. At the same time, however, his speech ended. Not because he was finished, but because the membership refused to hear him any longer.

"Have you no shame, to attack a man when he wants to help you?" "Sit down, you phony!" "Shame!" The noise rose and drowned out the committeeman though he had the advantage of a mike. He sat down to a chorus of boos.

The motion was then put to a voice vote, and carried overwhelmingly. But still the Stalinists were not satisfied, and they demanded a standing vote. This time they were crushed. Out of some 2,800 members present, about 12 stood up to vote against the motion.

Harry Bridges sat silent through the entire incident. Either he did not like the Stalinist line or he did not think it popular to side with them. His following inside the union was no longer as big as it was during the war when he attacked aid to the Minneapolis defendants.

After the meeting everyone was talking about it. The prevailing sentiment was: "They sure did a job tonight—not on Kutcher, but on themselves."

A year or so later I heard that the chief Stalinist spokesman in this local admitted to other members that their attack on me that night was the "worst mistake" they had ever made in Local 10, and that they still had not recovered from it.

The New York Conference for Civil and Human Rights, the San Francisco Conference Against Thought Control and other regional meetings taking place around that time were designed as preparatory steps in the mobilization of a national organization to defend the Stalinists. This was given the name, the Conference to Defend the Bill of Rights, and was called into session in New York on July 16–17, 1949. The conference call set forth this principle: "Free speech, free press, freedom of religion and assembly have no meaning if they apply only to those with whom we agree. They have meaning only where they apply also to minority and dissident groups with whom the majority are in disagreement."

A considerable number of liberals and other non-Stalinists, agreeing with this thought, sponsored and participated in this conference. Members of my party in New York, deciding to test the conference to see if it really believed what it proclaimed, attended and introduced the same proposal on my case and the Minneapolis defendants that had been rejected by the Civil Rights Congress conference a month before. An important struggle began to take shape between those who did and those who didn't believe in civil liberties for all.

Three days before the conference the *Daily Worker* printed an editorial warning that any movement which defended the civil liberties of the "Trotskyists" would not be supported by the Communist Party and could expect its active opposition. It denounced as "disrupters" those liberals like I.F. Stone, Thomas I. Emerson, Albert Deutsch, Harlow Shapley, Frederick Schuman and others who had never hesitated to defend the Stalinists from persecution but who rejected the Stalinist factionalism that stood in the way of a united defense movement. The editorial was plainly designed to stiffen the Stalinist followers to resist action by the conference in accord with the principle stated in the conference call.

That was what happened. A battle took place in the resolutions committee, which ended in the majority of that committee voting for a resolution, introduced by Prof. Emerson, calling for support of the rights of members of my party as well as those of the Communist Party. But the Stalinists had a mechanical majority of the conference and they rammed through their own line after a hot debate (in which Paul Robeson, defending the Stalinist position, demagogically demanded: "Would you ask the Negroes to give freedom of speech to the KKK? Would you give civil rights to Jefferson Davis?").

These proceedings disgusted so many of the non-Stalinist elements that they withdrew, and the Conference to Defend the Bill of Rights, instead of becoming a permanent organization, died an immediate death. The Stalinists had known that this would happen, but with them it was rule or ruin when it came to the rights of their revolutionary socialist opponents. In this case it proved to be rule *and* ruin of the organization they originally expected to help defend their own rights.

No open opposition to support of my case was voiced at this conference, however. While attacking my party as "fascist," the Stalinists did not think it was tactically wise to refuse openly to support me. So when an amendment in my behalf was offered, it was rejected, not on the ground that I did not deserve support, but on the ground that a resolution had protested "all" victimizations under the "loyalty" program, and therefore it was not necessary to have anyone designated by name.

Actually, the Stalinist line had not changed at all. Three days after the conference, when the Stewards Council of Local 430 of the United Electrical Workers adopted a resolution asking the forthcoming national convention of their union to aid me and "the other victims of President Truman's loyalty purge," the leading Stalinist in the local denounced me and my party as "fomenters of war, fascists, agents of Wall Street and fingermen for the FBI."

But in the public press, the Stalinists were more careful of what they said about my case. This brings me to Mr. Howard Fast, the novelist.

After I.F. Stone had sharply rebuked the Stalinists for their behavior at the first of the two conferences in New York, the Stalinists needed some luminary to answer him. Mr. Fast filled the bill, and on July 11, 1949, the *New York Daily Compass* printed a letter signed by him that contained more fiction than all of his novels put together. I will quote only the part referring to me:

"Mr. Stone is quite right when he states that the Kutcher case is a thoroughly disgusting and revolting example of the operation of our loyalty act. Certainly no member of the Civil Rights Congress could disagree with him on that. When questioned on his beliefs, Kutcher said quite frankly that he supported the overthrow of the government by force and violence. For all I know, this may be a part of the

Trotzkyite program. But I would say, along with Mr. Stone, that in the broadest sense of American freedom, a person has the right to think as he pleases, so long as these thoughts are not carried out in terms of criminal action.

"But Mr. Stone should also inquire into the intent of this Trotzkyite in raising the Kutcher case at this particular meeting. The Kutcher case is only one of many, many cases of the violation of civil liberties of Americans by one branch or another of the Truman government. Any one of a dozen or two dozen of these cases could have been raised at the same meeting as amendments to the resolution on the trial of the eleven Communists.

"Any one of these many cases, so raised, would have been opposed in the same way that the amendment of the Kutcher case was opposed—as a watering down of the central intent of the resolution itself. Why then was the amendment on Kutcher raised?

"If James Kutcher desires civil rights support of his case, there are very simple channels for communicating his desire to the Civil Rights Congress. But when James Kutcher and Farrell Dobbs use his case, as well as the case of other Trotzkyites who are admitted pro-fascists, as a device to disrupt a meeting in the interest of civil rights, then I think Mr. Stone makes a serious error in accepting the whole cloth of the particular goods they weave."

Perhaps Mr. Fast did not know that while I was in Los Angeles I had written to the Civil Rights Congress, asking it to hear an appeal for my defense, and that the Congress never even answered my letter. But he certainly knew that the Communist Party had been openly opposing my defense, and that in this respect my case was different from "the many, many cases" he referred to, and therefore merited consideration at a conference "for civil and human rights" that was dominated by the Communist Party. He also knew that there would have been absolutely no "disruption" (that is, discussion) and no "watering down of the central intent of the resolution" if the conference had merely voted to support me, in that resolution or in a separate resolution.

But these evasions were not what angered me most about his letter. As soon as I got a copy of it on the West Coast, I wrote a letter to the *Compass,* parts of which follow:

"Mr. Fast feigns agreement with Mr. Stone that my discharge 'is a thoroughly disgusting and revolting example of the operation of our loyalty act.' He then goes on to say: 'When questioned on his beliefs, Kutcher said quite frankly that he supported the overthrow of the government by force and violence.' This is a complete fabrication. I have never said anything of the sort. On the contrary, at Loyalty Board hearings and in the press, I have repeatedly stated that neither I nor the Socialist Workers Party advocate violence to achieve socialism. . . .

"This is not a mere slip of the pen by Mr. Fast. In the first place, this same false accusation of preaching violent overthrow of the government is Attorney General Clark's pretext for political blacklisting of the SWP and other organizations and for ordering my discharge. By putting this position in my mouth, Mr. Fast not only lies about my views but aids the loyalty purgers in excluding me from my job. In the second place, Mr. Fast's falsification coincides with the standard slanders spread by the Stalinists to prevent support for my fight. . . .

"Mr. Fast provides further evidence that the Stalinists, who shout so loudly about assaults on their rights, are unwilling to join in protecting the civil liberties of their left-wing political opponents. That is why I cannot refrain from characterizing Mr. Fast's letter as 'a thoroughly disgusting and revolting example of the operation' of the Communist Party.

"Farrell Dobbs, SWP national chairman, in his reply to Mr. Fast, demanded that Fast submit his alleged evidence against me and my party to an impartial Commission of Inquiry to be headed by I.F. Stone. I am eager to appear before such a body. Unless Mr. Fast does likewise, he publicly exposes himself as a conscienceless slanderer."

The *Compass* did not print my letter, but Mr. Fast received a copy. He did not agree to the establishment of an impartial Commission of Inquiry at which he could produce his "evidence" against me. He never retracted his lies either. And the Communist Party continued for several months after that to do everything it could to prevent other organizations from helping me.

Then, toward the end of 1949, the Stalinist line, or rather the tactical application of their line, was changed. Their public opposition to me proved to be very unpopular not only with non-Stalinists but even with members and sympathizers of the Communist Party, who began to balk, violate discipline and get up and speak in favor of motions to endorse my case. Consequently, the Stalinist leaders handed down a new policy: to remain silent when my case was brought up for consideration. They followed this policy until the end of 1952. During this time I saw many union leaders enjoy themselves by trying to bait Stalinists into entering the discussion when my case came up.

At the start of this chapter I said there was an important lesson to be learned from the role of the Stalinists. I tried to draw this lesson in the talk I gave at the 1949 Bill of Rights celebration sponsored by our committee in New York. After describing the role of the Communist Party, I went on:

"I want to say one more thing about the Stalinists. In one or two cases I was asked by officers at meetings where I spoke to omit all remarks about [the need to defend the constitutional rights of the Stalinists too]. 'Don't mention them,' I was told, 'because they are so discredited that the members are liable to react unfavorably against your own appeal for support.' Perhaps that was the reason; perhaps they just didn't want to defend the Stalinists' civil rights themselves.

"But in all cases I said that I would prefer to let the members know exactly what I stood for, even if it might be a little unpopular. Of course I was not demanding that the various meetings must express support for the Communist Party's civil rights if they wanted to defend mine; but I wanted to make it clear to everyone I spoke to that I believed it would be inconsistent for them to take the position that everyone's civil rights needed defense except the Stalinists'.

"And that's a point I want to make here too. As you know, the Stalinists hailed the conviction of the eighteen Trotskyists in Minneapolis under the Smith Act, and continue to sabotage all efforts to get a presidential pardon to restore their civil rights. Today they are the victims of the same repressive law whose enforcement they applauded eight years ago. I think there is a big lesson to be learned from that.

"And so I say to you tonight and especially to the leaders of the great labor movement, don't make the mistake the Stalinists made in 1941. Don't be blinded by your political differences with the victims of the witch-hunt, as the Stalinists were in 1941. Don't make the error of thinking that it's not your neck in the noose, as the Stalinists did in 1941. For if you permit the precedent to be set against the Stalinists, as the Stalinists did against the Trotskyists in 1941, then it will be your own turn next.

"And your fight against repression will be all the harder to win then, if it can be shown that you stood aside and refused to uphold civil rights for Stalinists because these scoundrels refuse to support the civil rights of their political opponents. What I say about the need to defend the rights of minorities applies not only to racial and political minorities but also to moral and religious dissidents, such as the conscientious objectors and the Jehovah's Witnesses. . . ."

15

Into the courts

Toward the end of 1949 my attorneys were ready to take the case into the federal courts. But we ran into a hitch: our suit had to be filed in Washington, D.C., and therefore required the services of a Washington lawyer. We quickly learned that this was something sooner said than done. This hitch cost us some time but proved to be a real blessing in disguise, because it led George Novack to make the acquaintance of Joseph L. Rauh, Jr., of the firm Rauh and Levy. Mr. Rauh is one of the outstanding labor and civil liberties lawyers in the capital, and was then chairman of the national executive committee of Americans for Democratic Action, which had previously endorsed my case. He studied the record carefully, agreed to serve as counsel with Mr. Myer, and assumed a major role in preparing the civil suit that was filed in the U.S. District Court in Washington on February 9, 1950.

Mr. Rauh has worked diligently at my case through hearing after hearing and brief after brief since that time because he believed and believes that a real infraction of civil liberties and a grave injustice is involved. At the outset he told George and me that he agreed with few, if any, of the tenets of the Socialist Workers Party and he reserved the right to make his disagreements clear at all times. He has even informed me that there are lots of things in this book that he does not agree with, but that too, he feels, is my business. He gave his time and energy in my case—all without compensation—in an effort to vindicate my right to free speech and free association without losing my government job.

Named as codefendants in this suit were VA Administrator Carl Gray, Jr.; Attorney General J. Howard McGrath (who had taken Mr. Clark's place); United States Civil Service Commissioners Harry B. Mitchell, Frances Perkins and James M. Mitchell; and twenty-one members of the Loyalty Review Board, headed by Seth Richardson.

Among other things the suit asked that my discharge be declared in violation of Section 9A of the Hatch Act and Executive Order 9835; that this law and this order be declared unconstitutional and of no effect as applied to me by the defendants; that my discharge be set aside and held illegal; that a mandatory injunction be issued directing Mr. Gray and his agents to reinstate me to my job with back pay; that all proceedings relating to my discharge be expunged from all records of the defendants; and that the attorney general be directed to destroy all lists purporting to classify the Socialist Workers Party under Executive Order 9835.

"Frankly," I told George Novack after reading the suit, "there are some things about this that I don't get. We have been saying all along that the executive order and Section 9A of the Hatch Act are unconstitutional, and we say it again in this suit. But we also say that my discharge is a violation of the order and the act. What difference does that make, or how important is that fact alongside of the bigger one of unconstitutionality? Why do we want to bother with a side issue like that?"

George laughed and said my question proved I wasn't cut out to be a lawyer. "In legal cases of this kind, where you are suing government officials, the odds are against you, and you must use every legal weapon or technicality available," he explained. "Bad as the executive order is, it still says that every government employee has the 'right to an administrative hearing.' Our complaint charges—correctly—that the defendants denied such a hearing to the plaintiff (that's you) when they refused to accord him 'a hearing on the very issue on which he was discharged,' namely, that your party 'advocates the overthrow of our constitutional form of government.'

"The inconsistency of this and the language of the executive order may seem like a side issue or technicality to you compared with the bigger issue of constitutionality. But legal history shows that judges are very fond of such things and grasp at them in preference to constitutional decisions. We're looking for a favorable verdict, and we want to offer the courts every legal handle they are willing to use for such a purpose. It would of course be wrong to hinge our entire suit around such a point, and we don't do that. But it would be even more wrong to neglect any legal point that might help us."

This reassured me. So did Mr. Rauh's statement to the press immediately after the suit was filed. My case, he told the reporters, is "an almost perfect example of what's wrong with the loyalty program. . . . Mr. Kutcher was discharged without a hearing. He got what appeared to be a hearing, but he was not allowed to show that the Socialist Workers Party, to which he belongs, does not advocate violent overthrow of the government. Thus he was not permitted to present evidence, nor did the loyalty boards make any decision, on the main issue involved in his discharge."

The influential *Washington Post,* commenting editorially on the suit, declared: ". . . Mr. Kutcher is the victim of a dual arbitrariness. The organization to which he belongs has been arbitrarily held to advocate what it denies advocating. And the advocacy imputed to the organization has been arbitrarily imputed to Mr. Kutcher through the mere fact of his membership—an assumption of guilt by association which the Supreme Court in the *Schneiderman* case denounced as invalid and repugnant to American law. As a result, Mr. Kutcher has been severely punished not only by the loss of his job and a blacklisting that may close all other avenues of employment to him but also by an official finding that he is 'disloyal' to his country in whose service he was grievously wounded. . . .

"One cannot help wondering, anyway, why the United States goes to so much trouble to punish James Kutcher. The loyalty program is supposed to protect the national security. But the national security needs no protection from a legless file clerk working in the Newark branch office of the Veterans Administration. The punishment of Mr. Kutcher serves no national interest. It serves no interest save vindictiveness. And Mr. Kutcher is made a target of this vindictiveness solely because he entertains certain unorthodox and unpopular political opinions. . . ."

As we drove back from Washington I expressed satisfaction to George that the case at last was in the courts, and asked him how much longer he thought it would take before the whole thing was wound up. "I'd like to say soon," he answered, "but I'm not making any predictions this time." I remember saying, "It shouldn't take more than a year now."

But it took almost a year and a half to get a decision from the district court, and that was still a long way from the final decision. Time went by slowly, and it became plain that the Department of Justice was in no hurry to have the courts rule on my case. We heard that they preferred to have some other appeal than mine serve as the first test case of the constitutionality of the "loyalty" program and blacklist. Whether or not this was true, the Department of Justice lawyers acted as if they had all the time in the world on my case.

While things were dragging in this manner before the courts, we kept doing what we could to keep the case alive and the public informed of its significance. We had some success in this despite the development of other civil liberties cases as vital as mine and more sensational. I spent part of my time speaking now and then, part of it studying history, and especially the history of the fight for civil liberties in this country, and part of it trying to find things to keep myself occupied. Through Carl Holderman and the New Jersey employment service I twice succeeded in getting a clerical job in private industry, paying an average of $35 a week. But after a few weeks I lost each of them, either because my work was not satisfactory or because my employers found out who I was.

While we were waiting, the U.S. Supreme Court, on April 30, 1951, handed down its first decisions on the "loyalty" program. The issues raised were not exactly like those in my case, but they were closely related.

The Joint Anti-Fascist Refugee Committee had entered court to protest its inclusion on the "subversive" list. It claimed that the attorney general's designation had caused it to lose reputation, "business and patronage," its tax-exemption status, meeting places and other facilities to conduct its activities, etc. Two other organizations, the International Workers Order and the National Council for American-Soviet Friendship, registered similar protests.

Bypassing the administrative machinery of the Loyalty Boards, these three organizations reached the courts with a constitutional challenge to the blacklist ahead of me. But in the federal district and circuit courts their complaints were dismissed when the government insisted that they had failed to state a claim upon which relief could be granted.

By a vote of five to three, the Supreme Court ruled that the lower courts had erred, and returned the cases to the district court for further action. The majority decision, written by Justice Burton, and concurred in by Justices Black, Jackson, Douglas and Frankfurter, did not deal with the constitutionality of the "loyalty" program. But it ruled that the blacklisting of the three organizations was "patently arbitrary" and that the attorney general had exceeded his authority in designating them as "communist" without first giving them a fair hearing. As a whole, the decision was undoubtedly a stinging rebuke to the newest member of the Court, Mr. Justice Tom Clark, who did not participate in the consideration of these cases.

Justice Burton wrote: ". . . the Executive Order does not authorize the attorney general to furnish the Loyalty Review Board with a list containing such a designation as he gave to each of these organizations without other justification. Under such circumstances his own admissions render his designations patently arbitrary. . . . The situation is comparable to one which would be created if the attorney general, under like circumstances [without a hearing, etc.], were to designate the American National Red Cross as a Communist organization. . . ."

Justice Jackson said he doubted that organizations were deprived of any legal rights when they were listed, but he joined with the majority because he believed their members were deprived of rights: ". . . the real target of all this procedure is the government employee who is a member of, or sympathetic to, one or more accused organizations. He not only may be discharged, but disqualified from employment, upon no other ground than such membership or sympathetic affiliation. And he cannot attack the correctness of the attorney general's designation in any loyalty proceeding." He also said: "To promulgate with force of law a conclusive finding of disloyalty, without hearing at some stage before such finding becomes final, is a denial of due process of law."

Justice Douglas, also concurring, said: "An organization branded as 'subversive' by the attorney general is maimed and crippled. The injury is real, immediate and incalculable." Although no charge nowadays is more serious, he noted, there are no standards to determine what "subversive" means: "These flexible standards, which vary with the mood or political philosophy of the prosecutor, are weapons which can be made as sharp or blunt as the occasion requires. Since they are subject to grave abuse, they have no place in our system of law. When we employ them, we plant within our body politic the virus of the totalitarian ideology which we oppose . . . [This procedure] condemns without trial. It destroys without opportunity to be heard. The condemnation may in each case be wholly justified. But government in this country cannot by edict condemn or place beyond the pale. The rudiments of justice, as we know it, call for notice and hearing—an opportunity to appear and to rebut the charge. . . . I do not mean to imply that but for these irregularities the system of loyalty trials is constitutional. I do not see how the constitutionality of this dragnet system of loyalty trials which has been entrusted to the administrative agencies of government can be sustained. . . ."

But to me the most interesting part of Justice Douglas' statement was something I had not known before. In a footnote he pointed out: "The International Tribunal tried Nazi organizations to determine whether they were 'criminal'. . . . That procedure, *unlike the present one*, provided that accused organizations might defend themselves against that charge." (My emphasis.)

Justice Black's concurring opinion was, in my opinion, the strongest and the one which gave the fewest concessions to the witch-hunters because he denied the right of the government to proscribe organizations under any circumstances: ". . . in my judgment the executive has no constitutional authority, with or without a hearing, officially to prepare and publish the lists challenged by petitioners. In the first place, the system adopted effectively punishes many organizations and their members merely because of their political beliefs and utterances, and to this extent smacks of a most evil type of censorship. This cannot be reconciled with the First Amendment as I interpret it. . . . Moreover, officially prepared and proclaimed governmental blacklists possess almost every quality of bills of attainder, the use of which was from the beginning forbidden to both national and state governments. . . . I cannot believe that the authors of the Constitution, who outlawed the bill of attainder, inadvertently endowed the executive with power to engage in the same tyrannical practices that had made the bill such an odious institution. . . ."

Those were the views of the majority of the Supreme Court. The minority's views were expressed in a dissenting opinion written by Justice Reed, in which Chief Justice Vinson and Justice Minton joined. The essence of Justice Reed's position was that neither organizations nor their members are denied any of their rights when they are listed. But the reason he gave for this opinion was very significant: "The employee's association with a listed organization does not, under the Order, establish, even *prima facie*, reasonable grounds for belief in the employee's disloyalty. . . . It seems clearly erroneous to suggest that 'listing' determines any 'guilt' or 'punishment' for the organizations or has any finality in determining the loyalty of members. . . . Listing of these organizations does not conclude the members' rights to hold government employment. It is only one piece of evidence for consideration. . . ."

In other words, even the minority of the Court, with the friendliest of feelings for the "loyalty" program, found it necessary to rely on the language of the original executive order. But what would these members of the Court say about Memorandum 32, which explicitly repudiated the "one piece of evidence" approach and made membership in certain organizations *mandatory* cause for the dismissal of its members? They said nothing about Memorandum 32 in these decisions, but I did not see how they would be able to ignore it in my case.

I felt like dancing with joy as I read the news of these decisions in the press. The "loyalty" program was not declared unconstitutional, but its methods were certainly given a black eye. The "subversive" list was condemned in some of the same terms I had been using to describe it. "McGrath will have to withdraw the list after this," I thought. "Why, he'll have to withdraw it even before the Court hears my case, and he'll have to withdraw all actions based on the list, including my discharge!"

This showed that two and a half years' experience with my case had still not rubbed away all my naivete. For the attorney general did nothing of the kind. The Court had condemned his procedure with respect to the blacklist at the same time that it returned the three cases to a lower court, but the Department of Justice acted as if it hadn't heard the news. It retained the list, and still retains it to this day. I ask myself: What would happen if one of the blacklisted organizations should disregard a decision of the Supreme Court? The newspapers would howl, the super-patriotic organizations would clamor for punitive action, and the government would claim that this was additional proof of the organization's "subversive" character. But the Department of Justice is apparently in a separate category—or acts as if it is.

The situation was further confused because on the same day that it ruled in the above-mentioned three cases, the Supreme Court handed down a decision in the case of Dorothy Bailey, a former employee of the Federal Security Agency who was fired for "disloyalty" after I was. Miss Bailey was charged with being a Communist and with being active in a "front" organization. She denied the charges and appealed the case to the courts, complaining that she had been dismissed without a hearing at which she could cross-examine and confront her accusers. When her lawyer asked the Loyalty Review Board for some information about her accusers, the chairman of the Board answered: "I haven't the slightest knowledge as to who they were. . . ." When he was asked if the accusers had submitted their charges against Miss Bailey under oath, the chairman said, "I don't think so." As Justice Douglas said: "The accused has no opportunity to show that the [unknown] witness lied or was prejudiced or venal. Without knowing who her accusers are she has no way of defending. She has nothing to offer except her own word and the character testimony of her friends."

The Circuit Court of Appeals ruled against Miss Bailey by a two-to-one vote. The case went to the Supreme Court, which ended in a four-to-four deadlock on her appeal. When there is a tie, the lower court decision stands, and Miss Bailey's appeal was lost. The Supreme Court, in the Joint Anti-Fascist Refugee Committee case, said in effect that it is illegal to brand an organization disloyal without a hearing; on the same day, in the Bailey case, it said in effect that it is all right to stigmatize and discharge a government employee without a fair and full hearing. The two rulings were so inconsistent that Justice Jackson wrote:

". . . Also beyond my understanding is how a Court whose collective opinion is that the designations are subject to judicial inquiry can at the same time say that a discharge based at least in part on them is not. By the procedures of this Loyalty Order, both groups and individuals may be labeled disloyal and subversive. The Court grants judicial review and relief to the group while refusing it to the individual. So far as I recall, this is the first time this Court has held rights of individuals subordinate and inferior to those of organized groups. I think that is an inverted view of the law—it is justice turned bottom-side up."

My case differed from Miss Bailey's in a number of ways, most of all because I did not deny membership in a blacklisted organization. "Your case poses the issue most sharply," George Novack told me, "and it will be harder for the Court to avoid taking a definite stand on the constitutionality of the 'loyalty' program than in the Bailey case. Besides, yours is now the only case challenging the constitutionality of the purge in the federal courts. Legally speaking, it is now more important than ever."

If the legal fate of the "loyalty" program hung in the balance, the Department of Justice seemed to be in favor of letting it hang there indefinitely. But finally June 26, 1951, was set for the hearing on "Civil Action 636-50" and District Judge Edward M. Curran was picked to hear and decide the case.

The brief filed by my attorneys naturally made full use of all the favorable implications of the Supreme Court decision in the Joint Anti-Fascist Refugee Committee case. The government attorneys filed a counterbrief contending that case was "irrelevant" because it did "not involve federal or state employment" and dealt merely with "injuries to the organization in its relation outside the field of government employment of its members." I thought that was splitting hairs pretty fine, but I guess such things must be expected as a matter of course in legal disputes.

What I did not expect, however, was to find a deliberate lie in the government brief, as follows: "In his own testimony, the plaintiff admitted before the Branch Board [in Philadelphia] that he personally advocated the overthrow of the government by unconstitutional means of force and violence, when, in the judgment of the organization to which he belonged, the use of force and violence was necessary and justified to achieve its aims." I never said that, and not even the quotations they tore out of context from my testimony to include in their brief could be twisted enough to prove that I had said that. I guess I should have expected something of the kind; it is hard to sustain a thought-control program without lies. I began to hope that the judges in my case would take the trouble to study what I actually said and refuse to be misled into accepting the government's lawyers' distortion of my views.

In court, the government attorneys declared that I had no right to a hearing other than those I got in Philadelphia and New York, and that these were adequate. They denied that my membership in the Socialist Workers Party was the only ground on which I was fired. They admitted it was the only ground given by Mr. Gray and the Loyalty Review Board, but said that didn't matter because the Branch Loyalty Board had promised to consider my case "on all the evidence" and had taken my "personal beliefs" into consideration in reaching its conclusion. This brought up the question: who had fired me, the Branch Loyalty Board or Mr. Gray or the Loyalty Review Board?

This question may seem relatively unimportant, but it isn't to lawyers and courts. The government said I was fired by the Branch Loyalty Board, and that Mr. Gray and the Loyalty Review Board merely upheld the Branch Loyalty Board decision. Their aim in making this contention was to get around the inconsistency of the Branch Loyalty Board decision (that I was discharged "on all the evidence") with the subsequent decisions of Mr. Gray and the Loyalty Review Board (that my discharge was made mandatory by membership in the Socialist Workers Party—reliance on Memorandum 32 rather than "all the evidence").

My attorneys quoted the regulations to show that the Branch Loyalty Board was empowered only to make recommendations on my dismissal, and that after their decision I was only suspended, not dismissed. According to these regulations, they showed Mr. Gray made the actual decision to discharge me, while the Loyalty Review Board affirmed his decision, and only then was my name removed from the rolls. If this was correct, then only my membership in the Socialist Workers Party was considered, because Mr. Gray and the Loyalty Review Board made no pretense of considering anything else. In that case, my lawyers argued, "all the evidence" had not been considered and I had not received the hearing I was entitled to.

My head was still swimming from these technicalities—I hated to think that my fate might depend on such things—when Judge

Curran handed down his ruling. In a brief statement he sided completely with the government attorneys:

"The Administrator of the Veterans Administration and the Loyalty Review Board only affirmed the action of the Branch Loyalty Board No. 3, located at Philadelphia, Pennsylvania, in removing the plaintiff from employment with the Veterans Administration. . . . Now, it is true that these appellate tribunals, so to speak, that is, the administrator of the Veterans Administration and the Loyalty Review Board in affirming the suspension stated that he was removed because of plaintiff's membership in a designated organization, which was the Socialist Workers Party, but plaintiff was initially removed by the Branch Loyalty Board. . . . The important thing is, was that action correct? It has been affirmed. The grounds for the affirmation were immaterial. . . ."

We had lost again. Our next step was an appeal to the U.S. Circuit Court of Appeals for the District of Columbia Circuit, the last stage before the U.S. Supreme Court.

While the necessary briefs were being prepared for this step, the U.S. Circuit Court of Appeals for the Second Circuit (New York), ordering a retrial of the Remington perjury case on August 22, 1951, termed the attorney general's blacklist "a purely hearsay declaration by the attorney general. . . . It has no competency to prove the subversive character of the listed associations. . . ." I did not become as excited by this ruling as I had been by the Supreme Court's initial denunciation of the blacklist procedure. The proof of the pudding is in the eating, and so far the Department of Justice had simply ignored the courts' rebukes on the blacklist.

We filed our appeal against Judge Curran's decision on September 7, 1951, but argument did not take place in court until April 10, 1952. The case was heard by a three-man bench, Circuit Court Judges James M. Proctor, E. Barrett Prettyman and Wilbur K. Miller. Judge Prettyman wrote the decision which the deadlocked Supreme Court failed to change in the Bailey case, and Judge Proctor had concurred in that decision. Mr. Rauh presented my case, while the time allowed for Mr. Myer was ceded to Herbert M. Levy, appearing for the American Civil Liberties Union as amicus curiae to ask for my reinstatement and for a court order directing the attorney general to cease the "illegal" practice of blacklisting organizations without notice or hearing. The government attorneys were Edward H. Hickey and Joseph Kovner.

Judge Prettyman showed a lively interest in the argument, interrupting Mr. Rauh for more information, asking Mr. Hickey some pointed questions about the legal contradictions in the government's case. Of course I couldn't tell what went on in Judge Prettyman's head but his questions seemed to indicate doubts about certain aspects of the government's position.

Six months passed. Then late in the morning of October 16, 1952, after driving my mother to the market on her weekly shopping trip, I came home to find the telephone ringing. It was a reporter: "Have you heard the news yet? It just came in from Washington. The Court of Appeals has just handed down a verdict on your case—and it's unanimously in your favor!" I was so dazed I almost dropped the phone. It seemed too good to be true. When he asked me for a statement, I stammered something about it being a great victory for civil liberties.

16

Back to the beginning

It *was* too good to be true. A few minutes later a call came through from Mr. Rauh's office in Washington, then I read the newspaper stories and the text of the court decision itself, and the whole thing came into perspective again. It was a victory for civil liberties all right, but not as big a victory as I first thought. The government suffered a setback—this was the first judicial defeat the "loyalty" program ever got—but that didn't mean I had my job back. Far from it. In fact, the total effect of the court decision was to roll back my fight for reinstatement to the position it was in four years before.

The chief positive feature of the unanimous decision, written by Judge Proctor, was its junking of Memorandum 32. It ruled that the memorandum was inconsistent with the provisions of Executive Order 9835 and therefore was "without validity or force and should be disregarded." On this basis it reversed Judge Curran's decision and vacated the order removing me from the VA's rolls. Mr. Gray was given to understand that he had no right to discharge me on the sole ground of my membership in the Socialist Workers Party, and that he was required to resume consideration of my case, this time taking "all the evidence" into account.

But this reversal of my discharge did not automatically restore me to my job, with or without back pay. What the court restored me to was the status I received after the Philadelphia Branch Loyalty Board recommendation in October 1948. That is, I was put back on the VA's rolls, but as a suspended employee, pending "consideration and determination by the Administrator (Gray) of the ultimate issue as to whether on all the evidence reasonable grounds exist for belief that Kutcher is disloyal."

On the more basic issues raised by my appeal, the court either refused to take a position or favored the government. It expressed no direct opinion on the constitutionality of the "loyalty" program. It ruled that while membership in a listed group could not be cited as the sole reason for firing a government employee, it might serve as the basis for "disbelief in the loyalty of an employee," justifying his discharge when the authorities stated they had considered all the evidence. It also reaffirmed its previous decision in the Dorothy Bailey case that the attorney general's list was "competent evidence" and that loyalty proceedings "do not require the constitutional and traditional safeguards of a judicial trial."

And so I was faced with the prospect of going through the same rigamarole as before, almost from the beginning. The main difference was that Mr. Gray could no longer fire me solely for my membership in the Socialist Workers Party. But there was nothing in the decision to stop him from firing me on this very same ground if he accompanied his decision with the statement that he had considered "all the evidence"—even if all the evidence consisted of nothing more than my membership.

Thus the decision did not at all mean an end to the use of guilt by association in the "loyalty" program. As I.F. Stone put it, the voiding of Memorandum 32 tended to "reduce the orbit of guilt by association," not to abolish it. In a general sense, it was a step forward, but only a small one (at the same time that, in a personal sense, it was a four-year step backward for me).

I stress the narrowness of the gain because some commentators tended to overemphasize its significance. The *New York Times*, in its first editorial on my case, "welcomed" the decision and hailed the court for having "acted in a way to strengthen the cause of civil liberties." I was glad that the editors of the *Times* thought the invalidation of Memorandum 32 was a good thing. I couldn't help wishing that they had said so in 1948 when I first began to fight against that memorandum: if they had told people then to support my fight against it, my efforts to get the case into the courts might have been a little easier. Of course, the *Times'* retroactive semisupport was better late than never. But that didn't give it any warrant to exaggerate the meaning of what the court actually did.

Another striking by-product of the decision was the new line on my case that it evoked from the Stalinist *Daily Worker*. As I have shown, for about one year the Stalinists actively opposed my efforts to get support and finances from labor and other organizations to take the case into the courts. Discredited and isolated by such behavior, they then adopted a policy of silence and apparent neutrality toward me, and practiced it for the next three years.

After the Circuit Court of Appeals decision, however, the *Daily Worker* ran an editorial saying: "In these days of wholesale wrecking of America's democratic heritage and legal protections by witchhunters, even the pale decision [in my case] has a certain meaning for the progressive forces defending the U.S. Constitution against the red-baiters. At least it casts doubts on the czarist-like decrees of the attorney general. . . . These 'subversive organization' lists are sheer lawlessness. . . . The latest court decision only proves this again, even (though) the judges failed completely to uphold the Constitution in their approval of dismissals for 'loyalty' opinions. Wherever there is resistance to the illegal blackmailing of Americans for belonging to organizations or for having certain views, the fight for saving America's heritage goes on . . ."

This was a far cry from the *Daily People's World* lie in 1949 that my case did not have "the remotest connection with the defense of civil rights" and an indirect admission that they had slandered me. I shall never forget the way the Stalinists sniped at me when I was trying to mobilize support for a fight against the purge, and I don't think anyone else should forget it. But I welcomed their avowed change of attitude even though I think they should have come right out in the open and admitted they were wrong before. If the decision helped to teach them or anyone else a lesson about the need for defending the rights of all, then that was another thing to be said in its favor.

Mr. Rauh said there was still a possibility that I might be returned to my job pending Mr. Gray's second decision on my case because the court decision did not bar him from reinstating me temporarily. But before that could happen the Department of Justice had to make up its mind about appealing the latest decision to the Supreme Court. This, together with some other legal technicalities, took a few more months; the delay was probably increased by the Republican victory in the November 1952 election, and the appointment of a new attorney general, Mr. Herbert Brownell, Jr. In the end the Department of Justice came to the conclusion that it would be better not to appeal, and the case was turned back to Mr. Gray. I waited as patiently as I could; then, suddenly, the witch-hunters gave me something else to think about for a while.

Ever since I was discharged from the army, my parents and I had been living in a federal low-rent housing apartment in Newark's Seth Boyden project. It was not a luxurious apartment, but it was comfortable, my parents had made friends among the neighbors, and I expected that we would remain there permanently. My parents, both 73 years old now, also expected that—until a few days before Christmas 1952 when my father got a letter from the Newark Housing Authority directing him to sign a so-called loyalty oath within three days as a condition for continued residence.

We then learned for the first time that Congress, in July 1952, had adopted an amendment to the Independent Offices Appropriation Act introduced by Rep. Gwinn, a New York Republican. The Gwinn Amendment required all heads of families living in federal low-rent housing to sign an oath swearing that no one occupying their apartment belonged to any of the 203 organizations on the attorney general's "subversive" list. Failure to sign the oath (which actually had nothing to do with loyalty as such) would mean eviction.

My father felt terrible. His first impulse was to blame me. "There— I hope you're satisfied now. I've told you a hundred times to leave your party. Now we have to move because you're so stubborn. And where will we go?"

It really was a dilemma for him. He didn't belong to any group on the attorney general's list and he was perfectly willing to sign the oath. But he could not do so without perjuring himself because of my membership in the Socialist Workers Party. He did not want to undergo the hardship of searching for new lodgings. And yet the only way he could keep his present home was if I left it. The price for keeping the apartment would be to break up the family.

I tried to calm him, to show him where the blame really belonged. And I offered to move out and get a room somewhere else. That set my mother weeping. She was sure I couldn't take proper care of myself. I withdrew the offer and promised to begin looking for a new apartment.

But when I began to think about the situation, I got angrier and angrier. Maybe I am stubborn, but on the other hand the last thing in the world I wanted was to go into court with a new case. So it wasn't mere stubbornness that led me to the conviction that we would have to fight this move.

What confronted me, I realized, was an extension of the same evil that I had been resisting—guilt by association. This time it was guilt by association with a new twist. I remembered an old saying, and I looked it up in a reference book. About 2,400 years ago Euripides, the Greek dramatist, wrote: "The gods visit the sins of the fathers upon the children." This was the view of justice that prevailed in ancient Greece, and that modern civilization has rejected as barbaric. But now the heresy-hunters were going even further than the ancients and were saying in effect: "The sins of the children are to be visited upon the fathers."

Furthermore, the discriminatory aims of the housing oath seemed to me to be highlighted by the recent Circuit Court of Appeals decision on my case. The court said that membership in the Socialist Workers Party or any other group on the attorney general's list was not sufficient cause by itself to justify discharge of any government employee. Yet, in clear contradiction to this ruling, the government was now proceeding from the view that membership in one of these groups was sufficient cause by itself to justify eviction of tenants from federal housing projects.

In some ways this oath was even worse than the federal "loyalty" program. At least a federal employee got some kind of hearing, no matter how inadequate, and his membership in a blacklisted group was supposed to be considered as only one piece of evidence. In the case of housing tenants there was not even the pretense of a hearing, and membership was considered the only evidence.

So, little as I relished the prospect, I felt I would have to engage in another court case. The first thing was to convince my father that his rights were worth defending too. It proved not to be as hard as I had feared. Maybe if I have a stubborn streak, I inherited it.

Anyhow, my father sent off a letter to the Newark Housing Authority, saying: "I am a loyal American citizen. I love my country and my home. I want to comply with all requirements for remaining in my home . . . I have begged (my son) again and again to leave this organization, but he refuses, saying that it is not subversive and he is not subversive . . . What should I do? I want to sign the certificate, I do not want to move, I do not want to break up my family because my son needs help to take care of him. Please help me, please tell me what to do, so that I can keep my home."

This letter was not answered. And so, three days after the first deadline set for filing the oath, I went to the American Civil Liberties Union for advice on how to ward off the threatened eviction move. The ACLU, through its New Jersey counsel, Emil G. Oxfeld, had announced that it was interested in challenging the constitutionality of the new oath.

Mr. Oxfeld said that the ACLU would be willing to represent both my father and me, since we were in a different status, in a court test of the oath. He told me that he had already arranged to act for another disabled veteran living at the Seth Boyden project, a teacher named Harry L. Lawrence. Mr. Lawrence did not belong to any organization on the blacklist, and as a teacher had already signed two loyalty oaths. But he felt the thing was now being carried too far and refused to sign the housing oath because it "infringes on my personal and civil liberty."

My father knew about the ACLU as a liberal organization and had great respect for it, so he readily agreed to participate in the suit. On February 2, 1953, Mr. Oxfeld filed suit in the New Jersey Superior Court on behalf of Mr. Lawrence, my father and me. We asked that the Gwinn Amendment be declared unconstitutional and that the Newark Housing Authority be restrained from evicting or threatening to evict tenants for failing to sign the oath.

This was the first legal test of the Gwinn Amendment, and Patrick Murphy Malin, executive director of the ACLU, said it was of national significance because its outcome might affect the enforcement of the oath all over the country. He also said:

"The Kutcher-Lawrence case marks the beginning of an ACLU effort to have the courts reverse this unwise and unconstitutional oath. We are undertaking this effort solely because of the fundamental civil liberties issues at stake. The cherished traditions of American democracy, free speech and association, and due process of law, must be actively defended if our high democratic ideals are to have real meaning. We hope that the courts will uphold these constitutional protections, which are the heart of our democratic society."

Six weeks later Superior Court Judge Walter J. Freund issued a restraining order preventing the Newark Housing Authority from evicting the eleven families who had not signed the oath, pending a ruling by the judge on the constitutionality of the Gwinn Amendment. That is where the housing case stands as this book is sent to the press [June 1953].

Around the time President Eisenhower was inaugurated in January 1953, we learned that the Department of Justice would not appeal my case to the Supreme Court, and disposition of my appeal was turned over to Mr. Gray. Mr. Rauh at once wrote him a letter, reviewing the history of the case and asking him to meet with us to discuss its future handling. Mr. Gray curtly denied us even the courtesy of a meeting.

I then sent an appeal directly to President Eisenhower, under whose command I had served in World War II, asking him for the "justice that has been denied to me by the preceding administration" during fifty-three months of litigation. The letter was much like the one I had sent President Truman in 1948. It urged the new president to do two things: "1. Advise the Veterans Administration to reinstate me without further delay to my job, with back pay and seniority; and 2. Direct the new attorney general to withdraw the 'subversive list' which was prepared without notice or hearing and the Department of Justice to dissociate itself completely from the arbitrary procedures connected with it." I also offered to meet with the president and discuss my case at his convenience.

The president did not answer me directly, but one of his secretaries must have sent my letter to Mr. Gray, who acknowledged its receipt and informed me that my appeal would be heard by the VA Loyalty Board of Appeals in Washington on March 9.

So we went to Washington again. (By my reckoning, this was my ninth appeal: The Philadelphia Branch Loyalty Board was first, President Truman second, Mr. Clark third, Mr. Gray fourth, the Loyalty Review Board fifth, the Federal District Court sixth, the Circuit Court of Appeals seventh, President Eisenhower eighth.) The chairman of the board of VA functionaries who heard the case was Mr. George H. Lynch. There was really only one new development at this hearing.

The original charges against me included four points: (a) my membership in the Socialist Workers Party; (b) my "employment" (that is, voluntary and unpaid service as recording secretary) in the Newark Branch; (c) my financial contributions to the newspaper, *The Militant;* and (d) "Evidence of record of your association and activity with persons, associations, movements and groups designated by the attorney general as subversive in nature." This last point was extremely mystifying and irritating because it made it appear that the charges were based on a variety of associations and activities aside from those that would normally result from membership in the Socialist Workers Party. In Philadelphia Mr. Myer tried unsuccessfully to get point (d) stricken from the charges after being refused a bill of particulars so that we would know just what it meant. Here is what was brought out in Washington under Mr. Rauh's skillful questioning:

> Mr. Rauh: As the charges from the previous hearing now stand, they come down to the simple proposition he was a member and that is all. If there is something else, something more specific, we believe that it should be so stated in the charges. If you will examine these, you will see that (a) is the charge of membership, (b) and (c) are charges that he did what a member would do, and (d) is the charge of association. So as to make possible a defense, I move, therefore, that we be given at this time orally or in writing an indication what the charges are above and beyond membership.
>
> Mr. Lynch: Mr. Rauh, the charges well could have been drafted more explicitly, there is no doubt about that. . . . Mr. Rauh, the charges against Mr. Kutcher in substance are to the effect that there are reasonable grounds for the belief that he is disloyal, and the charges find their basis in the fact, at least to a large extent, that one who is a member of the Socialist Workers Party and one who has association and activity with persons, associations or groups designated by the attorney general as subversive in nature, may be a person who is disloyal to the government. . . . Accordingly, Mr. Rauh, your motion is denied.
>
> . . . Mr. Rauh: Is it fair to say that the decision is that membership in the Socialist Workers Party, plus the normal incidences of membership, such as working in the branch headquarters, making a pledge to the paper and associating with members is in essence the charge against Mr. Kutcher? I think that is a fair question, Mr. Chairman.

Mr. Lynch: The answer to that question is no, Mr. Rauh. The essence of the charge is that there are reasonable grounds for the belief that he is disloyal . . .

. . . Mr. Rauh: I will refer now solely to (d) and see if we can clarify (d), which to my mind is the most difficult to understand, and ask whether (d) refers to association and activity with other members of the Socialist Workers Party?

Mr. Lynch: The answer is, Mr. Rauh, that the association and activity referred to in that subparagraph (d) refer to associations and activities within the Socialist Workers Party.

Reluctantly, but unmistakably, the government had been forced to admit that the sinister-sounding point (d) was merely a restatement of the previous points. It was clearer than ever that my "offenses" consisted of nothing but my membership in a legal party and my expression of opinions disliked by government bureaucrats.

On Friday, April 24, I received a telegram requesting me to appear at the personnel division of the Newark regional office of the VA on Monday morning, April 27, "on a matter of importance to you." Inadvertently, my parents saw the telegram and got all excited. Somehow, they interpreted it to mean that I was to be reinstated. (If they live to be a hundred, they will never abandon the notion that everything that happened to me was a "mistake.") On Saturday a registered letter arrived, repeating the same request. Again my parents were carried away with the wildest hopes. I steeled myself against it but I couldn't help being infected a little by their optimism when I entered the VA building Monday morning.

The VA manager shook my hand, asked after my health and handed me a "personal and confidential" letter from Mr. Gray's office in Washington. (It turned out that the reason for the telegram and so on was that the Washington office did not have my home address.) The letter said that both the VA Loyalty Board of Appeals and Mr. Gray, after duly considering my appeal, had reached the conclusion that on the basis of "all the evidence, there is a reasonable doubt as to your loyalty to the government of the United States, and that the case is within the purview of Section 9A of the Hatch Act. You have the right to appeal this decision to the Civil Service Commission Loyalty Review Board within twenty days after receipt of this letter . . ."

On my way out of the VA building, I phoned home to tell my parents they had nothing to celebrate. Then I went across the street to Washington Park and sat on a bench in the sun musing about the ups and downs of the last four years and eight months. I bought a paper when I left the park. Its headlines revealed that President Eisenhower had just issued a new executive order, revoking President Truman's Executive Order 9835 and announcing the coming abolition of the Loyalty Review Board which I had just been told I could appeal to.

But the revocation of Executive Order 9835, which I had sought so long, gave me no satisfaction, because President Eisenhower's Executive Order 10450 is even worse. It contains all the most reactionary features of the old order and adds some new ones. Among other things it directs the attorney general to continue issuance of a "subversive" list; it authorizes continuation of the practice of firing government employees on the basis of secret accusations, denying them the traditional right to confront and cross-examine their accusers; and, like the revoked order, it has no provisions for judicial review.

The new features of the Eisenhower program extend the purge far beyond the sphere of "loyalty." Now it is possible, in the name of "security," to fire any employee who does not measure up to his superior's "standards" of sobriety, morality, mental capacity, honesty, reliability, sex habits, etc. Under President Truman, an employee could be purged if there was a "reasonable doubt" as to his loyalty; under President Eisenhower, no one is safe unless it can be shown that his employment or retention of employment "is clearly consistent with the interests of the national security." This so-called standard is so much more rubbery than the old one that almost anything can happen under it—including the firing of Democrats so that loyal Republicans can get the benefits of patronage that would otherwise be impossible under civil service regulations. (I had warned that the purge started by the Democrats against their opponents on the left would eventually be extended and used against the Democrats themselves by their opponents on the right.)

Moreover, President Eisenhower did away with the Loyalty Review Board, allowing it only a brief period in which to clean up pending appeals. Previously, an employee fired by the head of his department could appeal to the Loyalty Review Board, made up of lawyers not employed by the government, and if the board ruled in his favor he could get his job back. Now the heads of departments are prosecutor, judge, jury and court of appeal. A purged employee has the right to appeal the department head's decision to a "hearing board" of three or more government officials, but its decision is not binding on the department head who did the purging, and the employee can remain fired even if the "hearing board" rules in his favor.

Appropriately enough, President Eisenhower, before issuing this order, "cleared it" with Senator McCarthy, who in great part owes his present dominance in American political life to the hysteria unleashed by President Truman's "loyalty" purge. The Senator endorsed the new program enthusiastically. He can recognize grist for his mill.

Two days later Attorney General Brownell issued his first "subversive" list. It included 192 organizations on previous lists, among them the Socialist Workers Party, and 62 new groups—many of them whose only "crime" was the help they had extended to victims of the witch-hunt, such as raising money for their legal expenses and for the care of their families.

Mr. Brownell also said that he had worked out a "hearing" procedure for the blacklisted groups which "conformed" with the Supreme Court's ruling in the Joint Anti-Fascist Refugee Committee case in 1951. This was a lie. The Supreme Court did not merely say that the groups on the list were entitled to a hearing. It said that they must have a fair hearing *before* being blacklisted. Mr. Brownell's procedure was a shabby evasion of the Supreme Court's decision, not conformance with it. First he put 254 groups on his list and publicly smeared them as "subversive." Then he sanctimoniously turned around and said that if they didn't like it, they could appeal to him for a "hearing." But who can have any confidence in a procedure where the judge pronounces you guilty before you have even had your day in court? It remains to be seen if the Supreme Court will reject this mockery of fair procedure, or if it will submit once again to an attorney general high-handedly defying its clear directives.

We decided to make our tenth appeal to the Loyalty Review Board, although its days were numbered and although I would not get my job back even if it ruled completely in my favor because the Eisenhower order provides that everyone who has been cleared under the old Truman program must be reprobed and regrilled under the more drastic provisions of the new one.

The hearing was held before the Loyalty Review Board in Washington on June 4, 1953. Its members were plainly in a hurry as they listened to the arguments presented by Mr. Daniel H. Pollitt, Mr. Rauh's able associate. The hearing lasted less than an hour.

The members of the Board made little pretense that they were actually considering the merits of my appeal. Exactly one day later—June 5—they sent Mr. Rauh a letter stating that they had again upheld my discharge. The verdict was reached in indecent haste, but its authors sought to cover themselves by ruling against me in two ways. Their conclusions were: "(a) that there are reasonable grounds to believe that Mr. Kutcher is disloyal to the government of the United States, and (b) that there is a reasonable doubt as to Mr. Kutcher's loyalty to the government of the United States . . . Accordingly, the decision of the administrator of the Veterans Administration is in all respects affirmed and Mr. Kutcher's separation from the service has been requested."

The actual date on which my name was again removed from the rolls of the VA was June 16, 1953—which will be better remembered as the day when the workers of East Germany began their inspiring political uprising against their Stalinist rulers.

Our next steps were back into the federal courts. But the whole situation was greatly complicated by the new Eisenhower order. As this book goes to the printers, a few weeks before the fifth anniversary of the start of the case, the Kutcher Civil Rights Committee and my attorneys are studying all the complications to find a way to continue the case in the courts. I personally do not see much chance of winning it until after the Supreme Court has ruled on it. And one thing I have learned is how hard it is for someone in my position to get even a hearing from the Supreme Court, let alone a favorable decision.

17

Lessons from American history

In June 1950, a few days before the Korean War began, Judge Learned Hand of the U.S. Circuit Court of Appeals asked: What would happen to Thomas Jefferson if he were living in the United States today?

The question came up during a hearing on the appeal of the eleven Stalinist leaders convicted under the Smith Act in 1949. Judge Hand said he was troubled about the government's contention that the defendants had not been convicted because of their beliefs. He wanted to know what would have happened, under the Smith Act, to 18th century "liberals or democrats" who conspired to overthrow the government when it "got oppressive enough." He asked what about Jefferson, who "again and again in his encyclicals advocated the propriety of overthrowing a government that had become utterly offensive"—would he have come under the provisions of the Smith Act?

The government attorney was embarrassed by the question. The only answer he could think of was that "Jefferson was a man who had lived under an oppressive government" and would never have thought of advocating the right to revolt against a government like the present one. The question was not really answered in the court-room. But it is a vital question, worth serious thought, because it illustrates what has been happening to the American tradition of free speech under the impact of the "loyalty" program and associated measures that have been instituted since the start of the cold war.

Thomas Jefferson was a democrat and not a socialist, but he was a revolutionary democrat. He did not merely "conspire to advocate" the right of revolution (as the charge reads in the Smith Act indictments)—he actually advocated that right in the Declaration of Independence, which says it is the right of the people to alter or to abolish any form of government that becomes destructive of the rights of life, liberty and the pursuit of happiness. And he not only advocated the right of revolution—he practiced it too.

It is for this that we honor Jefferson today, and hold him up as an example to our schoolchildren. Yet he would surely be indicted under the Smith Act today for advocating such ideas.

With his ideas, would the author of the Declaration of Independence be able today to hold a job as a Hollywood or radio script writer?

With his ideas, would the founder of the University of Virginia be able to sign a "loyalty" oath such as is required for any teaching post in many of our institutions of higher learning?

With his ideas, would the founder of the Democratic Party be able today to form any organization that would not be included on the "subversive" blacklist?

I don't go as far as Jefferson, who said in 1787: "God forbid we should ever be twenty years without . . . a rebellion. . . . What country can preserve its liberties, if its rulers are not warned from time to time, that this people preserve the spirit of resistance? Let them take arms. . . . What signify a few lives lost in a century or two? The tree of liberty must be refreshed from time to time with the blood of patriots and tyrants. . . ."

I don't advocate a bloody revolution but a peaceful one—a radical change in our economic, political and governmental institutions when a majority of the people favors it, and I would not advocate any forcible actions whatever unless the opponents of such a change resorted to violence themselves, as they did in Spain. For holding and expressing these ideas, I am barred from a clerical job with the Veterans Administration. Would Thomas Jefferson, holding and expressing the ideas he did, be able to qualify today for the posts of secretary of state, ambassador to France, vice president and president, which he held at one time or another—or even for my clerical job?

As a socialist, I don't regard the Constitution as sacred or unchangeable. Constitutions reflect relationships and ideas among their authors, and they have to change as times and conditions change. There are many things I think should be changed in the Constitution, including the procedure for amending it, which in my opinion is too undemocratic. Nevertheless, there is one thing in the Constitution that I am opposed to changing: the Bill of Rights, and especially the First Amendment ("Congress shall make no law respecting the establishment of religion, or prohibiting the free exercise thereof; or abridging the freedom of speech, or of the press; or the right of the people peaceably to assemble, and to petition the government for a redress of their grievances."). In fact, the abolition of this provision would signify the end of democracy in the United States.

If I read our history correctly, the Bill of Rights was not granted to the American people, but was asserted by them. The authors of the Constitution were conservative men, and the original Constitution did not contain any bill of rights. That was one of the reasons for the strenuous opposition to the proposed Constitution after the American Revolution. Jefferson, writing from France to Madison in 1787, said: "I will now add what I do not like [about the Constitution]. First the omission of a bill of rights providing clearly and without the aid of sophisms for freedom of religion, freedom of the press, protection against the standing armies, restriction against monopolies, the eternal and unremitting force of the *habeas corpus* laws, and trials by jury. . . . Let me add that a bill of rights is what the people are entitled to against every government on earth . . . and what no just government should refuse or rest on inference."

In the end, the supporters of the Constitution were able to get it accepted only by pledging to add a bill of rights. That is why I hold that the Bill of Rights was not given to the American people as a gift, and why it cannot be taken away from them.

Now of course no one is proposing to remove the First Amendment from the Constitution, and there is not much danger of that happening even if such a demand should be raised. But there is a danger of the First Amendment being emasculated, deprived of its content, even while it remains on the books. Hitler did not repeal the democratic Weimar Constitution when he came to power; he let it remain on the books while proceeding systematically to destroy all the democratic liberties it was supposed to guarantee. It can happen here too. I go further and say it is happening here. The danger to freedom of speech is not remote but present, and growing more menacing every day.

Look at the things that have been happening since the beginning of the cold war. Teachers have been fired because of their views. Clergymen have been removed from their church posts because of their associations. Union officials have been ordered to sign noncommunist affidavits before their unions could enjoy privileges of the National Labor Relations Board. People have been convicted for their ideas under the Smith Act. Workers have been fired out of their jobs in private industry because of their alleged politics. Actors have been barred from the screen or airwaves because of organizations they used to belong to. Lawyers have been terrorized into refusing to defend clients with unpopular views. Special "loyalty" oaths have spread like a plague from educators to students and even to doctors. Political parties, appearing on the ballot for decades, have been ruled off the ballot because their names appear on a list in Washington.

"But," some people say when these outrages against free speech are cataloged, "but you are exaggerating the danger. After all, only a tiny fraction of one per cent of the population is involved. The situation is deplorable, but freedom of speech for the great majority of the people has not been infringed at all."

It is true, if we take the "loyalty" program as an example, that only a small proportion of government employees has been discharged as "disloyal." But what about the 99 odd percent of government employees who are not discharged—what is the effect of the "loyalty" program on them? A preliminary investigation of this question has been made by New York University Professors Maria Jahoda and Stuart W. Cook; their findings are printed in the March 1952 issue of the *Yale Law Journal*. They show that the effect of the "loyalty" program has been to intimidate and frighten all government employees, including those never remotely suspected of disloyalty. The fear of being charged with disloyalty has been enough to make them shy away from all "controversial" discussion, to quit reading liberal books, to break off associations Senator McCarthy would disapprove of, to stop thinking thoughts that some day might be labeled dangerous. Their findings led the two professors to the cautious "hypothesis" that "Federal loyalty and security programs are undermining the great traditions of American democracy which they should seek to preserve."

So while the "loyalty" program has cost only a few thousand government employees their jobs, it has had the added (and much more damaging) effect of frightening two million other government employees, admittedly not disloyal, so badly that they dare not exercise the rights guaranteed them by the First Amendment.

Teachers are affected the same way. If they see only one or two teachers fired for their ideas, only three or four denied a promotion because of their associations, that is enough to intimidate them into keeping quiet about their ideas and discontinuing any associations that might lead to trouble. And similarly with the rest of the population. The people are becoming "afraid of the good old American habits of speaking one's mind and joining organizations one believes in," as the American Civil Liberties Union put it in a letter to President Truman asking him to modify the "loyalty" program in July 1951. The First Amendment remains on the books, but its spirit is being vitiated by a government-sponsored pressure to conform.

Here is how the present situation was described by Supreme Court Justice William O. Douglas in an article entitled "The Black Silence of Fear," printed in the *New York Times* on January 13, 1952:

> There is an ominous trend in this nation. We are developing tolerance only for the orthodox point of view on world affairs, intolerance for new or different approaches. . . . There have been eras of intolerance when the views of minorities have been suppressed. But there probably has not been a period of greater intolerance than we witness today. . . . It means that the philosophy of strength through free speech is being forsaken for the philosophy of fear through repression. . . .
>
> Fear has many manifestations. The Communist threat inside the country has been magnified and exalted far beyond its realities. Irresponsible talk by irresponsible people has fanned the flames of fear. Accusations have been loosely made. Character assassinations have become common. Suspicion has taken the place of good will. . . .
>
> Suspicion grows until only the orthodox idea is the safe one. Suspicion grows until only the person who loudly proclaims that orthodox view, or who once having been a Communist, has been converted, is trustworthy. Those who are unorthodox are suspect. Everyone who does not follow the military policymakers is suspect. . . .
>
> Fear even strikes at lawyers and the bar. Those accused of illegal Communist activity—all presumed innocent, of course, until found guilty—have difficulty getting reputable lawyers to defend them. Lawyers have talked to me about it. Many are worried. Some would not volunteer their services, for if they did they would lose clients and their firms would suffer. Others could not volunteer because if they did they would be dubbed "subversive" by their community and put in the same category as those they would defend. This is a dark tragedy.
>
> Fear has driven more and more men and women in all walks

of life either to silence or to the folds of the orthodox. Fear has mounted—fear of losing one's job, fear of being investigated, fear of being pilloried. This fear has stereotyped our thinking, narrowed the range of free public discussion, and driven many thoughtful people to despair. This fear has even entered our universities, great citadels of our spiritual strength, and corrupted them. We have the spectacle of university officials lending themselves to one of the worst witch-hunts we have seen since early days. . . .

Justice Douglas might have added that the courts too have contributed to the spread of this fear that saps the tree of democracy. The First Amendment expressly forbids Congress from passing any laws abridging freedom of speech, without any ifs or buts, but the Supreme Court has been steadily weakening this categorical injunction by voting to uphold as constitutional measures like the Smith Act and the New York Feinberg Law whose chief target is freedom of speech. He might also have added that the spearhead of this drive to compel conformity was the "loyalty" program.

Over and over I have asked myself: What is behind this trend to the suppression of free speech? I know that the standard answer of its apologists is "the menace of communism." Usually, this is a reference not to a foreign menace but to the threat of a fifth column practicing espionage or sabotage here. But then the question arises: Why don't they use the anti-espionage and anti-sabotage laws already on the books, instead of introducing new measures and pressures that damage the liberties of the population as a whole? Spies and saboteurs do not hesitate to falsely sign "loyalty" oaths, and they know better than to join organizations that are regarded with hostility by the government. The powers-that-be know this. That is why their insistence on measures and procedures that spread "the black silence of fear" must be construed as deliberate, and their references to "the menace of communism" as a pretext.

I have my own answer to the question. I believe the witch-hunters are using "the menace of communism" in this country as a bogey to divert attention from other problems and to facilitate the silencing of the American people so that they will be unable to question or challenge certain unpopular measures and policies undertaken by the authorities. I believe the political and economic rulers of this country are convinced that eventually they will go to war against the Soviet Union. Such a war will be so horrible and will impose so many burdens on the American people that the authorities want to insure in advance against any protests or rebellions by the people.

They fear that the capitalist system itself will be at stake in the next war, and that the main threat to this system and to their profits and privileges will come from the working people of this country. Their fears are justified: the events of my lifetime testify that war produces crises and convulsions that make it possible for the working people to rid themselves of oppressive governments and seemingly invincible social systems. World War I created the conditions for a revolution that tore the mighty Russian empire out of the capitalist system; World War II produced the Chinese and Yugoslav revolutions, and the Soviet domination of Eastern Europe that crushed the capitalist system by military-bureaucratic means in a half dozen other countries. Thanks to these wars, one-third of the world's population has been removed from the orbit of capitalism, weakening that system to the point where it now has only one section that can boast of any strength or stability—the United States.

But American capitalism itself will not be immune to the shocks and strains of a grueling war in which it will have few strong or dependable allies. The American people today, although they have powerful labor unions, are not yet consciously anticapitalist in their political thinking. But will they remain that way if they are dragged through the inferno of an atomic war which will be fought on American soil too next time and will necessarily produce the highest taxes, prices and casualty lists in our history? Wall Street, the Pentagon and Capitol Hill have few illusions on this score; they know that what the people think and how the people act depends on the conditions they live under, and that the next war may breed conditions fatal for the capitalist system in this country too. That, as I see it, is the reason for the witch-hunt—to intimidate everyone who is opposed to war and the evils that accompany war, to silence every voice that questions or proposes another course, to isolate every group that can supply answers to the people's aspirations for peace and prosperity.

I know that many of my readers will reject this explanation as the product of socialist dogma, and so I merely present it here rather than argue it. But whether this explanation is accepted or rejected— and that is beside the point I am trying to make here—there can be no doubt about the fact that there is a witch-hunt, that it presents grave dangers, and that these dangers must be fought.

Some will grant, for sake of argument, that my analysis may be in accord with the facts, but they say: "This is a crisis, and in times of crisis we are justified in restricting the rights of individuals, even the right of free speech, because such steps are necessary in order to preserve democracy." Another way of stating the same thought is: The means are justified by the end; in order to save democracy in the long run, it is permissible to restrict it in a crisis.

But what evidence is there to support the notion that the restriction of democratic rights (temporarily) will lead to the maintenance of democracy in the long run? Give the power to silence people into the hands of bureaucrats, civil or military, through a crisis period that they assure us will last for decades—and how much democracy will be left then, and how ready will those bureaucrats be to return the right of free speech to the people? Bad means lead inevitably to bad ends; and the end in this case would be a police state, whose rulers would never willingly surrender their dictatorial power.

Use the methods of totalitarianism in order to preserve democracy? Morally, it's weak; practically, it won't work out. I say: No. People who preach such a course have no faith in the democratic process. I say the answer to our problems in times of crisis as well as in normal times is more and not less democracy.

In fact, that is one of the chief paradoxes of my case. I believe in the Bill of Rights; those who fired me don't; and they fired me precisely because I believe in it and they don't. I and others like me are purged and stigmatized as "subversive" because we want to uphold the democratic liberties that *they* are subverting in the name of a crusade to preserve democracy. In other words, they are guilty of what they accuse me.

I think that the danger to the Bill of Rights is great, and that it comes primarily from those who pretend that the way to avoid totalitarianism is by imitating it. But great as the danger is, I think it can be overcome by the people when they see how their own rights are affected and when they join hands in militant self-defense to preserve the Bill of Rights for all.

To the best of my ability I have been telling everyone who would listen to me since 1948: "If it can happen to me, why not to you? If I can be penalized for my ideas, why can't you for yours? If my party can be put on a blacklist at the whim of the attorney general, for reasons he has kept secret, why can't your party or *the party you may want to form some day* also be put on a blacklist by whoever happens to be attorney general then? For your sake, as well as mine, you must speak out and act against this despotic procedure."

I know that my appeal has convinced some; I hope it has convinced many. But I never expected that my appeal alone would arouse the majority of the people to action against the witch-hunt. Their own experience will do that, and the spread of the witch-hunt is just the thing that is going to provide them with the experience to convince them, as it convinced me, that it is necessary to fight back.

When they make that decision, they will have great historic models to guide them.

In 1798, the Alien and Sedition Acts were adopted, ostensibly to combat "the menace of France," actually to suppress the opposition to the ruling Federalist Party. When President John Adams invoked these laws to silence the people, they saw through his game, arose in political revolt, repudiated the Federalist Party and drove it out of office so decisively that it never came to power again.

In the 1850s the Southern slaveholders used their control of the federal government in an attempt to make the American people enforce the slave system. The Fugitive Slave Law provided savage penalties for aiding escaped slaves and for failing to inform on them and their helpers. It aroused popular defiance and helped inspire the formation of the Republican Party, whose victory in the 1860 election was followed by the Civil War that ended the slave system.

In both these cases, political action supported by a majority of the people was needed to repulse the forces of reaction. Political action is needed again today, and it must be *independent* political action because the Democratic and Republican parties share equal responsibility for McCarthyism and McCarranism. The next big political step in the fight to preserve the Bill of Rights is the formation of a new party—an independent labor party, based on those sections of the population who have the most to lose from restrictions on democratic liberties: the labor movement, the working farmers, the Negro people, the housewives, the youth and the small shopkeepers.

Such a party, running its own candidates for office, could quickly win a majority of the voters and set up a government that would truly operate in their interests. It would be able to grapple successfully with all the major problems facing this country, such as war, economic insecurity and discrimination. Almost in passing, it would sweep aside all the witch-hunters and thought-controllers and make it impossible for them to do any more damage.

I don't know if the Supreme Court will ever hear my case or how it will rule if it does hear it; after the four-to-four decision in the Dorothy Bailey case, nobody can be sure.

But I am certain that if the Court rules favorably on my appeal and against the "loyalty" program, it would be a significant setback for the witch-hunters. I don't pretend that it would single-handedly reverse the ominous trend toward a police state—more than one court victory will be needed for that—but I do believe that it could be a turning point and that it would encourage renewed resistance to all efforts to impose thought control on the American people.

Similarly, I am certain that if the Court rules against me, the

American tradition of free speech would receive another nail in its coffin. I don't mean that a defeat for me would constitute the end of democracy and the victory of totalitarianism, but it would represent a long step in that direction. Those who want to regiment and gag the people would be emboldened to move further and faster toward their goal.

I hope with all my heart for a victory, but I don't know what to expect. The most disappointing thing of all would be a decision that skirts the main issues in my case and rests on some narrow procedural question, leaving the fundamental issue unresolved.

Whatever the Supreme Court does, my conscience is clear. I have done everything in my power to preserve the Bill of Rights for all. My faith in the democratic future of this country will remain unshaken even if the Court rules against me.

For I have appealed to two courts—the court of public opinion as well as the Supreme Court. The latter may decide that I cannot be restored to my job, but the court of public opinion will have the final say on the larger issues in my case. With all due respect to the Court, it will be the American people themselves who will decide whether or not this shall become a police state.

I return now to the case of Dred Scott, with which I compared my own case at the beginning of this book. The Supreme Court ruled against Dred Scott; it declared that slaves have no rights and that Congress had no constitutional right to abolish slavery in the territories. That decision, made in 1857, was a victory for the slaveholders and a defeat for the opponents of slavery. But the Supreme Court had misjudged the temper and the aspirations of the American people, and the Dred Scott decision, instead of bolstering slavery, helped to hasten its doom. Four years later, the slaveholders, refusing to recognize the democratic election of Lincoln, resorted to a violent civil war in defense of slavery. In 1865 the 13th Amendment, prohibiting slavery, was adopted, and in 1868, eleven short years after the Dred Scott decision, the 14th Amendment, granting the rights of citizenship to the Negro people, became a part of the United States Constitution.

I hope that the Supreme Court will read the temper and aspirations of the American people correctly today. Whether it does or not, I face the future with absolute confidence that in the end, and soon rather than late, the American people will hand down a favorable verdict on my case and on the larger struggle to retain the democratic liberties they have shed their blood to win.

18

The second five years

The previous chapters of this book were completed in 1953, when my case was almost five years old and I was forty.[*] These last two chapters are being written twenty years later, early in 1973. In them I tell the rest of the story about my case and try to draw certain conclusions about civil liberties in the United States. Although I was the one with the best reason to remember the details, I find that my memory of some has begun to fail after all this time; where there is no written record to consult I shall skip over some things. In com-

---

[*] The first edition of this book, bearing the same title, was published in Britain by New Park Publications in 1953 and distributed in this country by Pioneer Publishers. (For an explanation of why it was published in Britain, see Appendix A of the present edition.) Besides the first seventeen chapters, the first edition contained a lengthy appendix, "Comment on the Case," consisting of excerpted statements, editorials, letters and articles by various organizations, periodicals and individuals. This material was useful ammunition while the case was active, but I omit it from the present edition because the general information it contained may also be found in the text itself. A second appendix in the first edition, "Finances," which gave an audited accounting of the finances of the Kutcher Civil Rights Committee through December 31, 1952, has been replaced here by an audit account that runs through the end of the case and the disbanding of the committee (Appendix D).

pensation, the narrative, touching only the high points, will probably move faster. And the conclusions of course should benefit from the advantages of further hindsight.

I have left the first seventeen chapters exactly as they were printed. Not because they couldn't be improved by rewriting, but because they accurately express a certain reaction to events shortly after they had occurred; rewriting might alter that to some degree despite my intentions. The disadvantage is that I forego the opportunity to update some of the terminology current in the 1940s and 1950s. In the preceding chapter, for example, I wrote about the need to create an independent labor party based, among other forces, on "the Negro people, the housewives [and] the youth." Writing now, I would use the terms Black people or Afro-Americans or African-Americans, I would have mentioned other oppressed national minorities such as the Chicanos, Native American Indians and Puerto Ricans, I would have included among the progressive forces of our society not just housewives but all women engaged in struggle for liberation, and I would have spoken of the students in particular as well as the youth in general. I would have entitled Chapter 13 "My *First* National Tour," because I made another in 1954. In fact, we probably would not have given the Kutcher Civil Rights Committee that name if it had been formed a year or two later; the term "civil rights" was usually used in this country to designate "civil liberties" in the broader sense until around 1949; it is only since then that it has come to be used primarily for the rights of racial and ethnic minorities.

Let me return first to my housing case. As I said in Chapter 16, in February 1953 the American Civil Liberties Union filed suit in the New Jersey courts to have the Gwinn Amendment declared unconstitutional and to stop the Newark Housing Authority from evicting my parents and me. On March 19, Superior Court Judge Walter J. Freund stayed the eviction, pending a ruling on the Gwinn Amendment's constitutionality. At the same time, however, he indicated that the ruling might be delayed until the tenants had shown that the threat of eviction resulted from their failure to sign the housing oath.

This was a concession to the Newark Housing Authority which argued that it had the right to evict its tenants at any time and for any reason that it chose, and that our refusal to sign the oath was really beside the point!

Six months later, in October, when final briefs were filed in the New Jersey Superior Court, the Newark Housing Authority was still engaged in the same kind of legalistic flim-flam. It contended in its brief that no constitutional rights were infringed by excluding public housing tenants who refused to sign the oath. It even pretended to be indignant over what it called a case where "the selfish few would prevent the court from protecting the rights and happiness of many." It did not explain how the rights and happiness of many would be protected by depriving them of the right to belong to legal organizations of their own choice.

In the strange world inhabited by the Newark Housing Authority, we who didn't want to be dictated to were transformed into people who wanted to dictate to others: "Non-signers should not be permitted to dictate under what rules they will accept the bounties of Congress."

Judge Freund said he would render a decision on the basis of the written briefs by both sides. That was October 1953. Time marched on. First 1953 went off into history. Then 1954. I sometimes thought of Judge Freund and wondered what he was doing about our case. Was it bothering him? Was he thinking about it at all, or was he too busy with other matters? If he was thinking about it, from what angle? Were there complex legal principles disturbing him, or was he paralyzed by resentment at having been handed a hot potato? By the time 1955 rolled around I privately subscribed to the theory that one of his clerks had mislaid the file and the whole thing had been forgotten.

If so, eventually somebody must have found the file, because on March 18, 1955, a decision was handed down. It was not from Judge Freund (I can't remember why) but from his colleague on the Superior Court, G. Dixon Speakman. Judge Speakman issued an injunction forbidding the Newark Housing Authority to evict the families that refused to sign the oath. But he did not rule on the Gwinn Amendment. Instead, he relied on a narrow technical point—that the Newark Housing Authority had demanded oaths pertaining to all organizations on the blacklist, including so-called "front organizations," and not just those that were labeled "subversive" by the attorney general. The implication was that the Gwinn Amendment was fine, and our eviction would have been fine too if the Housing Authority had demanded that we swear an oath about a fewer number of blacklisted organizations.

But the Newark Housing Authority didn't like the decision either; its I-am-the-law doctrine had in effect been rejected or impaired. So on October 10, 1955, it appealed to the New Jersey Supreme Court, asking it to overrule the Speakman injunction.

The Supreme Court acted quite promptly, as such things go. On December 19 (three years after the housing case began) its four justices unanimously rejected the appeal and affirmed the injunction. They too refused to rule on the constitutionality of the Gwinn Amendment.

The next day Newark Housing Authority officials revealed that they were conferring with higher authorities in Washington about appealing the decision to the federal courts. They let it be known that they were also considering rewriting the oath to conform to the Speakman position and then making a new attempt to evict us on that basis.

But the Newark Housing Authority did not go to federal court and it did not circulate a rewritten oath. By the middle of 1956 Public Housing Authority officials around the country had lost about two dozen court cases involving attempts to evict tenants because of the oath, some of them in the federal courts. And although the Gwinn Amendment was not ruled unconstitutional in any of these cases, the Justice Department decided to give up its campaign to evict nonsigners of the oath. On August 3, 1956, the Public Housing Authority in Washington announced that the Justice Department had ruled that the Gwinn oath was "temporary legislation" and that it had expired.

So that's how my housing case, and all the other housing cases that had been challenged, came to an end.* We did not succeed in getting the Gwinn Amendment declared unconstitutional, but we did succeed in stopping its enforcement. It was not an unqualified victory (few victories are, I have learned), but it was most welcome in our home where, in the meantime, my father, suffering from diabetes, had had his right leg amputated.

Before resuming the story of my job fight, I must relate another episode which for a few weeks overshadowed the job issue but probably had an important effect on its outcome. That was the government's decision to cut off the disability pension which was my sole income. I learned about it in a letter from the VA during the third week of December 1955, just when the New Jersey Supreme Court was rejecting the effort to evict us. The rest of the country learned about it just before Christmas, a matter of timing that probably increased the public indignation with which the news was greeted.

Nobody's indignation was greater than mine. I had been relatively stoical about the loss of my job and the threat to our home, but this struck me as a really foul blow. I still remembered clearly the discussions among the disabled veterans at Walter Reed Hospital, and

---

* But the arrogance of public housing bureaucrats continues unabated. On December 8, 1972, the *New York Times* reported that the New York City Housing Authority was evicting a couple from a housing project in Harlem because their son had been jailed for an attempted robbery. The couple was Mr. and Mrs. Joseph Tyson, Jr., occupants of the St. Nicholas Houses at Eighth Avenue and 129th Street. Their main income is a disability allotment Mr. Tyson gets because of emphysema. "We'll have no place to live," Mrs. Tyson said. "We'll be out on the street." The American Civil Liberties Union was representing the Tysons, and promised to take the case to court if necessary. It seems that the Housing Authority keeps dossiers on public housing tenants and screens out or evicts those whom it finds "undesirable," allegedly in the name of protecting the other tenants against violent crimes. (They always commit these atrocities in the name of something else.) ACLU lawyers pointed out that the Tysons had committed no crime, and that their son, Joseph Jr., who is soon to be released from prison, had signed an affidavit that he would not become part of the household after his release.

the several lectures we had received there from army officers explaining the philosophy behind the disability pension. It was not charity, they emphasized, and it was not a privilege, but a *right*—an obligation of the government based on the recognition that it had to partially make up for the damage done to people while they were in government service. When I was making up my mind about fighting for my job in 1948, a question about the effect such a fight might have on my pension had entered my mind briefly, but I quickly dismissed it because no one could recall any case of a veteran ever being deprived of his pension for political reasons. And because the question never was raised by anyone during the next seven years, it was all the more shocking when the government not only raised it in 1955 but proposed to do something about it without delay.

I assumed that the motive for this new move was personal vindictiveness. I had been an embarrassment to the government, or at least a nuisance, and I thought they had decided to make me pay a heavier price for all this. But while this may have been a factor, it wasn't all that personal. For I soon learned that similar action was being taken against the veterans' pensions of two disabled leaders of the Communist Party, Robert Thompson and Saul Wellman, and that the government had gone to the lengths of suspending the meager old-age pensions of other Communist Party leaders, including William Z. Foster, and even of demanding the repayment of some of these pensions.

So there was a "principle" behind these attacks, as well as a dislike of the people attacked. And the principle was an extension of the line taken in the housing case earlier: No rights of wrong-thinking or wrong-speaking or wrong-acting people were to be respected—not the right to live in public housing, nor the right to receive disability pensions, nor the right to draw social security benefits, nor—once the logic that such things are government "bounties" is accepted—the rights to receive unemployment compensation, go to public schools, walk on the public streets, vote in public elections, etc., etc.

The first VA letter I got was from P.H. Moss, acting chairman, Central Committee on Waivers and Forfeitures, dated December 12, 1955, and it said:

> Dear Mr. Kutcher:
>
> The records in your claim have been submitted to this committee for a determination as to whether a forfeiture will be declared against you under Section 4, Public Law No. 144, 78th Congress, which reads as follows:
>
> "Any person shown by evidence satisfactory to the Administrator of Veterans' Affairs to be guilty of mutiny, treason, sabotage, or rendering assistance to an enemy of the United States or of its allies shall forfeit all accrued or future benefits under laws administered by the Veterans Administration pertaining to gratuities for veterans and their dependents: Provided, however, that the Administrator of Veterans' Affairs, in his discretion, may apportion and pay any part of such benefits to the dependents of such persons not exceeding the amount to which each dependent would be entitled if such person were dead."
>
> The evidence shows that you are and have been an active member of the Socialist Workers Party since 1938; that the Socialist Workers Party has been determined to be, by duly authorized officials of the United States of America, an organization which seeks to alter the form of government of the United States of America by unconstitutional means; that your numerous activities over the years which have been instrumental to furthering the aims and objectives of the Socialist Workers Party appear to constitute a violation of the above-cited statute, in that it also appears that you rendered aid and assistance to an enemy of the United States or of its allies by espousing and defending the Socialist Workers Party cause and thereby giving aid and comfort to the enemy by your influence upon others in undermining public interest and cooperation and confidence in the United States government's administration of the war effort and hampering and obstructing such effort.

The evidence also shows that in July 1950 and the summer of 1951 you attended a camp owned and operated by the Socialist Workers Party known as Mountain Spring Camp, Washington, New Jersey, at which time you stated that you liked the "red" system of government; that in this country half of what a worker earns goes to the government and under the "red" government the worker gets all he earns; that the government of the United States is composed of people who are cheaters and crooks who oppress the working people. It is further shown that you urged and advocated that the members in attendance at the camp cause strikes and get in key positions and get the Socialist Workers Party in control of the government of the United States. It is further shown that you stated that the party members couldn't wish them in, think them in, or vote them in; therefore they should be overthrown and killed and then get a new government.

In view of the above, it appears that you have violated the provisions of the above-cited statute.

You are hereby given an opportunity to furnish any evidence which in your opinion might explain your position in this matter. You may also avail yourself of the right of a formal hearing on the matter with representation by counsel, if desired. If you desire to avail yourself of this privilege, a reasonable extension of time will be granted to you for the purpose of assembling and forwarding such evidence. If no word is received from you within thirty days from the date of this letter, it will be assumed that you do not care to submit any further statements and the Central Committee of Waivers and Forfeitures will proceed with the consideration of your case on the basis of the evidence of record.

Despite the offer of "a reasonable extension of time," the government was unable to wait even for a reply before stopping my pension. Together with the December 12 letter came another from William Keller, VA Adjudication Officer, dated December 15, which went right to the point:

Dear Mr. Kutcher:

Your compensation award has been suspended effective the date you were last paid by this administration [November 30]. This action has been taken pursuant to Veterans Administration's regulations and procedures pending determination by the Central Committee on Waivers and Forfeitures, Washington, D.C., as to whether a forfeiture may be declared against you under the provisions of Section IV, Public Law 144, 78th Congress.

So, along with suspension of my pension, I was confronted with a serious escalation of the charges against me—from reasonable doubts about my loyalty to that of rendering aid and assistance to the enemies of the United States (which is very much like the charge of treason as defined in the U.S. Constitution: giving "aid and comfort" to its enemies); and with the rather difficult task of disproving statements attributed to me by persons unknown, whom the government would probably refuse to produce so that they could be cross-examined under oath.

But my first reaction, I must admit, did not revolve around these political questions. Instead, according to a newspaper of the time, I asked a friend if the December 12 letter I had just read meant that the government also planned to take back my artificial legs. Because the letter explicitly said "all . . . benefits" could be forfeited. All benefits in my case included not only the pension but the artificial limbs, free medical care, hospitalization at the VA hospital, etc. My friend told me not to get hysterical; it was most unlikely that even the most ardent witch-hunters would try to take my artificial legs, if only because of the bad publicity it would produce. He was probably right, but at the time I could not overlook the fact that only a week before an attack on my pension would also have been considered "most unlikely." And there were two numbers typed in at the top of the December 12 letter: one was my pension number, the other was my hospitalization number. That might mean nothing; on the other hand, it might mean that action on my hospitalization rights was next or already under way. I don't think I have any tendencies toward paranoia, but in such situations even normal people begin looking around over their shoulders.

This time I did not have to decide whether to fight; no other choice was possible. The committee in New York went into action, and so did Mr. Rauh and his partner, John Silard. On December 22 they fired off a letter to the Central Committee denouncing the new charges and all the circumstances surrounding it. They demanded immediate dismissal of the charges and resumption of the pension payments or a hearing at the earliest possible moment and the appearance in person at the hearing of any people the government intended to use as witnesses against me.

The new developments were made known to the news media the same day, with very favorable results. Especially effective was the treatment given in the December 23 issue of the *New York Post,* which carried a big headline on its front page, a sympathetic story by Murray Kempton, the full text of the two VA letters, and a long editorial which ended by saying, "Surely the Kutcher decision must be reversed. Beyond that the country has a right to meet the men who made the decision, and to ask why the fate of the nation's veterans is in their hands."

Maybe it was the Yuletide spirit, or maybe the pension case just seemed to be qualitatively more outrageous than the job case. Anyhow, in the next couple of days the press, radio, and TV audiences of this country learned more about my troubles with the government than they had in all of the preceding seven years combined, and most of the publicity was of the kind that made the government very unhappy.

Exactly six hours after the first *New York Post* articles reached the street, the VA office in Washington held a press conference to announce that my pension was being restored at once, pending the outcome of the hearing. Whoever made the announcement had the nerve to add that this was being done out of "a sense of fair play." Perhaps it was, but in that case the press publicity did a lot to bring it to the VA's consciousness.

The *Post* then picked up the demand that my hearing should be public and open to the press. This won support from U.S. Senator Estes Kefauver and a number of other members of Congress. To my surprise the government capitulated to this demand too. This was a sure sign that the government realized it might have overreached itself a little.

Since it was the first public hearing in any "loyalty" case, the press was there in full force on December 30 when we arrived at the VA Building. Work ceased in all the offices along the corridor from the elevator to the hearing chamber as heads popped out of the doors to watch me hobble along. Over fifty reporters and cameramen jammed the five rows of seats provided for them, and the proceedings were delayed as they kept asking for more pictures.

Up front, facing the audience, were the representatives of the Central Committee—Peyton H. Moss, John A. Cumberland and George Hunter. At a parallel table, with our backs to the audience, sat Mr. Rauh, Mr. Silard and I. Assorted VA officials, including Morris Lipps, acting chief counsel of the VA, sat at tables on either side.

The hearing was opened by Mr. Moss, a thin, elderly man with a heavy Southern accent. He began by asking me to stand to be sworn and then, as I began the laborious process of rising, changed his mind and told me I needn't stand and could just hold up my hand while seated.

Mr. Moss's opening statement consisted mainly of a reading of the December 12 letter, but he also read replies to the various requests in the Rauh-Silard letter of December 22. Treason? How did that ever come up? Why, they weren't charging me with treason but with rendering assistance to an enemy of the United States. The former might require a jury trial but the latter need not. In support of this distinction he quoted a legal opinion from the VA general counsel: "While the words 'rendering assistance' have substantially the same meaning as 'giving aid and comfort,' it is the opinion of this office that those words are used in Section 4 to describe a different offense from that of treason. (Giving 'aid and comfort to an enemy' is *part* of the elements constituting treason.) If not used to describe a different offense there would have been no point in using the words in the same sentence in said Section 4 in which the word 'treason' was used," etc.

Produce the faceless government agents so that they could testify against me under oath and in public? Oh no, that couldn't be done, because "you are informed that under the directive of the president of the United States dated May 17, 1954, the sources of the evidence on which the charges in this case are based will not be disclosed."

Mr. Rauh asked Mr. Moss to give us a copy of the rules and regulations covering the hearing. Mr. Moss said he couldn't do that. Why not, did that mean there were no rules? Oh, certainly there are rules, said Mr. Moss, but "I am the acting chairman of this Committee, and I will, in a sense, determine what shall be done at the hearing." Mr. Rauh again asked for a copy of the rules, and was again denied it. Mr. Lipps intervened, and after further exchange said, "There are no written published rules . . ."

> Mr. Rauh: In other words, there are no rules for the conducting of this hearing. That is all I am trying to get at. Is that correct?
>
> Mr. Lipps: That is correct.
>
> Mr. Rauh: Thank you.
>
> Acting Chairman: Okay. I will make the rules as I go along then. Now go ahead [with your defense]. . . .

Before setting out to show that the charges against me were not true, Mr. Rauh told the hearing, he wanted to make the point that even if they were true that would not justify stopping my pension.

> Mr. Rauh: The first reason is that . . . I do not believe that this body, the Veterans Administration, has any authority to find a man guilty of treason or rendering assistance to an enemy of the United States. What it has authority to do is to decide if a court has convicted a man, and if the court has not convicted the man it has no authority to find him guilty here.

The word "guilty" means guilty in a court of law, not guilty before an administrative tribunal. It means guilty after an indictment under the Fifth Amendment after a jury trial and after all the fair play of a court room. I say that this body has no authority to find Mr. Kutcher guilty of anything. . . .

Acting Chairman: Your request for dismissal of the case on the ground stated by you is denied . . .

Mr. Rauh's next point, if I understood it correctly, was that I couldn't be punished, even if everything alleged in the December 12 letter were true, because no crime had been committed. What is giving "aid and assistance" to an enemy, once you say that it is something different from giving "aid and comfort" to an enemy—especially when no attempt is made to show any intent to help an enemy? The only thing really involved here was the right of free speech; the Veterans Administration was trying to punish me for exercising my right of free speech, and this was dangerous ground. Mr. Rauh then read two statements against the Truman administration's foreign policy made by General Eisenhower when he was campaigning for the presidency in 1952, which he termed "every bit as detrimental to the war effort as anything Mr. Kutcher said." To his motion to dismiss on these grounds came the reply, "Your motion is denied."

Continuing his efforts to have the charges made more specific, Mr. Rauh asked the name of the country I was supposed to have aided, and here some new ground was broken.

Acting Chairman: I think I can answer that, Mr. Rauh. Communist China and North Korea.

Mr. Rauh: Mr. Kutcher is now charged with rendering aid and assistance to Communist China and North Korea, is that correct?

Acting Chairman: That is correct, sir.

Mr. Rauh: Now will you kindly state any act that he did that is alleged in this document in which he gave aid and assistance to Communist China or North Korea?

Acting Chairman: I can only repeat what we have already written to Mr. Kutcher. Mr. Rauh, I will just simply read this over again, since it appears that you didn't understand it. . . . [Reads from December 12 letter passage ending, "It is further shown that you urged and advocated that the members in attendance at the camp cause strikes and get in key positions and get the Socialist Workers Party in control of the government of the United States."] Now if you are going to cause strikes during time of war, you aid an enemy. That is our view of it.

Mr. Rauh expressed astonishment at this statement which, after the hearing, elicited angry comment by a number of labor papers that nobody would call radical. While "patriotic" pressure had been used to prevent and break certain strikes during the Korean War, exercising the right to strike had not been legally declared treasonable, and even conservative union leaders supporting the war rankled at suggestions that strikes constituted aid to an enemy. But Mr. Moss did not want to pursue this subject. Instead, he turned to me and began to ask questions.

One was whether I had been in Los Angeles to make speeches on July 8 and 9, 1949. Mr. Silard objected: "Mr. Chairman, there has got to be some limit. This country was not in war in July 1949." Overruled. Another set of questions concerned a letter I had sent to *The Militant* on April 18, 1949, supporting the Socialist Workers Party's defense of Communist Party leaders then on trial under the Smith Act in New York. Mr. Rauh objected to the question on the ground that it suggested that opposing Smith Act convictions made one guilty of rendering aid to an enemy of the United States. Actually, he pointed out millions of Americans, along with organizations such as the American Civil Liberties Union and the CIO, were opposed to the Smith Act trials. But Mr. Moss was not to be deterred: "Was not the purpose of your defense of the eleven communists prompted by the Socialist Workers Party to do whatever it could to the damage of our present constitutional government in this country?"

From the tone of his voice I gathered that Mr. Moss considered

George Weissman and James Kutcher looking over the pension hearing document in 1956, the eighth year of the case.

Joseph L. Rauh, Jr.

his next point to be a bombshell. This threw me off stride a little, so that when he asked me if I had attended the national convention of the Socialist Workers Party in New York City, I said I had, instead of first asking which one.

> Acting Chairman: We have information that at that convention a portion of the program was to be broadcast over the radio and the American flag was on the table next to the red flag, and that seeing it, you remarked, "Why do they have that God damn flag there?" referring to the American flag. Then it was explained to you that they could not make the broadcast unless the American flag was there, whereupon you remarked, "After they go, tear the S.O.B. up," and that following the program the American flag was removed. What have you to say in regard to that?

The whole thing was a fabrication. I have never been a flag-waver, but I am not a flag-hater either; symbols and symbolic gestures simply don't get me excited. I wondered whether the story had been concocted by an informer present at the convention or by the FBI authorities who paid his salary.

> Acting Chairman: Among your many speeches in different parts of the country in [furtherance] of the Socialist Workers Party, do you recall a speech you made in behalf of that party before a night class at Fenn College in Ohio in November 1949? . . .
>
> Mr. Kutcher: What did I say?
>
> Acting Chairman: There is information before this committee that one of the students asked you if the Socialist Workers Party was in favor of violent overthrow of the present government of the United States, and you answered that the party would take over the government legally when the time came, that the advocates of the present form of government would start the bloodshed and that the Socialist Workers Party would definitely defend itself.
>
> What did you mean when you said that you would take over when the time came? By that, did you mean that you would take

over forcibly whenever you felt that you were strong enough to do so?

Mr. Kutcher: I never made any such wild statements, but I can make a statement on that: We believe in using constitutional measures in order to achieve socialism, through the organization of a labor party and so on. Through the course of time we believe that we could become the heads of the labor party, and in that way be elected by regular constitutional measures into the government.

Acting Chairman: That is a little inconsistent with what you told the students then?

Mr. Rauh: Just a moment. Mr. Kutcher didn't testify he told the students that. You have a secret informer that you haven't the nerve to produce who said that. Mr. Kutcher didn't say he said that. Don't put those words in his mouth here in front of God and everybody.

Acting Chairman: I will say this: That that is inconsistent with the information we have as to what you told the students.

Mr. Rauh: By a secret informer that you won't produce face to face with us.

Acting Chairman: Did you address a meeting of the Student Bar Association of the Western Reserve Law School on November 7, 1949?

Mr. Kutcher: Yes, I probably did.

Acting Chairman: The committee has information that following your speech, the meeting was opened to questions and answers, and further that a student asked you, "If there is force and violence used to overthrow the government when the Socialist Workers Party attempts to take over, whose fault will it be?" You answered, "It won't be our fault if the majority want socialism and the minority don't want it. We aren't responsible for what happens." Did you make that statement?

Mr. Kutcher: All I said was that probably after we came into power, that the minority of capitalists would organize a coup d'etat. That has happened to other countries, and it could happen here.

This sequence dribbled away into a number of feeble attempts by Mr. Moss to put words into my mouth: "Isn't it true that you intend to take over whenever you think it is possible to do so, and take over by force without regard to the Constitution of the United States?" "It is not your intention to do so?" "It is not the Socialist Workers Party's intention to do so?"

Mr. Moss then declared a ten-minute recess, during which a number of reporters came to our table to talk with me. George Weissman, our committee's treasurer and its chief executive after George Novack moved to the West Coast in 1953, had sat near the press row and mingled with them during the recess. Remarks he overheard were: "So this is what they call a security hearing." "So this is what goes on." "'I'll make the rules as I go along.'" "Two-to-one the next charge is that he trampled on Old Glory with his wooden legs." The government had no trouble denying our motions, but it wasn't doing such a good job in persuading the press.

After the recess, Mr. Silard and Mr. Rauh asked me questions for the record that enabled me to refute the lies, clarify my political views, and underline the government's arbitrary procedure. The only thing we didn't get into the record was my low opinion of the unknown informers and their inability to make up statements that even sound like what a socialist would say. (In more than twenty years I had never heard a single radical say he liked "the 'red' system of government," whatever that may be; or present such a pathetic caricature of the Marxist theory of surplus value; or advocate the killing of government officials.)

Farrell Dobbs, then the national secretary of the Socialist Workers Party, who attended the hearing and watched the reactions of the audience closely, told me later that the emotional high point came with the last two questions asked by Mr. Silard.

> Mr. Silard: If your pension is denied you, Mr. Kutcher—and I assume you will have no other means of livelihood, or your parents—will you give up your membership in the Socialist Workers Party?

Mr. Kutcher: No, sir.

Mr. Silard: If your pension is retained, if this board should decide that you may retain your pension, will you give up your membership in the Socialist Workers Party?

Mr. Kutcher: No, sir.

Dobbs said that at this point there was audible a collective intake of breath by the audience, as if it had suddenly realized how futile and powerless the witch-hunt was to make a convinced revolutionist quit his party or renounce his ideas.

Mr. Rauh summed up, needling the Central Committee by stressing that I had been the only witness to testify under oath, and asked it to act on my case favorably and before the new year. Mr. Moss closed the hearing by saying the decision could not be made that quickly but would be made as quickly as possible.

The next day's papers were encouraging. "Kutcher got a hearing yesterday," reporter Murray Marder wrote in the *Washington Post* ". . . [but before it ended] the press saw a type of proceeding unlike anything that has come into public view. In this hearing there were no rules of procedure, no witnesses (except for the accused, Kutcher), nor any facts to back up the charges against him except the charges themselves." The *Philadelphia Inquirer* headline was "Legless Veteran Sticks to Socialist Beliefs Despite Pension Threat."

The Central Committee really did move fast for a governmental body. Only one week after the hearing, on January 6, 1956, it decided the case in my favor. Not in such a way as to clear me completely, however.

It admitted that some of the charges against me were irrelevant because they dated from before the Korean War, but defended their introduction on the basis that they were "background information." It also admitted that "the records of this committee do not reveal that a forfeiture under Section 4, Public Law 144, 78th Congress, has ever been declared against a veteran within the jurisdiction of the United States courts who had not been convicted of charges involving subversive activities," but defended its right to pronounce an administrative forfeiture "upon satisfactory evidence."

> This has been a very difficult case for the Committee to decide, as it is realized that, in order to support a forfeiture, it must be established beyond a reasonable doubt that the veteran did knowingly and intentionally render assistance to an enemy of the United States. While it is the opinion of this Committee that the utterances alleged to have been made by the veteran in July 1950 and the summer of 1951, if established beyond a reasonable doubt, would constitute a violation of the forfeiture statute, the Committee determined that all the available evidence does not measure up to this quantum of proof. . . . There is at least a reasonable doubt that he did, during the essential period here in question, individually or in concert with others, perform any act indicating a clear intent to aid an enemy of the United States or any of its allies.
>
> Therefore . . . it is the decision of the Committee that the veteran, James Kutcher, is not shown, beyond a reasonable doubt, to have been guilty of any of the offenses proscribed by Section 4, Public Law 144, 78th Congress, and that, therefore, no forfeiture under said statute is in order.

Despite their reluctance to back off from this "very difficult case," the witch-hunters did have to give in on the pension issue. It was another victory worth celebrating, and it served as a precedent in reversing other political pension cases. It also revived attention in the fight to recover my job, and probably contributed to speeding up further action in my court appeal.

As I reported earlier, my name was taken off the VA employment rolls for the second time after the Loyalty Review Board ruled against me in June 1953. Trying to get the case back into the courts, our lawyers on August 14 sent a formal appeal for my reinstatement to Eisenhower's new VA Administrator, Harvey V. Higley. He rejected the appeal two weeks later and that exhausted the administrative channels.

On October 16 our lawyers filed suit in the U.S. District Court in Washington. Around Christmas the government replied by filing a motion to dismiss our suit, but withdrew it after our side filed a memorandum in opposition to dismissal. At this point the government assigned a new attorney to handle the case. He took some time reading the record and deciding on the government's next steps, but finally, on August 11, 1954, he filed a motion for summary judgment. As I understand it, the granting of such a motion puts the whole case in the record without the formalities of a trial and lets the judge make a decision on the basis of the record. Our lawyers did not object to the summary judgment motion because it would save us time and money; for them, going to the district court was only a way of getting back to a higher court, where they hoped for more favorable results.

But the thing about the government's motion that most interested our lawyers was the collection of documents in the case filed as exhibits with the motion. One of these we had never seen before. It was a long memorandum (sixteen printed pages) from the VA Loyalty Board of Appeals to the VA administrator, presenting in detail the reasoning behind its decision against me on April 20, 1953. It bore the notation, "Approved: Carl R. Gray, Jr., 23 April 1953."

Technically this was very important, our lawyers explained to us, because *after* our hearing before the VA Loyalty Board of Appeals on March 9, 1953, this board had asked the Department of Justice to tell it why the Socialist Workers Party was on the attorney general's list. The Department of Justice complied on April 1, 1953, with a summary transmitted by Deputy Attorney General William P. Rogers, who later became Nixon's secretary of state. When the VA Loyalty Board of Appeals made its decision, it was based in part on this summary and on consideration of such things as a court decision in the Minneapolis "sedition" trial of the Socialist Workers Party (*Dunne* v. *United States,* 1941)—none of which was brought up at our hearing, and which therefore we never had a chance to answer. This later caused embarrassment for the government attorneys.

Along the way to a summary judgment at the district court level, the government ran into a maverick. On November 3, 1954, Judge Alexander Holtzoff denied the motion because it appeared to him that the government had failed to comply with the Court of Appeals' 1952 decision. So the government introduced its motion again on February 7, 1955, and to get the thing moving faster, our lawyers filed a cross-motion for summary judgment on May 9. On June 10, Judge Burnita Shelton Matthews "adjudged, ordered and decreed that the plaintiff's [our] motion for summary judgment herein be and hereby is denied, and it is further adjudged, ordered and decreed that defendants' [the government's] motion for summary judgment be and hereby is granted."

This meant that the government had won its case in the district court, and that all the documents were part of the record. On July 1 we went to the Circuit Court of Appeals with a motion that it reverse Judge Matthews' June 10 decision. By August this motion was placed on the Court of Appeals calendar, and that was how things stood legally when the pension fight broke out in December.

I shall omit most of the nonlegal developments for the three years following the Court of Appeals decision in 1952. It was not a happy time, for me personally, or for civil liberties generally. The witch-hunt became even more rabid and widespread after Eisenhower won the election in 1952. Joe McCarthy was the center of American politics for the next two years, and pretty much had his own way until mid-1954, when the U.S. Senate finally voted to censure him (he had gone "too far," attacking not only the army establishment but the Republicans too).

Hardly anyone thought there was any chance of my winning my job back. One of the lawyers associated with our case expressed the opinion that it was hopeless and we might as well quit; I don't give his name here because I know he meant well, and was only saying what most lawyers would have said. I didn't have much hope of victory myself, but didn't think we should throw in the towel as long as there was even the smallest chance. In addition, I wanted a court decision, whatever it would be. Even if unfavorable, it would provide educational ammunition. Meanwhile, I started to attend a printing school so that I could learn proofreading and increase my chances of getting a private job sooner or later.

But there is one episode from this 1953–55 period that I want to relate because it helps to complete and possibly correct an aspect of the picture presented earlier in this book. This concerns the role of the organized labor movement in relation to my case.

My fight would not have gone anywhere, it would not have lasted a year, without the aid I got from the unions, especially those in the CIO—this I firmly believed while the case was being conducted, and this I firmly believe today. In a 1953 footnote near the end of my chapter about my 1949 tour I called attention to disturbing changes that were beginning to affect the labor movement at that time. But the point was so vital that it deserved more than a footnote, and my failure to discuss it more adequately left my account one-sided and therefore inaccurate.

In 1948, when my case began, the libertarian traditions established during the radicalization of the 1930s still survived in the CIO, despite the fact that the cold war had already begun and the union leaders were beginning to feel the pressures of anticommunist conformity. The response from the unions to my initial appeals for help was very heartening, but of course it was not universal. Even then, a number of union leaders refused to have anything to do with me. I should have told in those chapters about some of these people and how they wiggled when approached, and how many of them backed out at the last minute after initially promising support.

At the end of 1949 the cold-war pressure on the union leaders came to a head at the national CIO convention in Cleveland where a number of unions were expelled for being "communist dominated." This was the same convention where I was allowed to sit at a table in the lobby and pass out literature and talk to the delegates about my case. I should at least have mentioned this in my remarks about that convention, but I am afraid that my mind was too narrowly concentrated on my case. In addition, I was hoping that the CIO's purge was only a temporary error or sign of weakness, and that the union members themselves would stop and reverse the purge, as my party was urging them to do.

I remember that at the end of that tour George and I had a discussion about whether or not, in my future talks to the unions, I should include some remarks expressing opposition to the CIO purge. The conclusion was that I should not introduce such remarks, because this would be condemned as "outside interference in internal union affairs" and I would rapidly find myself without any union audiences to talk to. Instead, we agreed, I would express my opposition obliquely, by never failing in any union talk I gave to voice my opposition to the government's infringements on free speech and its persecution of Communist Party members because of their views or associations. (Most CIO unions still held that position, at least on paper.) I was very conscientious about this point in all my talks to unions, even when union leaders advised me that I would be better received if I said nothing on the subject. Meanwhile, my party and *The Militant* were unequivocal in their condemnation of the union purges.

So the unions were in a state of transition, starting around the time my case began. A retreat from a wholehearted commitment to civil liberties had begun, but how much of a retreat was not clear to many of the union leaders themselves, who continued to pass excellent resolutions even as they were beginning to bend and adjust to the demands of the cold warriors. I didn't fully sense this during my national tour in 1949, but it was impossible not to see it when I made another tour in 1954, while we were waiting for the case to drag its way through the courts and seeking additional help to finance the costs.

This time some of the union leaders who had helped in 1949 were simply unwilling to have anything to do with the case; and many of those who did help were not willing to do as much as they had before. Formalities that had been waived in 1949 were now transformed into impassable barriers. Some local union officials who had acted on their own in 1949 now claimed they had to consult their national organizations before they could do anything. Bureaucratization of the unions had made enormous strides in those five years.

That, and the impact of McCarthyism, had frightened some and served as a pretext for others.

Early in June 1954, shortly after I began my tour, I drove from Detroit across the state to Grand Rapids to attend a Michigan CIO convention. So far as getting help was concerned, the trip was wasted, but I did learn something important. A rumor was being circulated, apparently originating in the national CIO office, that I had been misrepresenting the CIO's relation to my case, and that funds collected through the sale of my book were going to the Socialist Workers Party, instead of to the Kutcher Civil Rights Committee.

Gus Scholle, president of the Michigan CIO, who was personally friendly and had often helped our committee, told me that "information" of this kind had been transmitted to the Michigan CIO executive board through a telephone conversation between its secretary, Barney Hopkins, and a Mr. Kessler in the national CIO office. Until this was cleared up, he said, I might encounter some difficulty getting support even from such unions as the United Auto Workers, who had been among our principal supporters.

This was pretty dirty stuff. Not only were the charges untrue, but it was almost by accident that I learned about them and had any chance to reply. I never did learn the precise origins of these knife-in-the-back slanders, or who Kessler was. But it was not too difficult to figure out what was happening.

Philip Murray had died shortly after the November 1952 elections, and his place as CIO president had been taken by Walter Reuther, president of the United Auto Workers. In 1954 Reuther, who had belonged to the Socialist Party in the 1930s when I belonged to its youth affiliate, was trying to ingratiate himself with the witch-hunters in Washington and with the right-wing elements in both the CIO and the AFL (a year later he was to lead the CIO into its merger with the AFL). Cutting off connections with civil liberties cases like mine was a cheap way of demonstrating that the Reutherites were as respectable anticommunists as anyone else. Because nothing in my case had altered since it got promises of support from both the CIO and the UAW, the desired change could be brought about only through innuendo and behind my back.

After consulting with our office in New York, I sent a letter to John V. Riffe, executive vice president of the CIO who was in charge of the state and regional CIO councils. I really had to grit my teeth while preparing this and subsequent correspondence. I would have liked to tell the bureaucrats in the national CIO what I thought of them and their methods. But that would have been a luxury. It would have made me feel better, but it would also have played into their hands and deprived me of further local CIO support. So I remained polite and followed the tactic of making it as difficult as possible for them to repudiate their past declarations of support.

The correspondence is reprinted as Appendix B to this book, and I will not repeat here what is said there. Supporters of our committee in the labor movement circulated copies of this correspondence to every appropriate CIO body and official, which had the effect of partially counteracting the smear campaign, and eventually even the national CIO office issued a "clarification" explaining that it was not trying to "pass judgment on the merit" of my case.

I hope that my report of this episode will help to correct the perhaps idealized account of the unions' role that I wrote earlier. The help I got from the unions was indispensable. But it was not constant; it rose and fell with changes in the overall political situation. And it was not always given for the best reasons; sometimes the union leaders had to be shamed into it. It showed, in a very concrete way, how injurious it is to the cause of civil liberties when the leadership of the labor movement becomes intimidated and conservatized.

The pension victory in January 1956 spurred public interest in the job fight. Typical was the resolution passed by the New York Dress and Waistmakers Joint Board of the International Ladies Garment Workers Union, demanding that the VA "act in a consistent and logical way after restoring his pension by restoring his job to him." And, perhaps coincidentally, action in the courts began to move along a little more rapidly.

First there was the announcement that the U.S. Circuit Court of Appeals would hear the case on February 10. The hearing itself was rather routine. The judges on the bench were E. Barrett Prettyman, Wilbur K. Miller and John A. Danaher. When Mr. Rauh pointed out that the charges against me were the same as they had been in the case acted upon by the Court of Appeals in October 1952, the judges indicated that they remembered that decision. Their questions to Mr. Rauh seemed to me to be friendlier than the ones they directed to Benjamin Forman, the government's attorney. Mr. Forman distinguished himself by attacking my credibility, charging that the Socialist Workers Party and I had supported the Stalin-Hitler Pact of 1939 (!), and trying to make a big thing of my statement before the VA Loyalty Board of Appeals in 1953 that I would not inform the FBI about members of the Communist Party.

The Court of Appeals decision was handed down on April 20, 1956. The vote was two to one in favor of restoring my job, Judge Prettyman writing the decision, Judge Danaher concurring, and Judge Miller dissenting. Being more readable than most such documents, it is reprinted at the end of this book as Appendix C.

The decision was a victory for our side, and we made the most of it. But it avoided the basic constitutional issues we had raised and was based on questions of procedure followed by the government in firing me. It cited a 1944 law requiring that veterans employed by the government "have at least thirty days' advance written notice . . . stating any and all reasons, specifically and in detail, for any such proposed [removal] action," and a 1954 Court of Appeals decision (*Mulligan* v. *Andrews*), which held that "only findings upon the charges, specifically identified, can constitute the 'reasons' required to be stated in the ultimate adverse ruling." Summarizing, the charges against me were that I was "a member of, employed by, and made a contribution to an organization listed by the attorney general," while the reasons for my discharge given in the April 20, 1953, report of the VA Loyalty Board of Appeals were that the Socialist Workers Party "was found to advocate the overthrow of the government by unconstitutional means, and [I] was found to be aware of that aim and to support it consciously and actively." Therefore "the reasons stated in the report differ substantially from the charges made. Since only findings on the charges, specifically identified, can constitute reasons for removal, a reading of the charges must demonstrate the reasons for dismissal, assuming all the charges are sustained. This is not so here." That is, the four charges against me were not valid reasons for dismissal, or not sustained, or too vague and lacking in specificity. Therefore, "Under the rule in the *Mulligan* case, *supra,* the judgment of the District Court must be reversed."

In a final paragraph the decision indicated another reason for ruling against the government, namely, that the statement of the reasons for dismissal, as embodied in the report of the VA Loyalty Board of Appeals, had not been given to me at the proper time. "However in our view of the case it is unnecessary to discuss that point." But it did not even mention the constitutional questions raised by the case, let alone discuss them.

The effect of the decision was to return the case to the district court, where, on May 21, 1956, it fell to the lot of Judge Burnita Shelton Matthews, whose 1955 decision against me the Court of Appeals had reversed, to sign a document in which it was "ordered, adjudged and decreed that plaintiff's [my] separation from his position in the Veterans Administration was procedurally defective and therefore unauthorized, and it is further ordered that plaintiff be restored to the position from which he was separated by the Veterans Administration or, in the event such position no longer exists, to another position of like grade and seniority, with such rights and privileges as he may be entitled to under the law."

Then we braced ourselves for the government's next move. Would it appeal the decision to the Supreme Court? Or would it do the same thing it had done with the first Court of Appeals' decision—pretend to comply with it by reinstating me to the rolls and refiring me simultaneously? It had ninety days in which to make up its mind. I announced that I was ready, willing and able to go back to work. The *New York Post* called on the government to "concede defeat in its long and inglorious war" against me.

And that is what the government did—it conceded defeat, shortly after taking note of a clear straw in the wind. On June 11, the Supreme Court ruled—in the case of Kendrick M. Cole, who had been fired from the Federal Food and Drug Administration because of alleged association with the Nature Friends of America, which was on the attorney general's list—that the procedures used in the "loyalty" purge were illegal when used against government workers in "nonsensitive" jobs. Nine days later VA Administrator Higley instructed the Newark VA to restore me to my job, and I walked back in and went to work on June 26.

That should have marked the end of the story, but unfortunately it did not. There was still the matter of my back pay for almost eight years. I wanted the money both as a matter of principle and because I hoped with it to buy one of the special homes built for amputees. But it must have been a matter of principle for the government too. It had conceded defeat, but it did not want to pay full reparations.

Mr. Rauh kept prodding the government, and in September 1956 the VA sent the back pay case to the attorney general for an opinion. Four months later *New York Post* reporter Fern Marja set out to learn what had happened. In an article entitled "After Six Months . . . Kutcher Still Waits," published December 12, she reported that a VA official in Washington had told her, "The court ruling said in effect that Kutcher should be given his job and given whatever he is entitled to. That last part leaves quite a loophole. We don't know exactly what it means. . . ." At the Department of Justice she got only a "no comment" response.

In February 1957 the VA in Newark belatedly awarded me a bronze medal for "ten years of faithful and meritorious service" (the equivalent of a good conduct medal in the army). The February 26 *New York Post* quoted me as saying, "I was happy to get the award because it recognizes what the court ruled in my case—that for almost eight years I was illegally deprived of my job and that legally I have been an employee of the VA since 1946. I hope the government follows the logic of giving me the award and gives me the back wages coming to me. If it can decorate me for ten years' service, it isn't too much to ask that it pay me for the same ten years." The rumor on this occasion was that the VA had now applied to the comptroller general's office for a ruling.

In August 1957 the comptroller general came through—with a really outlandish ruling: I could not get my back pay because I was a member of an organization on the attorney general's list and the Appropriations Act forbade payment of funds to members of such organizations. (Government employees' wages and salaries are paid from funds authorized by the Appropriations Act.)

We called a press conference to show how absurd this ruling was. I sent another letter to President Eisenhower on August 23 in an attempt to publicize the contradiction between the continuing payment of my current wages every two weeks and the continued refusal to pay my back wages. "Mr. President," I wrote, "this [ruling] is ridiculous. The government is paying me today and I belong to the Socialist Workers Party. The same appropriation and other acts apply to my pay today as apply to my back pay. Please don't make me use up my money in high-priced litigation in the Court of Claims to get my back pay. . . . If it is legal to pay me biweekly today, it is certainly equally legal to pay me for what I would have earned had I not been illegally dismissed."

But the government preferred to look ridiculous, and the comptroller general's office insisted that back pay would never be granted to me without a court order. So on December 5, 1957, Mr. Rauh filed suit in the U.S. Court of Claims in Washington for an order directing the government to pay me back wages of approximately $23,000. (That would be gross pay, and would include the modest automatic pay raises I would have received during the period of my suspension. However, taxes, retirement contributions and insurance payments would have to be deducted.)

When it became clear that this suit would be won, the government agreed to bargain with us about the amount to be paid. If it was a matter of principle with them, they also seemed strangely insistent on keeping the sum to the minimum. They were adamant about refusing to include automatic pay raises, and in the end we yielded on this point in order to get the thing over. So on June 4, 1958, a few months short of ten years after the case began, the U.S.

Court of Claims, noting that there had been a stipulation by the two parties agreeing to settlement and consenting to judgment, ordered that judgment in my behalf be entered for $13,589.94. (Taxes, etc., had already been deducted, but a substantial lawyer's fee had to be paid out of it.)

After the money was actually paid, the Kutcher Civil Rights Committee disbanded on October 24, 1958. I retired from the VA at the end of January 1972. Six months later, the U.S. Circuit Court of Appeals in Washington ruled that the 33-year-old Hatch Act's prohibitions on political activity by federal government employees are so vague and broad that they are unconstitutional.

19

Summing up

To help clarify certain matters for readers who did not live through the postwar witch-hunt period or who remember it only faintly, I asked half a dozen young people, some of whom were not born when my case began, to read the first edition of this book and then pose questions they would like answered or discussed. In some cases I have synthesized their questions for convenience.

Near the end of Chapter 17 you said, "The most disappointing thing of all would be a decision that skirts the main issues in my case and rests on some narrow procedural question, leaving the fundamental issues unresolved." But isn't that exactly the kind of decision that ended your case? Would you still call it "the most disappointing thing"?

Yes, unfortunately the Court of Appeals decision was primarily procedural. And no, it was not the most disappointing thing that could have happened.

By 1956 the decision-making circles of the ruling class had decided to curb what they considered "excesses" of the witch-hunt. They did not proceed in a frank and forthright fashion, but piecemeal and partly by indirection, snipping off a few rough edges here or there. They didn't do away with the purge entirely, but they imposed certain restraints on it. The subversive list remained on the books, but "nonsensitive" government employees (meaning most of them) were excluded from some of its consequences. After letting the witch-hunters run wild for several years, the courts began to remind them that they did not have a completely free hand, that they had to observe certain procedures, etc. The courts did not become opponents of witch-hunting in principle; their goal was moderation in the witch-hunt, greater observance of legal niceties, and avoidance of excesses that made the government look more repressive than was necessary. And so I went back to my job through a decision that avoided ruling on the constitutionality of the subversive list, the loyalty program and the Hatch Act.

This surely displeased the zealots of the witch-hunt who feared that moderation would lead inevitably and quickly to the overthrow of the government. (They had their own variant of the "domino theory": begin by letting the likes of Kutcher hold a clerical job in the VA and you surely encourage millions to rise up against capitalism.) But the zealots were put on a leash by the real rulers of this country, who have acquired a lot of experience in determining what best serves the overall interests of capitalism, and when, and how.

Of course I was disappointed that the court had evaded the issues of principle in my case. I probably would have been less disappointed if I had realized at the time (as I did not) that the decision in my case, defective as it was in many ways, represented part of a political turn away from all-out repression. It almost goes without saying that I would have been even more disappointed if the court had actually taken up the principled issues and ruled against me on that basis.

What do you think was accomplished by all the efforts made in your behalf? Did they really make any difference in what the ruling class decided to do about McCarthyism, the subversive list etc.? Wouldn't the same general changes have taken place if you hadn't fought the case?

If I don't answer all these questions completely or with complete assurance, it is not because I question their relevance or validity, but because some simply are difficult to answer with certainty.

In an immediate sense I can point to the recovery of my job as an achievement of our work. It obviously never would have happened without our defense activities. It was not a big thing, it did not shake the world, but several victims of the witch-hunt have told me that my fight encouraged them to resist. That is a factor that can't be measured or weighed exactly, but anything that induced the victims to resist or keep on resisting, and thereby created the possibility of educating and mobilizing broader sentiment and action against the witch-hunt, was a decidedly positive factor.

Our victory, partial though it was, also heartened and gave ammunition to those who had not been directly victimized themselves but wanted to stop the repression. It tended to undermine the morale and self-confidence of at least some of the witch-hunters and their followers or dupes. And it had a healthy impact on the great mass of the people who stood in the middle and had not actively committed themselves to either side, whose support both sides were trying to win.

Another factor that must not be overlooked in drawing up any balance sheet relates to the overall aim of the witch-hunt, which was to root out or prevent the development of movements that might oppose Washington's plans to make the world safe for capitalist investments. A corollary was the complete annihilation, if possible, of parties or groups seeking to pose a socialist or communist alternative in the United States. This last objective came closer to being reached than many young people today realize. The Socialist Workers Party, the Communist Party and all other radical groups in this country were very badly damaged. Part of their members and supporters were intimidated, and dropped away. Another part became demoralized, and dropped away. Worst of all was the isolation that surrounded them. Inability to get a response to their work strengthened the internal dangers that can destroy any radical movement: opportunist adventures to break out of isolation and sectarian adaptation to isolation.

Although both its ranks and influence were seriously reduced by the witch-hunt, my party managed to survive, with its revolutionary perspectives and integrity intact, until the 1960s when the political climate improved and it began to grow again. To tell how this all happened would take another book. But the leaders of my party think that one of the elements enabling it to survive was the defense campaign waged around my case, which, although it was "only" a civil liberties case, could not be separated from the right of revolutionary socialists to exist and function legally. At the very least it enabled us to break through the shroud of silence and reach millions of people with arguments in favor of that right. If it did nothing else, even if it had not ended with my winning back my job, this alone would have justified our defense work. I know of additional results, because some people have told me that their first interest in socialism was aroused by curiosity about my case and the ideas for which I was being persecuted.

But the main thrust of your questions concerns something broader. Did civil liberties fights like mine compel the ruling class to moderate the witch-hunt? My answer is that our resistance to the witch-hunt undoubtedly had some effect on the calculations of the ruling class. Its incentive to even reconsider the question would have been much smaller if there had been no resistance; in that event, the ruling class proponents of all-out repression would have had the powerful argument that there was no need to modify the postwar policy because the whole population had accepted it. How much effect our resistance had I cannot say. I think it must have been significant, but I cannot prove it. In any case, I readily agree that it was not the sole cause of the change that was made in the mid-1950s and may not have been the main cause. The ruling class decided on that change, in my opinion, only after a careful consideration of all factors convinced it that a continuation of the witch-hunt along the lines initiated after the war was neither necessary nor in its own best interests.

If this is correct, or approximately correct, does it follow then that our resistance was wasted effort, or, by implication, that it would be wasted if we were faced with a repetition of the conditions we faced in the years after World War II? Absolutely not! In the first place, we did not have the advantage of hindsight. At the time the government was definitely moving in the direction of a police state. We did not know that the ruling class would have second thoughts about this perspective some day, and I am sure the ruling class itself did not know that. The retreat from the police state perspective was not inevitable; it could have been forestalled, for example, by the outbreak of a world war, which at that time all sides considered possible. Not to have resisted with every resource at our command would have meant relying in the last analysis on the good will or rationalism of the ruling class. That is not the kind of "realism" I ever could recommend to anyone, nor the kind that genuine radicals can accept after the experience of the United States government's role in Indochina.

I welcome these questions insofar as they are motivated by a desire to put my case into its proper (modest) framework. But I cannot go along with any suggestion that struggle was unnecessary at that time or, by implication, next time. What alternative will there be except struggle (more massive and more effective than that of the 1950s) when the ruling class again turns in the direction of a police state? Wouldn't it be stupid, suicidally stupid, to abstain from struggle on the ground that the ruling class did not go all the way last time? I insist that there is nothing at all in the history of that period to provide any basis for believing that they will not try to go much farther or even all the way next time.

You seemed to think we were on the verge of becoming a police state, but it didn't happen that way. What happened to change the whole atmosphere in this country from the one described in your book to the quite different one that prevailed in the 1960s?

The police state danger in the 1950s was real, present and ominous; it is poor logic to assume that it never existed merely because the process was interrupted and in part reversed.

I have already said that I think the ruling class decided in the mid-

1950s to suspend the process. Not because of any devotion to democratic principles, abstract or concrete; it wouldn't have taken them so many years if that had been their main concern. They did it out of carefully calculated self-interest. Weighing all the factors, international and national, they concluded that continuing the police state process at that time would do them more harm than good, would cost more than it was worth, would hamper the kind of capital-labor relations that are most profitable for the capitalists. Changes in the balance of power after the Soviet Union acquired atomic and hydrogen weapons, and the effects these had on the imminence of war; the lessons of Korea, where U.S. military might had to settle for a draw; the desire to be able to present a democratic "image" in propaganda directed to the insurgent colonial peoples; the disadvantages, overhead costs and unreliability of demagogues like Joe McCarthy; the belief that the tested weapons of propaganda and corruption were superior to naked police coercion for keeping the masses in line at home (except in special situations); perhaps the feeling that domestic threats to their power had been exaggerated—these and no doubt other considerations figured in their decision.

While one part of the answer to the above question can be explained by a decision of the ruling class, the other and bigger part relates to something that happened independently of the will of the ruling class—a radicalization of a large strata of the American people in the 1960s.

This radicalization did not assume the same forms that previous American radicalizations had taken—for example, the radicalization in the early 1900s that is associated with Eugene V. Debs, or the radicalization in the 1930s that is associated with the rise of the CIO. But like them, the radicalization of the 1960s was a result of masses of people trying to grapple with the particular contradictions of capitalism as they were expressed and felt in their own time. It began with the Black people fighting against oppression, first through peaceful civil rights demonstrations and then through explosive urban uprisings. It spread among the youth, first of all students, who began with sympathy for the Black struggle and quickly began to question the other evils of capitalism and imperialism, especially after the victory of the Cuban Revolution and the extension of U.S. intervention in Indochina.

(An important date in the reversal of the witch-hunt atmosphere was May 1960, when students staged a successful demonstration against the House Un-American Activities Committee hearings in San Francisco. From that point on the red-baiters were put on the defensive and the tremendous anti-Vietnam-war movement, which was to dominate the latter part of the decade, owed its success in no small measure to its firm rejection of all red-baiting attempts to divide it.)

After the youth came the women, also influenced initially by the Black struggle. They were followed by the Chicanos, Native Americans, Puerto Ricans, Asian Americans. Men and women in the armed forces. Homosexuals and lesbians. Prisoners, political and otherwise. Intellectuals and artists. Teachers, perhaps infected by their students. Religious dissidents. Even the legal profession. Name almost any group, and it was pretty sure to be influenced in some ways by the widespread moods of questioning or rejecting orthodox and traditional views or conclusions. Even young workers were touched by the radicalization, although the union bureaucracies are still holding the fort against change and the young workers have not yet been able to put their own stamp on the unions.

I don't mean that the United States is on the eve of revolution—only that there is a larger audience for revolutionary ideas now than at any other time in my political life. And therefore a bigger reservoir of opposition to any attempts the government will make to return to the conditions of the 1950s. The government senses this too. Its postwar witch-hunt succeeded in intimidating a whole generation, and many of its effects survived even after the witch-hunt was suspended. But the young people who were born during and after the war, and who are the chief bearers of the current radicalization, have not so far been seriously affected by red-baiting, which receded during the 1960s for the simple reason that it no longer had much impact. That is the main reason why the government so far has not launched an all-out campaign of repression.

I can see that it was necessary for you to go through the courts and various administrative channels, but what was the point of your numerous appeals to Truman and Eisenhower, your meeting with Clark, and so on? Since these were not legally necessary, didn't they have the effect of creating illusions about these scoundrels by seeming to imply that they were perhaps not responsible for the loyalty purge?

Wouldn't it have been better to have a small defense committee that agreed with your political views than the large committee you actually had, which on the whole disagreed with them? It wasn't the members of that committee that did the basic work on your case anyway. With a smaller committee, but one that agreed with you politically, your propaganda could have been more political, more socialist in content.

I have grouped these questions together because I think they show a common lack of understanding about tactical problems in defense cases. In a defense campaign the main objective is to win the case if possible—to free the defendant, expose the injustice, regain the job, etc. The way to do this is to reach the widest number of people and persuade them of both the justice of your cause and the connections it has with their own interests. That takes effective educational work (in the jargon of the radical movement, propaganda). There is more to it than stating the facts or denouncing the persecutors. You have to state the facts in such a way that they can break through the silence with which the government usually tries to surround your case. You have to seek ways of exposing the persecutors that will seem plausible to people who are not already on your side.

I never had any illusions about Truman and Eisenhower, but many of the people I was trying to win as supporters did. My appeals to Truman and Eisenhower were first of all a means of trying to keep the case alive in the daily press and the radio, and therefore in the consciousness of people who knew about it only through those media. Secondly, they were a way of exposing Truman and Eisenhower in the eyes of many well-intentioned people who would say,

"I'm sure your firing was a mistake committed by lower-echelon officials and that Truman (or Eisenhower) would stop it if he knew the facts." I was surprised by the number of people who held such naive views, including experienced trade unionists. It would have given me deep satisfaction to blast Truman and Eisenhower all over the map, but then my press releases would not have been printed, and the people I wanted to reach would not have had the educational benefit of seeing that Truman and Eisenhower did not respond to appeals, no matter how reasonable or objectively presented. It was far better for such people to go through that experience than it would have been for me to confine myself to merely telling them that Truman and Eisenhower would not respond favorably.

Nothing but trouble can result from failing to understand the distinction between a defense committee and a political party. I already had a political party behind me, the Socialist Workers Party, doing everything within its means to help me; unfortunately, its means were restricted. What I needed was a broad committee through which I could reach out to influence people who did not already support my rights. I didn't need a committee to make political pronouncements or to express agreement with my political ideas. That would only have duplicated what the Socialist Workers Party already was doing, and it would not have opened any new doors to me. Furthermore, it was not my main task to present and defend the ideas of the Socialist Workers Party. We had a division of labor: the Socialist Workers Party presented our joint ideas to the public; my task was to explain why I, and the Socialist Workers Party, had the right to hold our socialist ideas without being persecuted for them. If, in the process, I also explained some of these socialist ideas or aroused interest in them (and that happened as frequently as it happened naturally), that was all to the good; but that was not my main job in our division of labor. Incidentally, none of the defense committee members who differed with my political views ever complained about the way I answered questions relating to my views or charged that I was using the committee as a political football.

A few years ago a Californian friend told me that he had tried to become active in a defense committee supporting Black Panther victims of police repression. He found it difficult, however, because when he attended a meeting of the committee, he was told that he could join only if he was in agreement with the Black Panther Party's program and tactics; and he was given a copy of Mao Tse-tung's little red book and told to study it. But my friend had not made up his mind about the Black Panther program—all he was sure about was that they should not be persecuted or murdered, and he wanted to help them on that basis. When he said that he was critical of Maoism, he was told not to come back. I do not question anyone's right to form committees of this type; perhaps they served a function in bringing together sympathizers of the Black Panthers. But I do question the correctness of calling such formations "defense committees." And I would not like to be in the shoes of anyone whose life or liberty depended on the ability of such a "defense committee" to win mass support.

Do you see the way your case was handled as a model to be followed in the many cases of repression against the Black liberation, antiwar and other radical movements today?

No, I do not offer it as a model. The nature of a defense campaign is largely shaped by the circumstances of the time when it takes place, especially the political climate. What you try to accomplish must be related to what seems possible. Your tactics are obviously different in a period of severe reaction and a period when millions are acquiring radical ideas. What a difference between 1948 and 1973! What a difference in the American people's reactions to the Korean War and the Indochinese War, although the basic issues were similar. At the time of my case it was quite difficult to find any lawyers to represent me, even when I consented to their making periodic declarations that they did not agree with my political views; today there are plenty of good young lawyers willing and able to defend radicals and nonconformists. Thanks to them, to a greater unwillingness among jurors to be treated as stooges in trials involving radicals, and to changes in court rules about evidence, wiretapping, etc., radical defendants today are less certain to be convicted automatically than was the case in the 1950s. When my case began it was still possible to gain significant support from the organized labor movement; today, when the unions have become more bureaucratized and conservatized, it would be difficult to get equivalent support. On the other hand, many millions outside the labor movement have been radicalized, and offer areas of possible support that did not exist in 1948.

Having said that, I still must add that I think there are useful lessons to be learned from our defense campaign. Today's conditions are different, and therefore new tactics must be considered, but there is still a distinct difference between a defense committee and a political party, and the two should not be mixed up in theory or practice. If a defense committee is to be effective in reaching out and mobilizing mass support for the victims of repression, it still must be nonpartisan, it must avoid sectarianism, and the thing it must demand is not agreement with the ideas of the defendants but agreement with their right to hold and express them. A broad defense committee of this kind not only makes sense; it also represents the wisest kind of politics.

If I were called on to make an evaluation of some defense committees I have observed in recent years, my major criticism would be that they are too unimaginative and too conservative about tapping the great potential for support that exists all around them. Patient and persistent work probably could make headway in the unions even under their present leadership, and certainly could win support among the younger workers.

What, in your opinion, are the present prospects for the United States to become (a) a police state, (b) a place where the democratic rights of all will be fully recognized and enforced?

The radicalization of the 1960s moved the country farther away from a police state than the ruling class had planned in the 1950s. The Nixon administration has tried to reverse this process, with partial success, but only partial success so far. It would be a bad mistake to take this threat lightly because the witch-hunt after World

War II showed how much initiative can be taken and how much damage can be done in this area by a determined administration. All I am sure of is that the outcome will be decided by bitter struggle. I also think there will be much more resistance this time than there was in the 1950s.

So long as the capitalists can maintain their rule and their profits without resorting to a totalitarian dictatorship, they will do so, because it is easier and cheaper for them. As soon as their rule and their profits are seriously challenged, they will not hesitate, or at least not for long, to try to destroy whatever democratic rights they think get in their way. Those are the two poles between which the coming struggle will unfold. Even this does not tell the whole story, because prior to any decision they make about establishing a police state the capitalists are not going to go out of their way to preserve or extend democracy. Some people talk as if "repression" were a recently developed device of the ruling class, dating approximately since 1968. Actually it has always been present, used more or less in different periods, but always on hand and in reserve. We have never had complete or consistent enforcement of democratic rights in this country, and I believe we are never going to have it under capitalism. Capitalism learned to live with fragmentary, partial and often deceptive forms of democracy when it was useful or when there was no alternative, but its continued existence is incompatible with the establishment of genuine rule by the majority. Only a socialist revolution that will do away with economic exploitation, racism, sexism and cultural degradation can hope to bring to life the full blessings of democracy that capitalism talks about but has always denied the great majority.

"Eternal vigilance is the price of liberty." This slogan of the early capitalist class is still timely today. I am sure it will be timely until capitalism goes, and I suspect that it will still come in handy after capitalism goes, until the last vestiges of oppression are eradicated in a new society.

New York, 1973

APPENDIX A

They were afraid to print my book*

My book, *The Case of the Legless Veteran,* which will be published on October 1 [1953], is the report of one man's experiences in modern America. It is by an American, it deals with crucial problems of civil liberties which affect all Americans, whether or not they are aware of it—and yet I could not get it published in my own country. It was finally published in Britain, against which this country made a revolution in the name of life, liberty and the pursuit of happiness. Shades of 1776!

I think there is a certain significance in this because, like the book itself, the reception it got from American publishers throws added light on the state of civil liberties in our country today. That is why I would like to report it to readers of *The Militant,* many of whom have given me inspiring support in my fight to recover the government job from which I was purged in 1948, and whom I count on for added support in the distribution of the book.

I wrote the book in the spring and summer of 1952, bringing it up to date in the spring of this year, after it had been accepted for

* Reprinted from *The Militant,* September 21, 1953.

publication in Britain. I began to circulate it among publishers in New York City, six copies at a time, in August 1952. At the end of eight months, I had covered thirty-six publishing firms, all of the big ones and many of the smaller ones. Most of the replies were received after Eisenhower's election.

I sent along a letter, making three points:

(1) The great importance of the issues dealt with in the book.

(2) The fact that eight hundred national and local organizations had actively concerned themselves in my case, and that the initial market for the book might be drawn from among them by an enterprising publisher.

(3) My recognition that as a writer I am an amateur (I added I never expected to write another book) and that I would have no objection to the book being edited, provided none of the basic facts were omitted or distorted.

Some of the replies were cold mimeographed rejection slips, expressing no opinion one way or the other. But most of them tried to explain why. Following are some typical responses:

"You have done a good job but after very careful thought, we have decided that this is the sort of book that we do not do well with."

"Whereas we feel the case is important, we cannot feel that enough people would read a book on the subject."

"While we found it very interesting, our sales department has told us that there is very little market for a book of this type."

"You have told your story well . . . I am not at all sure however that the sizable market exists which you point to in your note to the publisher."

"We found much that was admirable and moving in your script, but we really felt that it would not be something that would fit in with any ease on our list."

"As you know, we have done other good books on this theme (which is becoming all too familiar) and I'm sorry to say that they have not been good publishing ventures. We really offered them as public services but as we do have to sell the books we print we cannot do too much of this . . . I most sincerely hope that you can interest someone else in it soon."

"We are sorry to say that it does not seem to be a possibility for our list . . . In addition to the timeliness of and general concern with your case, we were particularly interested in your literary style and therefore disappointed in your statement: 'I am not a writer, and will never even try to write another book.' If you ever decide to write again, we would appreciate seeing additional work. A copy of our catalog is being sent to you under separate cover, which will give you an idea of the type of books we publish."

"We are grateful to you for making available to us your stirring story. It is, it can safely be said, one of the test cases in the great and terrible story of the fight for civil liberties, which we are all of us now engaged in. There is no question in our minds but that you have been badly treated, and at the same time become a symbol for all of us, a symbol of courage and strength and perseverance and self-abnegation which is particularly meaningful now . . . The above is not merely to assuage what must be your disappointment that we cannot make you an offer for your work. But it is to express to you something of the regret which I personally feel that this important story does not lend itself, in the opinion of this company, to successful commercial handling. And we are, after all, a business firm which has to show a profit. Probably only a foundation or otherwise subsidized organization could publish this book, significant as the story is and as crucial as it is for our lives. This is a story everyone should be familiar with, but unfortunately few people would pay money to become familiar with it. This, at any rate, is our analysis of the market . . . You can be sure that the majority of those who think are hopeful that the final decision concerning your case will be a favorable one for you—and for this country."

"Certainly your situation is worthy of more public attention than it has been given; personally I would agree with you and those who have come to your defense that there is a great deal of injustice and hysteria involved not only in your specific case but in the fact that these sorts of things are happening today . . . All in all, it does not seem that any purpose would be served by publication of this manuscript in book form; after all, few people other than those who already know and sympathize would be sufficiently aware of or interested in the matter to pay their money for a full book on the subject. This is undoubtedly cruel but true."

"We have read your story and were rather impressed by it. Although your presentation is a bit rough in spots, it seems to us that you might have a publishable book here. However, it is not the sort of book with which (X) as publishers have had any marked degree of success, and we are taking the liberty of sending it over to our colleagues The (Y) Company, who are better equipped to promote to the best advantage a book of this sort. You will be hearing directly from Mr. (Z) of that organization."

And later Mr. (Z) wrote: "We have read it with great interest and sympathy. After giving the matter considerable thought, however, we have very reluctantly concluded that we cannot justify its publication on commercial grounds."

I couldn't help wondering why they had turned me down. I have no author's pride, and know that many literary faults can be found with my book. But as a reader of books I know that many are published which are not at all superior to mine in style or human interest—to say nothing of the importance of theme. I noticed that if I wanted to, I could easily cull several "blurbs" from the publishers' letters of the kind that are often printed on the back of books.

I also thought it odd that although most of the replies related to the need for a market, none of them displayed the slightest interest in questioning me further about the details of my statement that there already was a substantial market for the book among the many organizations that had supported my fight for reinstatement. So I decided to personally visit some of the publishers and editors who had written me to try to find out what they really thought. I saw five editors and publishing company officials altogether.

One told me: "I was quite interested when I saw the title—it looked like it might be a mystery with a new twist. It had me fooled for a few minutes." Our discussion made it clear that his only interest was profit-making—he did not even pretend to be interested in performing public services—and that he had a very low conception of the intelligence of the people who bought his books.

I told him maybe the people would buy less trashy books if the publishers would offer them with the same crusading zeal and advertising that they expend on their present wares. But he was not impressed.

Another man said: "I'll be frank with you. With some expert editing, such as we can provide, I think your book would be publishable, and two, three years ago we might have been willing to take a chance on it. Not expecting that it would make a lot of money, you understand, but to fill out our list and reach a certain portion of the public. But things have begun to change since the Korean War, and now with the election [of Eisenhower], they are altogether different. I tell you frankly I wouldn't take the chance even if your book was five times as good as it is and even if it meant a decent profit."

He was not reticent about the reason, although he said he would not admit it publicly, and would deny having said it:

"Sooner or later McCarthy or those other congressional committees are going to start in on the publishing business. Hollywood, Broadway, the schools, the unions—sooner or later they will go to work on us. And no publisher today wants to be put on the spot and smeared for publishing any book that can be labeled as radical. You can call it cowardly if you want to, but I call it caution and common sense. I don't want censorship any more than you do, and the cleaner our skirts are, the less chance there is that those committees will be able to do lasting damage to our business."

I thanked him for his honesty, and pointed out that self-censorship could be just as harmful and destructive in the long run as outside censorship. But he thought this view was impractical, idealist and unbusinesslike, and assured me that if I had as much to lose as he did I would feel the same way.

One of the other three men I spoke to admitted the same fear of McCarthyism when I pressed him on it.

Convinced that this fear must have been at least one of the elements in some of the rejections I had received, and knowing that there was nothing I could do to overcome such a fear, I gave up hope of getting the book accepted by any commercial firm in the land of the free and the home of the brave.

Only one company of the thirty-six I sent the manuscript to offered to print it—Pioneer Publishers, whose aim is to spread the truth, not to make money. But their shortage of funds meant a long delay in publication. So I sent the thing off to a new company in Britain, New Park Publications Ltd., which accepted it at once. An arrangement was made for Pioneer to handle the American distribution.

Thus the efforts to get the book published—and read—fall into the framework of the same civil liberties fight as my effort to reverse the "loyalty" purge and recover the job that was taken away from me because of my political opinions and associations.

That is why I hope that the readers of The Militant will join me in a campaign to break through the mounting tide of reaction and censorship and enable this book to get the audience that its subject merits.

Thanks to the economies effected by the publisher, The Case of the Legless Veteran, which is of normal book length (about ninety thousand words), will be sold here for only $1. This extremely low price, plus its attractive format, will make mass sales of the book possible if enough people take a real interest in it and push it.

Those publishers claimed that their chief concern was the lack of a market for this book. I'm still betting that they don't know any more about this question than they do about a lot of others.

APPENDIX B

Correspondence with the CIO

Newark, New Jersey[*]

John V. Riffe
Executive Vice President, CIO
718 Jackson Pl., N.W.
Washington, D.C.

Dear Mr. Riffe,

It has been brought to my attention that Mr. Barney Hopkins, Secretary of the Michigan State CIO, reported to the Michigan State CIO Executive Board the contents of a telephone conversation he had with Mr. Kessler re the Kutcher case, in which he informed Mr. Hopkins of the following:

1. Kutcher had misrepresented the position of the CIO at some CIO gathering by stating that the CIO endorsed the politics and philosophy of Kutcher and his party, the Socialist Workers Party.

2. That proceeds from my book, *The Case of The Legless Veteran,* were going to the Socialist Workers Party and not to the Kutcher Civil Rights Committee.

---

[*] This letter, actually sent from Detroit, was mailed June 17, 1954.

I have never at any time represented the CIO as giving support to me in any manner other than what is published in my book; namely, the statement by the National CIO Committee to Abolish Discrimination, what the late Philip Murray wrote, and what the various International, State Council and local CIO bodies have done to help publicize and win my case.

Not one single cent from the proceeds of my book is going to the Socialist Workers Party.

As a means of raising the much needed funds to continue fighting my case, I have donated all royalties from my book to the Kutcher Civil Rights Committee. Unfortunately this is not very much, for the book consists of over ninety thousand words and sells for just $1.00. The fact that I had to have the book printed in England has added an additional expense to its publication. I am sure you will be able to clear up this misunderstanding. As you probably know, I am once again on national tour. It is especially important now to get all possible support behind my case because we are back in federal court and this time we will carry the fight straight to the Supreme Court.

I am looking forward to hearing from you soon.

Fraternally,
James Kutcher

P.S. Any communication addressed to my home address in New Jersey will be forwarded to me.

copies, per request:
Gus Scholle
Al Barbour

CONGRESS OF INDUSTRIAL ORGANIZATIONS
CIO
718 Jackson Place, N.W., Washington, D.C.
September 10, 1954

Mr. James Kutcher
Detroit, Michigan

Dear Mr. Kutcher:

I wish to acknowledge receipt of your undated letter to me concerning your efforts to attain reinstatement in your former government position, and actions that individual or organization members of CIO have taken relative to the same.

That there was delay in replying to your letter, I regret. It was caused by my extended absence from Washington, and the belief on the part of my office staff that your letter was of such a nature as to warrant my personal attention.

Attached you will find a copy of a letter sent from this office on August 5, 1954, to all CIO Regional Directors, over the signature of Carl A. McPeak, Assistant Director of Councils, which deals with the matter at hand.

This letter represents accurate presentation of our position.

I trust it will answer the questions your letter broached.

Sincerely yours,
John V. Riffe
Executive Vice President

P.S. I note that your letterhead carried among its list of endorsers the "National CIO Committee to Abolish Discrimination." For your information, there is now no committee so named.

John V. Riffe

CONGRESS OF INDUSTRIAL ORGANIZATIONS
CIO
718 Jackson Place, N.W., Washington, D.C.
August 5, 1954

To All Regional Directors:

We are receiving numbers of inquiries from councils about the country regarding CIO endorsement of James Kutcher, a veteran now touring the United States in an effort to finance his fight for reinstatement with the Veterans Administration in New Jersey.

Several years ago, when this man's discharge occurred, some CIO organizations, including councils, came to his defense in protesting against the method of, and the reasons given for, his discharge.

The groups and persons promoting the current campaign are using literature which implies that CIO is a present sponsor. On the basis of this implication some CIO councils may be persuaded to lend their names and facilities to the promotion.

Will you please inform the councils in your region that any attempt to indicate that the present financing efforts has the endorsement, sponsorship, or approval of the National CIO, or any of its committees or departments, would be misrepresentation. No such endorsement, approval, or sponsorship has been given, promised or authorized.

For your convenience, we are enclosing several copies of this letter in case you desire to forward them to your staff and to the councils by whatever means you consider appropriate.

Fraternally yours,
Carl A. McPeak
Assistant Director of Councils

Minneapolis, Minn.
Sept. 27, 1954

Mr. John V. Riffe
Executive Vice President, CIO
718 Jackson Pl., N.W.
Washington, D.C.

Dear Mr. Riffe:

Your letter of September 10, 1954, sent to Detroit, finally caught up with me here in Minneapolis, the latest stop in the national tour I am making to publicize my six-year legal fight for reinstatement with the Veterans Administration, to help finance that fight in the courts, and to promote the sale of my book, *The Case of the Legless Veteran,* all the royalties of which are being donated to the nonpartisan Kutcher Civil Rights Committee which is handling my legal fight.

I thank you for your courtesy in personally answering the letter I sent you in June, expressing my alarm over rumors I had heard that I was guilty of misrepresenting the relations of the CIO with my case. I was eager to clear up any misunderstandings, and that is why I have studied with care the copy you sent me of Mr. McPeak's letter to all CIO regional directors on August 5, 1954.

As Mr. McPeak said, "some CIO organizations, including councils, came to his [Kutcher's] defense in protesting against the method of, and the reasons given for, his discharge."

This is true. The support of CIO unions, leaders and members has been generous and vital to me; without it, I doubt that I ever would have been able to get my case into the courts, where it is still being litigated. To indicate that this feeling of mine is no exaggeration, I list the following CIO bodies that were so concerned about the civil liberties issues raised in my case that they took time from their regular business to extend moral and/or financial help to me in one form or another:

International CIO unions: Amalgamated Clothing Workers, Amalgamated Lithographers, Marine and Shipbuilding Workers, National Maritime Union, Transport Workers, United Automobile Workers, United Packinghouse Workers and United Retail, Wholesale and Department Store Employees.

State CIO Councils: California, Connecticut, Illinois, Ohio, Michigan, Minnesota, New Jersey, Pennsylvania, Rhode Island (and the Washington State CIO Political Action Committee).

Industrial Union Councils: a total of twenty-three, including those in New York City, Chicago, Los Angeles, Detroit, Philadelphia, Cleveland, the Twin Cities, Akron, Toledo and Newark.

In addition I received support from hundreds of CIO local unions, the exact number of which I can report when I am home again.

This list only partially reflects the warm sympathy and encouragement I have received from CIO unions, leaders and members all over the country. I have had the privilege of appearing at several state CIO conventions as an officially invited speaker. In addition, when I was on my first speaking tour in 1949 and my visit to Cleveland coincided with the holding of the CIO's Eleventh Constitutional Convention, I was invited by the convention arrangements committee, and I gladly accepted the invitation, to sit at a convention booth featuring the literature on my case and discuss it with all interested delegates.

Mr. McPeak also said, "The groups and persons promoting the current campaign are using literature which implies that CIO is a present sponsor. On the basis of this implication, some CIO councils may be persuaded to lend their names and facilities to the promotion.

"Will you please inform the councils in your region that any attempt to indicate that the present financing effort has the endorsement, sponsorship, or approval of the National CIO, or of any of its committees or departments, would be misrepresentation. No such endorsement, approval, or sponsorship has been given, promised or authorized."

It is unfortunate that Mr. McPeak did not consult me or the Kutcher Civil Rights Committee on this matter because it is plain that his warning is based entirely on the fact, to which your postscript refers, that the letterhead of the Kutcher Civil Rights Committee includes among its sponsors the name of the "National CIO Committee to Abolish Discrimination."

I was unaware until after I started on my current tour last May that this committee no longer exists. If we had known about this, we would automatically not have included the name of this committee on our list of supporters. As soon as I received your letter, I conveyed this information to the Kutcher Civil Rights Committee and urged that it delete the name of the no longer existent committee from the letterhead, and notify all its branches to follow suit. I am sure that this will be done without delay.

But I assure you that there was no element of misrepresentation in the listing of this committee on our letterhead, where it has been for almost six years, or any motive of deception involved. The relations between my case and the National CIO Committee to Abolish Discrimination are a matter of record. Both Mr. James B. Carey, chairman of the committee, and Mr. George L-P Weaver, director, personally assured me of the committee's support, as their files should confirm. In fact, the first presentation of the facts in my case outside of my home town was personally made by Mr. Carey himself when he introduced me at a *Herald Tribune* forum in New York City in 1948.

In addition, Mr. Philip Murray, in a letter to the Kutcher Civil Rights Committee dated May 22, 1950, and quoted in full in my book,[*] specifically referred to the National CIO Committee to Abol-

---

[*] The Murray letter, written on a CIO letterhead, was a devastating refutation of the Riffe-McPeak version of the CIO's past relations with my case. Since it was included in an appendix to the first edition of this book that is omitted in this edition, it is reprinted here:

Dear Mr. Novack:

I regret very much that your letter of May 2nd did not come to my attention until after the Steelworkers Convention had adjourned.

Since it is now too late for the Steelworkers Convention to take action with respect to it, I have referred your communication to our National CIO Comish Discrimination as the body which has "manifested the interest of the CIO in Mr. Kutcher's case." He also said, "I am sure that Mr. Weaver, the Director of this Committee, will continue to lend the support of our organization in view of the important civil liberties issues involved."

I hope that these facts will suffice to demonstrate that we have been scrupulously careful to make no claims with relation to the CIO that were not completely justified, and that the continued inclusion of the name of the National CIO Committee to Abolish Discrimination was due only to the fact that we were unaware it had gone out of existence.

My present tour is sponsored nationally by the publishers of my book and cosponsored by local branches of the Kutcher Civil Rights Committee, and I have never claimed anything else in the speeches I have made to local CIO bodies and other groups I have spoken to during this tour. No effort was ever made anywhere, any time, by anyone, to imply that this tour is endorsed, approved or sponsored by the national CIO. I never asked for such endorsement, approval or sponsorship from the national CIO, and it would be a violation of all the standards I have followed consistently for me to imply that I had them, or to permit any associate to make such an implication. I am proud of the support I have received from CIO unions, leaders and members, and I never fail to publicly express my gratitude for this. But I would be a fool, and I would sully myself in the bargain, to claim what I never asked for nor received.

I do not believe that it was the intention of Mr. McPeak's letter to cast any cloud of suspicion or doubt over my case, and I hope that it will not have this effect. I hope that the successor of the National

---

mittee to Abolish Discrimination which has heretofore manifested the interest of the CIO in Mr. Kutcher's case.

I am sure that Mr. Weaver, the Director of this Committee, will continue to lend the support of our organization in view of the important civil liberties issues involved.

Very truly yours,
Philip Murray

CIO Committee to Abolish Discrimination, which I believe is named the CIO Civil Rights Committee, will see fit to extend me support of the type mentioned in Mr. Murray's letter. And I hope that my relations with the CIO as a whole will be as friendly, as principled and as honorable in the future as they have been in the past, since 1948.

It is in this spirit that I continue my appeals to labor and liberal groups of all varieties to help me regain the job from which I was discharged solely because of my political views and associations. No matter how difficult it may be, I intend to keep fighting to win my case (now in the federal courts—for the third time) so long as there is any possibility that resistance against the attack on my democratic rights will help to promote and preserve democratic rights generally. I believe that a victory in my case would benefit not only me but the American people as a whole, and especially the labor movement whose future depends so greatly on the preservation of civil liberties for all. I am certain that this belief will continue to be shared by every person and every organization devoted to the Bill of Rights.

Trusting that I have cleared up any misapprehensions that may have arisen about my case, I am,

Fraternally yours,
James Kutcher

CONGRESS OF INDUSTRIAL ORGANIZATIONS
CIO
718 Jackson Place, N.W., Washington, D.C.
October 28, 1954

Mr. James Kutcher
Newark, New Jersey

Dear Mr. Kutcher:

I am writing in reply to your letter of September 27, 1954, addressed to Executive Vice President John V. Riffe, relative to the general situation surrounding your dismissal from the Veterans Administration, and your efforts to obtain reinstatement. Brother Riffe's schedule has been, and is, such that to await his ability to reply to your letter personally would result in additional and unnecessary delay in acknowledging receipt of your letter.

In addition, since my name and my actions have been featured prominently in the correspondence that has been exchanged between yourself and Executive Vice President Riffe, I welcome the opportunity that this referral of your letter affords me in the way of clarification of my position.

I want you to understand that whatever action I, or any representative of the councils department, have taken in this matter is in no way intended to pass judgment upon the merit of your case. My letter to the CIO Regional Directors of August 5, 1954, had as its intent bringing to their attention, and to that of the councils in their region, the fact that the current fund raising campaign of the Kutcher Civil Rights Committee had not been specifically endorsed by any agency of the National CIO.

The information that letter contained was factual at the time it was written. These facts remain unchanged.

For Executive Vice President Riffe and myself, I welcome your personal assurance that "no effort was ever made anywhere, any time, by anyone, to imply that this tour is endorsed, approved, or sponsored by the National CIO."

In closing, let me assure you again, that my letter to the Regional Directors was not designed to evaluate the validity of your position.

Sincerely yours,
C.A. McPeak
Assistant Director of Councils

APPENDIX C

The court's decision

UNITED STATES COURT OF APPEALS
FOR THE DISTRICT OF COLOMBIA CIRCUIT

No. 12831
JAMES KUTCHER, APPELLANT

v.

HARVEY V. HIGLEY, Administrator of Veterans Affairs;
PHILIP YOUNG, GEORGE M. MOORE, and
FREDERICK J. LAWTON, Members of the United States
Civil Service Commission, APPELLEES

Appeal from the United States District Court
for the District of Columbia

Decided April 20, 1956

Mr. *Joseph L. Rauh, Jr.,* with whom *Messrs. John Silard* and *Daniel H. Pollitt* were on the brief, for appellant.

Mr. *Benjamin Forman,* Attorney, Department of Justice, with whom *Mr. Leo A. Rover,* United States Attorney, and *Messrs. Paul A.*

Sweeny and *William W. Ross,* Attorneys, Department of Justice, were on the brief, for appellees. *Mr. Lewis Carroll,* Assistant United States Attorney, also entered an appearance for appellees.

Before PRETTYMAN, WILBUR K. MILLER, and DANAHER, Circuit Judges.

PRETTYMAN, *Circuit Judge:* Our appellant is a disabled veteran who was employed in clerical capacity in the Veterans Administration. He was discharged from that employment because the Administrator of Veterans Affairs concluded there are reasonable grounds to believe he is disloyal to the United States[1] and there is reasonable doubt of his loyalty to the Government.[2]

The controversy was here once before.[3] The judgment of the District Court sustaining Kutcher's discharge was then reversed. After the remand further proceedings were had before the administrative agencies, including full hearing before the Boards having jurisdiction in the matter. As a result Kutcher was again discharged.

The second discharge was premised upon findings and an opinion of the Veterans' Administration Loyalty Board of Appeals submitted to the Administrator on April 20, 1953. The Board's conclusions were embodied in two documents. One was a brief (one printed page) report, which simply identified the case and said that "Following careful review of the entire evidence of record," the Board had concluded that reasonable grounds existed for the belief that Kutcher was disloyal and further that reasonable doubt existed respecting his loyalty. The other document was a long report (sixteen printed pages), in which the Board described the proceedings in detail and made extensive findings and conclusions in support of its final recommendation. Kutcher was not given a copy

---

1. Exec. Order No. 9835, 12 FED. REG. 1935 (1947), 3 C.F.R. 129 (Supp. 1947).

2. Exec. Order No. 10241, 16 FED. REG. 3690 (1951), 3 C.F.R. 431 (Supp. 1951). And see Jason v. Summerfield, 94 U.S. App. D.C. 197, 214 F.2d 273 (D.C. Cir. 1954), *cert. denied,* 348 U.S. 840, 99 L.Ed. 662, 75 S.Ct. 48 (1954).

3. Kutcher v. Gray, 91 U.S. App. D.C. 266, 199 F.2d 783 (1952).

of this document until it was introduced as a defense exhibit[4] in the present proceeding in the District Court. However, in the record before that court, which is the record before us on this appeal, the long report stands as the statement of the reasons for Kutcher's discharge. The trial court granted a Government motion for summary judgment.

After the remand by this court upon Kutcher's first appeal, no change was made in the charges preferred against him. The charges were:

> "a. Evidence of record of membership in the Newark Branch, Socialist Workers Party. The Socialist Workers Party is contained in the list of organizations named by the Attorney General on November 24, 1947, as within the purview of Executive Order No. 9835.
>
> "b. Evidence of record of your employment in the Newark Branch Headquarters, Socialist Workers Party. The Socialist Workers Party is contained in the list of organizations named by the Attorney General on November 24, 1947 as within the purview of Executive Order No. 9835.
>
> "c. Evidence of record of your financial pledge to 'The Militant' Fund Drive. 'The Militant' is the official newspaper of the Socialist Workers Party.
>
> "d. Evidence of record of your association and activity with persons, associations, movements, and groups designated by the Attorney General as subversive in nature."

Section 14 of the Veterans' Preference Act of 1944, as amended,[5] requires that a preference eligible "shall have at least thirty days' advance written notice . . . stating any and all reasons, specifically and in detail, for any such proposed [removal] action." In *Deak* v.

---

4. By reference attached to the Government's motion for summary judgment.

5. 58 STAT. 390 (1944), STAT. 723 (1947), 5 U.S.C.A. § 863.

Pace[6] and in *Money* v. *Anderson*[7] we held that a person in the classified civil service is entitled to such notice of the asserted reasons for his proposed discharge as will enable him to prepare and present his defense to the charges.[8] The statute here involved contains as stringent requirements of specificity as does the statute which was involved in those cases.[9]

In *Mulligan* v. *Andrews*[10] we held, referring not only to the provisions of the statute relative to removal of employees from the classified civil service but also to the Civil Service Commission's regulations issued under that act, that only findings upon the charges, specifically identified, can constitute the "reasons" required to be stated in the ultimate adverse ruling. In substance this was a holding that the discharge of a classified employee must be based upon a charge preferred in advance. The employee must have a fair chance to defend himself upon the very grounds on which he may be discharged.

We come, then, to consider the long report of the Veterans' Administration Loyalty Board of Appeals. Our problem is whether the reasons for Kutcher's discharge therein stated could fairly have been anticipated from the charges preferred against him. The report showed that the charges were the result of F.B.I. reports and dealt very largely with Kutcher's membership and activity in the Socialist Workers Party. He admitted membership in the Party, indeed openly affirmed it. The report said that in view of the decision of this court upon the prior appeal the Board believed it advisable, if not requisite, that it be informed of the grounds upon which the Attorney General had listed the Socialist Workers Party, and that the Deputy Attorney General had transmitted a summary of the information

---

6. 88 U.S. App. D.C. 50, 185 F.2d 997 (1950).

7. 93 U.S. App. D.C. 130, 208 F.2d 34 (1953).

8. The same rule is implicit in Borak v. Biddle, 78 U.S. App. D.C. 374, 141 F.2d 278 (D.C.Cir. 1944), *cert. denied*, 323 U.S. 738, 89 L.Ed. 591, 65 S.Ct. 42 (1944).

9. Manning v. Stevens, 93 U.S. App. D.C. 225, 208 F.2d 827 (D.C. Cif.1953).

10. 93 U.S. App. D.C. 375, 211 F.2d 28 (1954).

in the hands of the Department of Justice which constituted the basis of the Attorney General's action. The information thus transmitted was set forth in the Board's report.

The Board examined the opinion of the Court of Appeals for the Eighth Circuit in *Dunne* v. *United States*,[11] in which case the court affirmed the conviction of eighteen members of the Socialist Workers Party for conspiracy to advocate the overthrow of the Government by force and to advocate insubordination in the armed forces. "This case," said the Board, "throws searching light on the character, nature, aims and purposes of the Socialist Workers Party." The Board said it did not draw an analogy between Kutcher and the defendants in the *Dunne* case or conclude it followed from his membership in the Party that there is reasonable ground for the belief he is disloyal. The Board was concerned with the *Dunne* case as throwing light upon the nature of the Party of which Kutcher was and is a member.

The Board was of opinion that Party membership alone would not warrant a finding adverse to Kutcher, if a showing were made that he was innocent of the subversive purposes and aims of the Party. It therefore addressed itself to the proposition: "Is this appellant, James Kutcher, aware of the purposes and methods advocated for the attainment of those purposes of the Socialist Workers Party in which be continues his membership and activity?" Finding a contradiction in Kutcher's statements as to the aims of the Party the Board concluded his original answers more nearly reflected his true intent and understanding. It considered Kutcher's statement that the Communist Manifesto, as expressive of the views of Karl Marx, did not contemplate revolution or destruction by force and violence of our present constitutional government.

The Board found that Kutcher has been and is an active worker in the Party. The Board said:

> "On the record before us, including the Attorney General's listing and viewed in the light of the decision of the U.S. Circuit

---

11. 138 F.2d 137 (1943), *cert. denied,* 320 U.S. 790, 88 L.Ed. 476, 64 S.Ct. 205 (1943).

Court of Appeals in the Dunne case, this Board is satisfied that the Socialist Workers Party advocates destruction of our present system of constitutional Government by force, if necessary, in the attainment of its Communist aims and purposes. Can one, who knowingly participates actively in the furtherance of such an organization over a period of years, stand without reasonable doubt as to his loyalty to our existing form of Government?"[12]

The Board said the view that Kutcher knowingly participated in activities which would destroy, if necessary, by unconstitutional means our system of government, did not rest alone upon the fact of his membership in the Party. It discussed a speech made by Kutcher, reported *verbatim* in the official organ of the Party, and his admission that the newspaper report was correct; in the speech Kutcher made statements as to Lenin and the program of the Party. The Board recited that Kutcher said, under oath, he would not report to the F.B.I. a member of the Communist Party known by him to be such. The Board also pointed out that Kutcher's position in the Socialist Workers Party was as great as those of at least two of the defendants in the *Dunne* case.

The Board said it gave full consideration to Kutcher's service in and honorable discharge from the Army; he lost both of his legs in World War II as a combat infantryman. The Board also said no acts

---

12. This key finding as to the purpose and program of the Party was made despite the ruling of the Chairman of the Board at the hearing that the Board would not in any sense undertake to try out the case of the character and nature of the Socialist Workers Party as such. He stated the proposition a number of times, once saying: "Well, I want to make it clear right here that the Socialist Workers Party is not before us." He later made an ambiguous reservation on the point, saying the Board might consider evidence as to the nature of the Party for the purposes of this case. He ruled that counsel for Kutcher would be given an opportunity to address himself to the nature of the Party if he desired to do so. Counsel put to Kutcher some questions as to his belief concerning the aims of the Party, and he was cross-examined on that subject.

13. We refer here to the first three charges; we discuss the fourth later.

of disloyalty on Kutcher's part had been shown and his efficiency on the job had not been questioned.

To summarize briefly, the charges against Kutcher[13] were simply: he was a member of, employed by, and made a contribution to an organization listed by the Attorney General. The reasons he was discharged were: the Party was found to advocate the overthrow of the Government by unconstitutional means, and Kutcher was found to be aware of that aim and to support it consciously and actively.

No elaboration of the foregoing is necessary to demonstrate that the reasons stated in the report differ substantially from the charges made. Since only findings on the charges, specifically identified, can constitute reasons for removal, a reading of the charges must demonstrate the reasons for dismissal, assuming all the charges are sustained. This is not so here. The first charge was that Kutcher was a member in the Socialist Workers Party, which had been designated by the Attorney General as subversive. This court held in the prior appeal that this charge could not constitute a valid reason for dismissal. Thus findings thereon, even if made, would not have been sufficient. The second charge was that Kutcher had been employed at the Newark Branch of the Headquarters of the Socialist Workers Party. In its report the Board made a reference to such employment but merely related it as an item leading to the more important finding that Kutcher was in close association with the Newark Branch of the Party, knew practically all of the members of that Branch, and so could hardly help knowing the aims and purposes of the Party. Employment, then, was not a reason nor, standing alone, even an important detail of the reasons for dismissal. The third charge was that Kutcher had made a financial pledge to the fund drive of *The Militant,* an official newspaper of the Socialist Workers Party. No findings whatever were made specifically relating to this charge.

The fourth charge was that Kutcher associated and was active with persons, associations, movements and groups designated by the Attorney General as subversive. This charge was wholly vague. It might be taken merely as a summary of the three preceding charges. If so it adds nothing to the case against Kutcher. It might also be taken as a broad and sweeping charge embracing numerous unspecified activities and associations. If so it was too vague and lacks even the specificity this court held necessary in *Deak* v. *Pace, supra.* If findings were made relating to this charge they could not be sustained.

Under the rule in the *Mulligan* case, *supra,* the judgment of the District Court must be reversed.

We note again that the statement of the reasons for dismissal, as embodied in the report of the Board, was not furnished Kutcher in the ordinary course but came to him when it was filed by the Government as an exhibit in the civil action which Kutcher brought in the District Court. However in our view of the case it is unnecessary to discuss that point.

Reversed.

WILBUR K. MILLER, *Circuit Judge,* dissents.

Finances

Some people have expressed curiosity about how a case like mine was financed and what the money collected was spent on. Below is a consolidation of three auditing statements of the Kutcher Civil Rights Committee books, from the day it began to function until almost ten years later when, its mission accomplished, it disbanded.

As the statement of receipts shows, more than two-thirds of the approximately $17,000 collected came from local branches of the committee and from unaffiliated organizations. Most of the latter were unions, and probably most of the money collected by the branches and sent to our national office in New York also came from local unions.

Of our disbursements, a little over one-third was for legal expenses, and another one-third went for transportation and tour costs, printing and postage. Our legal expenses were astonishingly low for what was done in the courts and administrative hearings; that was because the lawyers who helped me really believed in the cause of civil liberties enough to serve it without financial remuneration. Our legal expenses therefore were almost exclusively for what was needed to process this long case to the point where I regained my job. I feel sorry for any working class civil liberties defendant who has to pay lawyers' fees too. Travel and literature costs of course were justified by the fact that without them we would not have had any income at all. Another reason why we were able to get so much done with relatively little money was that all labor in the case was volunteered and therefore we did not make any expenditures whatever on wages or salaries.

I do not know, even approximately, how much money the government spent on its side to fight this case, and I have never found anyone who would even make an educated guess. But everyone with whom I have discussed the matter is sure that the government spent far more to fire and keep me fired than we did to regain my job. Maybe some day the government will release a figure; that will be the well-known day. And no one needs to ask where it got the funds.

Finally it should not be forgotten that $17,000 went a lot further in the 1950s than it does in the early 1970s. To accomplish today what our committee did then would take at least twice and perhaps three times $17,000, and then only if lawyers' fees were not paid. In criminal cases, requiring investigative work, etc., the legal expenses would be higher.

[Financial statement on following page.]

KUTCHER CIVIL RIGHTS COMMITTEE
Statement of Cash Receipts and Disbursements
October 20, 1948, to October 24, 1958

RECEIPTS

Local Committees	$6,881.27	
Organizations	6,492.29	
Individuals	2,960.58	
Loans Received	417.42	
Sale of Books	173.00	
Royalties on Books	137.90	
Refund of Typewriter	101.49	
Publication Fee	25.00	
Total Receipts		$17,188.95

DISBURSEMENTS

Legal Expenses	$6,035.31	
Transportation and Tour Expenses	3,392.26	
Printing	2,008.09	
Postage	1,099.84	
Office Expenses	961.80	
Publicity	937.73	
Telephone and Telegraph	916.81	
Furniture and Fixtures	458.41	
Loans Returned	417.42	
Books	212.60	
Auditing	150.00	
Bank Charges	97.14	
Miscellaneous Expenses	19.00	
Total Disbursements		$16,706.41
Balance as of October 24, 1958		$482.54 [*]

---

[*] This sum was turned over to me as a gift when the committee disbanded. In turn, I divided it up and contributed it to several defense committees.

INDEX

THE TEAMSTER SERIES

FARRELL DOBBS

Four books on the 1930s strikes and organizing drive that transformed the Teamsters union in Minnesota and much of the Midwest into a fighting industrial union movement. Written by a leader of the communist movement in the U.S. and organizer of the Teamsters union during the rise of the CIO.

Teamster Rebellion

Tells the story of the 1934 strikes that built a fighting union movement in Minneapolis. $16.95

Teamster Power

The 11-state Midwest over-the-road organizing drive. $18.95

Teamster Politics

Rank-and-file Teamsters lead the fight against antiunion frame-ups and assaults by fascist goons; the battle for jobs for all; and efforts to advance independent labor political action. $18.95

Teamster Bureaucracy

How the rank-and-file Teamsters leadership organized to oppose World War II, racism, and government efforts—backed by the international officialdom of the Teamsters, the AFL, and the CIO—to gag class-struggle-minded workers. $18.95

AVAILABLE FROM PATHFINDER. SEE FRONT OF BOOK FOR ADDRESSES.

Also from Pathfinder

Capitalism's World Disorder

Working-Class Politics at the Millennium

JACK BARNES

The social devastation and financial panic, the coarsening of politics and politics of resentment, the cop brutality and acts of imperialist aggression accelerating around us—all are the product not of something gone wrong but of the lawful workings of capitalism. Yet the future can be changed by the united struggle and selfless action of workers and farmers conscious of their power to transform the world. $23.95

The Communist Manifesto

KARL MARX AND FREDERICK ENGELS

Founding document of the modern working-class movement, published in 1848. Explains why communism is derived not from preconceived principles but from facts and from proletarian movements springing from the actual class struggle. $3.95

To Speak the Truth

Why Washington's 'Cold War' against Cuba Doesn't End

FIDEL CASTRO AND CHE GUEVARA

In historic speeches before the United Nations and UN bodies, Guevara and Castro address the workers of the world, explaining why the U.S. government so hates the example set by the socialist revolution in Cuba and why Washington's effort to destroy it will fail. $16.95

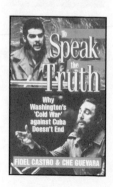

From the Escambray to the Congo

In the Whirlwind of the Cuban Revolution

INTERVIEW WITH VÍCTOR DREKE

In this participant's account, Víctor Dreke describes how easy it became after the Cuban Revolution to "take down the rope" segregating blacks from whites at town dances, yet how enormous was the battle to transform social relations underlying all the "ropes" inherited from capitalism and Yankee domination. He recounts the determination, internationalism, and creative joy with which working people have defended their revolutionary course against U.S. imperialism—from Cuba's own Escambray mountains, to the Americas, Africa, and beyond. $17.00

Thomas Sankara Speaks

The Burkina Faso Revolution, 1983–87

Peasants and workers in the West African country of Burkina Faso established a popular revolutionary government and began to combat the hunger, illiteracy, and economic backwardness imposed by imperialist domination. Thomas Sankara, who led that struggle, explains the example set for all of Africa. $19.95

Genocide against the Indians

GEORGE NOVACK

Why did the leaders of the Europeans who settled in North America try to exterminate the peoples already living there? How was the campaign of genocide against the Indians linked to the expansion of capitalism in the United States? Noted Marxist George Novack answers these questions. $4.00

The Changing Face of U.S. Politics

Working-Class Politics and the Trade Unions

JACK BARNES

Building the kind of party the working class needs to prepare for coming class battles—battles through which they will revolutionize themselves, their unions, and all of society. It is a handbook for workers, farmers, and youth repelled by the social inequalities, economic instability, racism, women's oppression, cop violence, and wars endemic to capitalism...and who are determined to overturn that exploitative system and join in reconstructing the world on new, socialist foundations. $19.95

FBI on Trial

The Victory in the Socialist Workers Party Suit against Government Spying

MARGARET JAYKO

The victory in the case fought from 1973 to 1987 "increases the space for politics, expands the de facto use of the Bill of Rights, increases the confidence of working people that you can be political and hold the deepest convictions against the government and it's your right to do so and act upon them" — from the introduction. $18.95

By Any Means Necessary

MALCOLM X

Speeches tracing the evolution of Malcolm X's views on political alliances, women's rights, intermarriage, capitalism and socialism, and more. $15.95

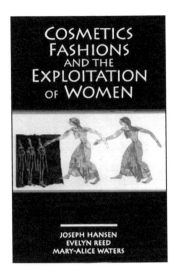

Cosmetics, Fashions, and the Exploitation of Women

JOSEPH HANSEN, EVELYN REED, AND MARY-ALICE WATERS

How big business plays on women's second-class status and social insecurities to market cosmetics and rake in profits. The introduction by Waters explains how the entry of millions of women into the workforce during and after World War II irreversibly changed U.S. society and laid the basis for a renewed rise of struggles for women's emancipation. $14.95

Making History

Interviews with Four Generals of Cuba's Revolutionary Armed Forces

Through the stories of four outstanding Cuban generals, each with close to half a century of revolutionary activity, we can see the class dynamics that have shaped our entire epoch. We can understand how the people of Cuba, as they struggle to build a new society, have for more than forty years held Washington at bay. Preface by Juan Almeida; introduction by Mary-Alice Waters. Also in Spanish. $15.95

The History of the Russian Revolution

LEON TROTSKY

The social, economic, and political dynamics of the first socialist revolution as told by one of its central leaders. "The history of a revolution is for us first of all a history of the forcible entrance of the masses into the realm of rulership over their own destiny," Trotsky writes. Unabridged edition, 3 vols. in one. $35.95

The History of American Trotskyism

Report of a Participant, 1928-38

JAMES P. CANNON

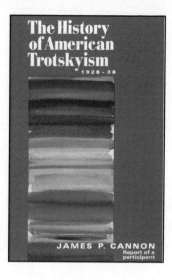

"Trotskyism is not a new movement, a new doctrine," Cannon says, "but the restoration, the revival of genuine Marxism as it was expounded and practiced in the Russian revolution and in the early days of the Communist International." In this series of twelve talks given in 1942, James P. Cannon recounts an important chapter in the efforts to build a proletarian party in the United States. $18.95

Democracy and Revolution

GEORGE NOVACK

The limitations and advances of various forms of democracy in class society, from its roots in ancient Greece, through its rise and decline under capitalism. Discusses the emergence of Bonapartism, military dictatorship, and fascism, and how democracy will be advanced under a workers and farmers regime. $18.95

Nelson Mandela Speaks

Forging a Democratic, Nonracial South Africa

Mandela's speeches from 1990 through 1993 recount the course of struggle that put an end to apartheid and opened the fight for a deep-going political, economic, and social transformation in South Africa. $18.95

Washington's 50-year Domestic Contra Operation

LARRY SEIGLE

As the U.S. rulers prepared to smash working-class resistance and join the interimperialist slaughter of World War II, the national political police apparatus as it exists today was born, together with the vastly expanded executive powers of the imperial presidency. Documents the consequences for labor, Black, antiwar, and other social movements and how the working-class vanguard has fought over the past fifty years to defend democratic rights against government and employer attacks. In *New International* no. 6. $15.00

Che Guevara Talks to Young People

The legendary Argentine-born revolutionary challenges youth of Cuba and the world to read and to study. To work and become disciplined. To join the front lines of struggles, small and large. To read and to study. To aspire to be revolutionary combatants. To politicize their organizations and in the process politicize themselves. To become a different kind of human being as they strive together with working people of all lands to transform the world. And, along this line of march, to revel in the spontaneity and joy of being young. Also in Spanish. $14.95

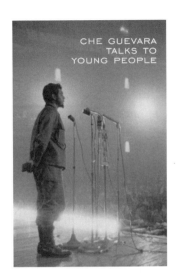

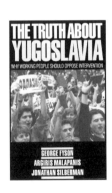

The Truth about Yugoslavia

Why Working People Should Oppose Intervention

GEORGE FYSON, ARGIRIS MALAPANIS, AND JONATHAN SILBERMAN

Examines the roots of the carnage in Yugoslavia, where Washington and its imperialist rivals in Europe are intervening militarily in an attempt to reimpose capitalist relations. $9.95

Cointelpro: The FBI's Secret War on Political Freedom

NELSON BLACKSTOCK

The FBI's spying and disruption against socialists and activists in the Black and antiwar movements. Includes FBI documents. $15.95

Write for a catalog. See front of book for addresses

U.S. IMPERIALISM HAS LOST THE COLD WAR. That's what the Socialist Workers Party concluded at the opening of the 1990s, in the wake of the collapse of regimes and parties across Eastern Europe and in the USSR that claimed to be communist. Contrary to imperialism's hopes, the working class in those countries had not been crushed. It remains an intractable obstacle to reimposing and stabilizing capitalist relations, one that will have to be confronted by the exploiters in class battles—in a hot war.

Three issues of the Marxist magazine *New International* analyze the propertied rulers' failed expectations and chart a course for revolutionaries in response to rising worker and farmer resistance to the economic and social instability, spreading wars, and rightist currents bred by the world market system. They explain why the historic odds in favor of the working class have increased, not diminished, at the opening of the 21st century.

U.S. Imperialism Has Lost the Cold War

JACK BARNES

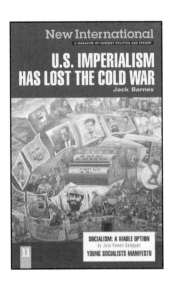

"It is only from fighters, from revolutionists of action, that communists will be forged in the course of struggle. And it is only from within the working class that the mass political vanguard of these fighters can come. The lesson from over 150 years of political struggle by the modern workers movement is that, more and more, to become and remain a revolutionist means becoming a communist." In *New International* no. 11. **$14.00**

Imperialism's March toward Fascism and War

JACK BARNES

"There will be new Hitlers, new Mussolinis. That is inevitable. What is not inevitable is that they will triumph. The working-class vanguard will organize our class to fight back against the devastating toll we are made to pay for the capitalist crisis. The future of humanity will be decided in the contest between these contending class forces." In *New International* no. 10. **$14.00**

Opening Guns of World War III

JACK BARNES

"Washington's Gulf war and its outcome did not open up a new world order of stability and UN-overseen harmony. Instead, it was the first war since the close of World War II that grew primarily out of the intensified competition and accelerating instability of the crises-ridden old imperialist world order." In *New International* no. 7. **$12.00**

ALSO AVAILABLE IN *New International's* SISTER PUBLICATIONS
IN SPANISH, FRENCH, AND SWEDISH

Che Guevara, Cuba,
and the Road to Socialism

ARTICLES BY ERNESTO CHE GUEVARA,
CARLOS RAFAEL RODRÍGUEZ, CARLOS
TABLADA, MARY-ALICE WATERS, STEVE CLARK,
JACK BARNES

Exchanges from the early 1960s and today on the
political perspectives defended by Guevara as he
helped lead working people to advance the transformation of economic and social relations in Cuba.
In *New International* no. 8. **$10.00**

The Second Assassination of
Maurice Bishop

STEVE CLARK

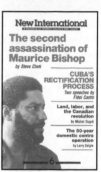

The lead article in *New International* no. 6 reviews
the accomplishments of the 1979-83 revolution in
the Caribbean island of Grenada. Explains the roots
of the 1983 coup that led to the murder of revolutionary leader Maurice Bishop, and to the destruction of the workers and farmers government by a
Stalinist political faction within the governing New
Jewel Movement. **$15.00**

The Rise and Fall of
the Nicaraguan Revolution

Lessons for revolutionists from the workers and
farmers government that came to power in Nicaragua in July 1979. Based on ten years of socialist
journalism from inside Nicaragua, this special issue of *New International* recounts the achievements
and worldwide impact of the Nicaraguan revolu-
tion. It traces the political retreat of the Sandinista National Liberation
Front leadership that led to the downfall of the revolution in the closing
years of the 1980s. Documents of the Socialist Workers Party by Jack
Barnes, Steve Clark, and Larry Seigle. In *New International* no. 9. **$14.00**

Distributed by Pathfinder